PRAISE & ENDORSEMENTS FOR

What's Done in the Dark
Affair-Proofing and Recovery from Infidelity

This is much more than a book about either avoiding or recovering from marital affairs. It is a celebration of the true meaning of marital unity. It is a guidebook about how to restore the joy of a God-blessed marriage.

—**Jim DeMint**, Former **US Senator**,
President of the Heritage Foundation,
and **Author** of *Falling in Love with America Again*

Dr. Williams takes on the painful issue of marital infidelity with great sensitivity and wisdom. He describes types of affairs and masterfully explains why people cheat. He outlines clear steps that couples can make to repair the damage and restore their marriage. **This book is a must for couples struggling with infidelity and also for the therapists who treat them.**

—**Stanley E. Hibbs, PhD**, Atlanta **Psychologist** and
Author of *Anxiety: Treatment Techniques That Really Work*,
Anxiety Gone: The Three C's of Anxiety Recovery,
and *Consider It Done: Ten Prescriptions for Finishing What You Start*

This book is a key resource that provides objective steps and facilitates trust in God to heal and restore a relationship from the wounds of betrayal. **It has great insights and tools for those who counsel these couples as well.**

—**Marsha Crowe, Women's Minister** at
Johnson Ferry Baptist Church, Atlanta, Georgia

My wife, Lynn, and I have had the privilege of knowing Dr. Williams and his wife, Dru-Ann, for almost forty years. He has, in my opinion, penned a book that not only effectively identifies the causes of marital betrayal, but also provides practical solutions for the affected partners. **I would highly recommend this reading as an important tool to prevent an affair or recover from one.**

—**James Minor, MD, FACC**, Orlando **Cardiologist**

In my twenty-seven years of practice, I can honestly say that this is the single best resource for any couple working to heal and reconnect from a breach of trust in their relationship. It is clear that Dr. Williams has spent decades "in the trenches" with couples, helping them work through the trauma of betrayal. This book is both for couples whose relationships have experienced a gradual erosion of intimacy and may be susceptible to outside threats, as well as those who have actually encountered betrayal. **It is an invaluable book and a road map back to an emotionally strong marriage.**

—**Mark E. Crawford, PhD**, Atlanta **Psychologist** and **Author** of The Obsessive-Compulsive Trap: Real Help for a Real Disorder and When Two Become Three: Nurturing Your Marriage after Baby Arrives

Dr. Williams combines over thirty years of professional experience with a compassionate heart and a desire to see individuals and couples develop resilience and healing. **I highly recommend this book and will be sharing it with my clients!**

—**Richard Blankenship, LPC, NCC, CCH, CPCS, CCPS, CCSAS**
Author of Spouses of Sex Addicts: Hope for the Journey
Founding Board Member of the Association of Partners of Sex Addicts Trauma Specialists, and **President** of the International Association of Clinical Sexual Addiction Specialists

Dr. Williams takes the most difficult situation a couple can encounter and offers hope. He provides a step-by-step guide to understanding and even regenerating the marriage covenant. Very refreshing.

—**Dr. R. Allen Stewart, Senior Pastor** at Hartwell United Methodist Church in Hartwell, Georgia

This is my dad's third book. He has been practicing marriage and family therapy for thirty years as a psychologist. He happens to be married to the most wonderful, kind, loving, godly woman I have ever known: Dru-Ann Kinsey Williams. I am proud and humbled to call them both my parents. I am also proud to recognize my father as the most intelligent and insightful man I have ever known. He also happens to be my all-time number-one hero in my life. I encourage you all to explore his insights.

—**Christopher Williams, MBA**
Terry College of Business, University of Georgia
Director of Business Development at Promethean

BOOKS AND ARTICLES WRITTEN BY D. CHARLES WILLIAMS, PHD

BOOKS

Forever a Father, Always a Son: Discovering the Difference a Dad Can Make. Wheaton, IL: Victor Books, 1991.

8 Toughest Problems Parents Face and How to Handle Them. Cowritten with Kent Brand LCSW. Carol Stream, IL: Tyndale House Publishers, 1989.

ARTICLES
(posted on www.drwilliamscoach.com)

"A Simple Test of a Good Relationship"
"Dating Relationships You Want to Avoid"
"Early Relationship Blunders: Look before You Leap"
"Don't Make Someone a Priority Who Only Makes You an Option"
"Premarital Counseling Decreases Disillusionment"
"Premarital Counseling: Prevention or Intervention?"
"The Life Cycle of Father-Son Relationships"
"Changing Your Spouse"
"How to Be a Boring Spouse"
"Complementarity in Marriage"
"Would You Rather Be Right or Close?"
"Marital Conflicts Can Bring You Closer"
"Men's Top-Ten Secrets for Making a Happy Marriage"
"Remarriage at Midlife"
"Arguments in Relationships: 15 Ways to Neutralize and Resolve Them"
"Does Your Relationship Lack Rituals of Affection?"
"Living with a Moody Spouse"
"When Men Don't Listen, Women Misinterpret"
"Ten Things I Love about My Wife"

WHAT'S DONE IN THE DARK

WHAT'S DONE IN THE DARK

AFFAIR-PROOFING AND RECOVERY FROM INFIDELITY

A Self-Help Guide for Couples
(Includes fifty homework exercises for couples)

D. CHARLES WILLIAMS, PHD

Alpharetta, GA

The names, persons, and situations described in this book are completely fictional and not related to any actual past or present clients. Any similarities to actual people or situations are merely coincidental.

Although the author and publisher have made every effort to ensure that the information in this book was correct at press time, the author and publisher do not assume and hereby disclaim any liability to any party for any loss, damage, or disruption caused by errors or omissions, whether such errors or omissions result from negligence, accident, or any other cause.

The questionnaires, inventories, exercises, assessments, categories, types of affairs, and homework assignments are those of the author except where otherwise noted. Permission is granted to copy or use this information as long as appropriate credit is ascribed to the author.

Copyright © 2017 by D. Charles Williams, PhD

All rights reserved. No part of this book may be reproduced or transmitted in any form or by any means, electronic or mechanical, including photocopying, recording, or any information storage and retrieval system, without permission in writing from the publisher. For more information, address BookLogix Permissions Department, 1264 Old Alpharetta Rd., Alpharetta, GA 30005.

ISBN: 978-1-61005-857-5
Library of Congress Control Number: 2016920579

10 9 8 7 6 5 4 3 2   0 2 2 4 1 7

Printed in the United States of America

∞ This paper meets the requirements of ANSI/NISO Z39.48-1992 (Permanence of Paper)

14 Signs you have crossed into an Emotional Affair (9/15/15) Posted on the Goodtherapy.org website. Goodtherapy.org staff.

Scripture quotations marked (NIV) are taken from the Holy Bible, New International Version®, NIV®. Copyright © 1973, 1978, 1984 by Biblica, Inc.™ Used by permission of Zondervan. All rights reserved worldwide.

Scripture quotations marked (ESV) are from the ESV® Bible (The Holy Bible, English Standard Version®), copyright © 2001 by Crossway, a publishing ministry of Good News Publishers. Used by permission. All rights reserved.

Scripture quotations marked (KJV) are taken from the Holy Bible, King James Version (Public Domain).

This book is dedicated to my brother, Hank Williams, my father, Bob Williams, and my mother-in-law, Jacquelyn Kinsey Lastition. We love and miss you every day.

I could never have written this book without the support and patience of my loving wife of over forty years, Dru-Ann Kinsey Williams. She has shown me true love and what a happy, faithful marriage can be. She has been God's gift to me, and my special angel. Without her, my life would never have been what it is. Her sons are blessed.

"A single lie discovered is enough to create contagious doubt over every other truth expressed."

—Unknown

CONTENTS

50 Checklists, Assessments, Inventories, and Homework Exercises	xix
Preface	xxi
Acknowledgments	xxv
Introduction	xxvii
Chapter 1—The End of Innocence	1
Are We All Susceptible?	1
The Temporary Insanity of Affairs	3
The Unanticipated Consequences	5
What Lies Beneath? The Danger in Affairs	6
The Loss of Innocence and Exclusivity from Affairs	10
Paying Now or Paying More Later	11
We Are Only as Sick as Our Secrets	12
Chapter 2—Why We Cheat	15
Twenty-One of the Most Common Reasons People Are Unfaithful	15
Seven of the Most Common Social Influences that Encourage Infidelity	34
Checklist: Twenty-Eight Reasons Why We Cheat	41
Chapter 3—What Kind of Affair Is It?	43
Five New Proposed Diagnostic Categories of Affairs	43
Category 1: Impulse Affairs	44
One-Night Stands	44
Retaliatory Affairs	45
Cheating-While-Dating Affairs	46
Engagement Affairs	48
Chapter 4—Category 2: Proximity Affairs	51
Emotional Affairs	51
Inventory: Signs of an Emotional Affair	53
Close-Friend Affairs	54
Celebrity or "Love the One You're With" Affairs	55
Mate-Poaching or Coveting Affairs	57

Workplace Affairs	58
In-Law Affairs	59
Family and Genetic Sexual-Attraction Affairs	60

Chapter 5 — Category 3: Avoidance Affairs — 63

Exploratory Affairs	63
Ulterior Motive Affairs	64
Dependency or "I Can't Be Alone" Affairs	66
Conflict-Avoidance Affairs	67
Intimacy-Avoidance Affairs	68
Financial Affairs	70
Sexual Identity Affairs	71

Chapter 6 — Category 4: Addiction Affairs — 73

Cyber Affairs	73
Fantasy Affairs	75
Serial Affairs	77
Swinging Affairs	79
Sex-with-Yourself Affairs (SWY)	81

Chapter 7 — Category 5: Stage-of-Life Affairs — 83

Midlife Affairs	84
Empty-Nest Affairs	85
Tripod Affairs	87
Entitlement Affairs	88
Sweetheart or Old-Flame Affairs	89
Exercise: What Type of Affair Are You Dealing with?	91

Chapter 8 — Traumatic Responses to Discovering Infidelity — 93

Shock, Devastation, and Depression	93
Denial and Disbelief	94
Anger and Retaliation	95
Pain, Anxiety, and Desperation	97
Feeling Paralyzed	99
The Final Straw: Ending the Marriage	99
Exercise: Which of These Traumatic Reactions Best Fits You?	101

Chapter 9 — Four Infidelity Recovery Stages: A Twelve-Action-Step Process — 103

Stage 1 — Discovery: "The Reality Check"	104

Action Step One: Recognition — 104
  When You Have Suspicions — 104
  Lies, Vagueness, Inconsistencies, and Deceit — 104
  What If I Suspect That My Spouse Is Cheating? — 105
    Exercise: Gathering the Evidence — 107
    Inventory: Infidelity and Cheating:
      Thirty Signs to Look for — 108
Action Step Two:
Typical Reactions of the Offending Spouse — 110
  Denial as the First Line of Defense — 110
  Defensive Anger, Blaming the Victim,
    and the Trickle-Out Approach — 111
    Checklist: The Invalidating Effects of an
    Affair on the Betrayed Spouse or Partner — 113
    Exercise: The Anger List — 115

Chapter 10—Action Step Three: Taking Responsibility — 117
  Boys and Men — 117
  Total Disclosure — 117
  Consequences of Not Disclosing — 119
    Exercise: Ending-the-Affair Agreement — 120
    Exercise: Full Disclosure — 122
    Exercise: Post-Traumatic Stress Disorder (PTSD)
    and Managing Triggers over the Affair — 123
  Best Times Not to Talk — 124
    Checklist: My Rationalizations for the Affair — 125
  What If My Spouse Won't Stop the Affair? — 127
    Staying Together — 127
    Separating — 128
    Letting Go — 128
    Cheating Is Cheating Is Cheating — 129
    Exercise: Taking Care of Yourself — 130
  Why Marriage to a Lover after an Affair Doesn't Last — 131

Chapter 11—Action Step Four: Relapse Prevention — 133
  Ten Ways to Ensure the Affair Will Not Reoccur — 133
    Checklist: What I Need to Rebuild Trust — 137

Action Step Five: Experiencing Remorse	140
Exercise: Remorse over the Affair	143
Exercise: What Is Worth Saving about Our Marriage/Relationship?	144
Chapter 12—Stage 2—What Is? What Isn't?	147
Action Step Six: Realizing the "Whys"	147
Why Did This Affair Occur?	147
Exercise: What Weakened Our Marriage?	149
How Core Issues Affect the View We Have of Ourselves and Our Spouse	150
Men and Women Who Are Cheated on Often	153
Exercise: History of Previous Relationships	155
Exercise: Our Relationship and Marital Life Timeline	156
Exercise: Inside and Outside Negative Influences	157
Exercise: Barriers within Me	159
Chapter 13—Action Step Seven: Reoccurring Forgiveness	161
The Silent Treatment	161
Forgiveness Is the Most Important Step	161
Why Don't We Forgive?	162
How Will Forgiveness Help Me?	164
What Is Forgiveness?	165
True Forgiveness Changes Lives	166
Exercise: Relationship Recovery	168
Exercise: A Daily Prayer of Appreciation	169
Exercise: Marital and Relational Forgiveness	170
Exercise: Letter of Apology	171
Chapter 14—Stage 3—Where Are We Going from Here?	173
Action Step Eight:	
Reevaluating Expectations of Each Other	173
Exercise: What Are My Fears about Our Relationship?	175
Changing Your Spouse	177
Frozen in the Pain of the Past: "How Do I Know It Won't Happen Again?"	178
Exercise: Identifying My Greatest Fears and Needs	181
Exercise: Reevaluating Expectations	183

Exercise: Character Self-Assessment	185
Exercise: The Kind of Person I Want to Become	187

Action Step Nine:
Repair and Restitution of the Relationship	188
Personal Changes	188
The Power of an Apology	190
Exercise: Amends Letter	191
Exercise: Daily Love Dare: Forty Days of Giving	192
Exercise: Relationship Validation	193
Action Step Ten: Reconciling and Recommitting	194
Changing Interactional Patterns	194
Exercise: Relationship Self-Assessment	196
Exercise: Love Language Inventory	198
Exercise: Gratitude Love Letter	199

Chapter 15 — Stage 4 —
Deepening Emotional Intimacy Together — 201

Action Step Eleven:
Rebuilding Trust and Reconnecting	201
Creating a Safe Place in Your Marriage	202
The Four As of Intimacy: Attention, Affirmation, Affection, and Attitude	206
Exercise: Little Things I Would Enjoy You Doing for Me	209
Checklist: Rituals of Affection	210
Exercise: Elements of Emotional Intimacy	211
Action Step Twelve: Reunion and Recovery	215
Betrayed but Unbroken: A Case Study of the Four-Stage, Twelve-Action-Step Process	216
Exercise: Emotional-Intimacy-Relationship Rebuilding	219
Exercise: Fun Things We Would Like to Do	223
Exercise: Marital Status Update	224
Exercise: Infidelity-Recovery-Stage Assessment	225

Chapter 16 — The Best Ways to Affair-Proof Your Marriage — 227
Five Principles That Ensure Faithfulness	228
Win Three Personal Battles Within	239

Chapter 17 — The Marital Boundaries Test — 245

Chapter 18—The Process of Becoming One   253
   Maturing into a Marriage Mindset: Becoming a Team   253
     Exercise: The Marriage Mindset Quiz   255
   Improving Your Marriage by Deepening Your Faith   256
     Locked in an Impasse   256
     We Are Our Own Worst Enemy   257
     Deepening Our Faith   257

Chapter 19—Rejuvenating Your Love Life   267
   How to Become a Boring Spouse   268
     Checklist: The Boring Spouse   269
   Emotionally Disconnected: The Key to a Sexless Marriage   271
     Checklist: Drifting Apart   273
   Enhancing Emotional Intimacy by
     Meeting the Needs of Your Spouse   275
     Checklist: Emotional Intimacy   276
   Taking It Slowly: Resuming Sex after an Affair   277
     Exercise: Sensate Focus   279
   You Need to Feel Loved to Make Love   280
   Listening Lights Up the Sheets   282
   For Your Eyes Only: How Exclusivity Heightens Attraction   284
     Exercise: Prayer of Gratitude   288

Epilogue   289
Bibliography   291
About the Author   295

50 Checklists, Assessments, Inventories, and Homework Exercises

Checklist: Twenty-Eight Reasons Why We Cheat
Inventory: Signs of an Emotional Affair
Exercise: What Type of Affair Are You Dealing with?
Exercise: Which of These Traumatic Reactions Best Fits You?
Exercise: Gathering the Evidence
Inventory: Infidelity and Cheating: Thirty Signs to Look for
Checklist: The Invalidating Effects of an Affair on the Betrayed Spouse or Partner
Exercise: The Anger List
Exercise: Ending The Affair Agreement
Exercise: Full Disclosure
Exercise: Post-Traumatic Stress Disorder (PTSD) and Managing Triggers over the Affair
Checklist: My Rationalizations for the Affair
Exercise: Taking Care of Yourself
Checklist: What I Need to Rebuild Trust
Exercise: Remorse over the Affair
Exercise: What Is Worth Saving about Our Marriage/Relationship?
Exercise: What Weakened Our Marriage?
Exercise: History of Previous Relationships
Exercise: Our Relationship and Marital Life Timeline
Exercise: Inside and Outside Negative Influences
Exercise: Barriers within Me
Exercise: Relationship Recovery
Exercise: A Daily Prayer of Appreciation
Exercise: Marital and Relational Forgiveness
Exercise: Letter of Apology
Exercise: What Are My Fears about Our Relationship?
Exercise: Identifying My Greatest Fears and Needs
Exercise: Reevaluating Expectations
Exercise: Character Self-Assessment
Exercise: The Kind of Person I Want to Become

Exercise: Amends Letter
Exercise: Daily Love Dare: Forty Days of Giving
Exercise: Relationship Validation
Exercise: Relationship Self-Assessment
Exercise: Love Language Inventory
Exercise: Gratitude Love Letter
Exercise: Little Things I Would Enjoy You Doing for Me
Checklist: Rituals of Affection
Exercise: Elements of Emotional Intimacy
Exercise: Emotional-Intimacy-Relationship Rebuilding
Exercise: Fun Things We Would Like to Do
Exercise: Marital Status Update
Exercise: Infidelity-Recovery-Stage Assessment
The Marital Boundaries Test
Exercise: The Marriage Mindset Quiz
Checklist: The Boring Spouse
Checklist: Drifting Apart
Checklist: Emotional Intimacy
Exercise: Sensate Focus
Exercise: Prayer of Gratitude

PREFACE

Chapter One, entitled "The End of Innocence," examines how susceptible anyone can be to infidelity. It describes the insidious influences and slippery slope most people encounter prior to an affair. It clearly details the loss and consequences that inevitably occur when unfaithfulness occurs in a marriage. The traumatic responses a betrayed spouse experiences are also examined.

Chapter Two, entitled "Why We Cheat," examines how essential it is for couples to learn why the affair occurred. It underscores the importance of understanding twenty-eight factors that contribute to infidelity in order for the couple to move forward. Clearly, no act of unfaithfulness is justifiable, despite whatever problems exist in a marriage. However, infidelity can reoccur if both spouses do not understand what led to the betrayal, as well as how they each may have inadvertently contributed to it.

Chapters Three through Seven are a first-ever effort made to define a nomenclature that identifies five categories and describes twenty-eight different types of affairs that exist. Details of the motivations and influences that contribute to why each type of affair occurs are included. Examples and vignettes are provided for illustration.

Chapter Eight, entitled "Traumatic Responses to Discovering Infidelity," examines the six most typical reactions to the realization that an affair has occurred. It details how the unknowing spouse emotionally responds to the betrayal.

Chapters Nine through Fifteen, encompassing the four-stage, twelve-action-step model for restoring a marriage after an affair, have come from many years of talking with couples in the throes of betrayal. They are trying to make sense of what occurred, why it happened to them, and whether their relationship can be restored. There are a number of models that have identified similar stages of recovery that have notable merit by authors such as Emily Brown, Shirley Glass, Janis Abrahms Spring, Dave Carder, Don-David

Lusterman, Snyder, Baucom and Gordon, Frank Pittman, Harley and Chalmers, and Liz Currin.

This twelve-action-step model has added even more detail to what a couple must do if they are to fully repair and affair-proof their damaged relationship. Many couples navigate through the discovery stage and the what-next stage, but prematurely exit therapy because the process is such a painful reminder of the past. The twelve-action-step model places particular emphasis on relapse prevention, repair, reconnecting, rebuilding, recommitting, deepening emotional intimacy, reunion, and rejuvenation within the marriage.

Chapters Sixteen through Eighteen, entitled "The Best Ways to Affair-Proof Your Marriage," "The Marital Boundaries Test," and "The Process of Becoming One," help individuals and couples rebuild and grow together. It offers tools to protect their marriage from the negative societal influences that adversely impact their relationship.

"The Marital Boundaries Test" assists couples in recalibrating healthy boundaries to protect their marriage from damaging outside influences.

"The Process of Becoming One" helps couples recognize that it is not enough for a marriage to just be repaired. In order to become affair-proof, emotional intimacy must be established. Some marriages have not experienced this type of closeness since the early years of their relationship, if ever. Couples who do not develop a deeper emotional and spiritual connection than they previously had may spend years fighting about the affair or even become susceptible to unfaithfulness again.

Chapter Nineteen, entitled "Rejuvenating Your Love Life," addresses key strategies for reconnecting emotionally and sexually from boredom, neglect, and the destructive effects of infidelity.

The twelve-action-step model and the affair-proofing strategies help couples who are emotionally broken learn to thrive together in spite of the infidelity. The entire book is user friendly and has fifty exercises, self-assessments, inventories, questionnaires, homework, and practical activities. These will help couples understand each other, repair wounds and hurts, rebuild their emotional lives together, reintroduce playfulness and sexuality, and ultimately affair-proof their relationship.

ACKNOWLEDGMENTS

A special acknowledgment goes to my sons, Chris and David. I couldn't be prouder of the young men you have become. You are both awesome!

I appreciate so much my loving mother, Betty Williams, who has always been the example of loyalty and commitment. I am also grateful for my wonderful, supportive brother, Ken Williams, and my always-generous sister-in-law, Fran Williams.

I am also in debt to my loyal friends and family whose marriages I have admired.

They include Joe and Vicki Hoffman, Dr. Jim and Lynn Minor, Ross and Kim MacKenzie, Bill and Ann Poole, Chuck and Dr. Ann Lucas, Daryl and Steve Gray, Tom and Debbie Kulsar, Sherwin and Debbie Mackintosh, Kevin and Noelle Broyles, Dr. Mark and Lin Ottenweller, Bob and Jackie Keene, Tom and Kelly Brown, Nick and Diane Ammons, Ken and Wendy Williams, Terry and Dianne Barnes, John and Barbara Rhodes, Joby and Sarah Scroggs, Jacob and Leigh Scroggs, Bill and Bonnie Pratt, Dave and Cheryl Matthews, Dennie and Emily Shepherd, Jim and Pam Hannah, Gene and Alyson Veal, Blake and Leann Neyland, Reese and Mary Kay Neyland, Steve and Betsy Gooch, Jim and Debbie Mackie, Mark and Michelle Brock, Dick and Jo Jayne Soule, Dr. Don and Janet Stevens, Cliff and Kathy Cox, Allen and Susan Anderson Bell, Paul and Wendy Kellet, Jerrund and Connie Wilkerson, Don and Suzie Shultz, Wayne and Donna Collins, Fernando and Donna Nasmyth, John O'Neill and Bobbie Busha, Don and Susan McLaughlin, Ken and Kay Truelove, Paul and Dianne Evans, Jack and Karen Stilts, Hal and Diane Opdyke, Jerry and Mary Ann Kapalko, Terry and Kathy Holesko, Craig and Mary Haverfield, John and Cindy Lawrence, Phil and Teresa Howard, Dr. John and Kathy Stroop, Mike and Brigid Richardson, Rich and Beth Mewborn, and Senator Jim and Debbie DeMint.

I have been proud to be associated with some of the most qualified and capable colleagues during my career.

They include Drs. Marsha Sauls, Stan Hibbs, Donna Ulrici, Susan Burleson, Sandy Hoffman, Randy Gerson, Bill Doverspike, Ted Ballard, Richard Blankenship, Major Boglin, Guy Sommers, Chuck and Dr. Ann Lucas, Lew and Finnette Fabrick, Bonnie Cooper , Linda Myrick, Phil Morris MD, Farris Johnson MD, Jim Minor MD, Mark Ottenweller MD, Paul Kellet MD, Anna Williams, Rose Padilla, Ted Goetz, Don Burroughs, Patty Brawner, Marilyn Vickers, Sylvia Knight, Greg Garcia, Justin and Anastasia Shewell, David Woodsfellow, Mark Crawford, Kent Brand, Allan Kennedy, David McAnulty, Keith Crawford DMD, Brenda Stewart, and Marsha Crowe.

A debt of gratitude goes to the staff of BookLogix for editing this manuscript. A special thanks goes to Dru-Ann Williams and Bobbie Busha for their guidance and editing of the initial manuscript.

I will be forever grateful to my wonderful clients, who over the years have taught me more than I could have ever taught them.

INTRODUCTION

"A fool is someone who gives up something he loves for something he desires."

—Unknown

WHAT IS BETRAYAL?

Jenny met Russell on Match.com, and he seemed to be the man of her dreams—until she discovered that he had a history of cheating on all the other women he dated.

Tina and Geri were close friends for years, until one day, Geri refused to accept her calls or talk to Tina over a seemingly minor misunderstanding.

Jim and Tony were co-owners of a mortgage business for ten years. Jim discovered that Tony had secretly started another company on his own and was funneling new clients to his new venture.

Sara and Katie had been friends for years and had always honored the girl code of not dating guys the other was interested in. Sara found out that Katie had gone out with a guy Sara had dated and was very fond of.

John and Tammy had sacrificed a great deal for their children over the years. Jack, their youngest son, had struggled to stay employed or demonstrate a consistent direction in life. He didn't like hard work, so he tended to job-hop. When he asked for another loan from his parents, they declined and suggested he get a temporary, part-time job to supplement his lifestyle. He cut them off and refused to talk with them for a year.

Dan had enlisted the support and direction of Stan, an older colleague whom he admired in his company, to provide some mentoring for him. When Dan heard from a peer that Stan had been making fun of him to some other colleagues, he was embarrassed and angry.

Have you ever known someone who portrayed themselves in one way and later discovered they were not who they said they were?

Has a close friend ever cut you out of their life and been unwilling to discuss what was wrong?

Has a trusted colleague ever taken advantage of you for his or her own personal gain in a business deal?

Have you ever been blatantly lied to and deceived by a close friend or spouse?

Has one of your adult children ever turned against you when they didn't get what they wanted?

Has a close confidant treated you with warmth and acceptance in your presence, but you found out later that he or she was critical of you to others?

If you have had any of these occur in your life, then you have experienced betrayal.

There are few things more painful than being betrayed by someone you love or care about. It hurts deeply, especially when that person is a close friend, a lover, your child, or your spouse. It can leave a scar that can be forgiven, but perhaps never forgotten. When trust is violated, we view that person differently than we ever have before. We scrutinize them more closely. The realization that we were deceived may cause us to question ourselves. The hurt and anger we experience can cause us to turn inward and become self-protective. We may feel foolish, naïve, gullible, or blame ourselves for ignoring the obvious. We may even lose confidence in our own judgment and question the trustworthiness of everyone else.

The greatest betrayal in marriages is caused by infidelity. It is by far the most devastating and negative affront affecting couples today. When emotional or sexual infidelity occurs in a committed relationship, it may never be the same. The offending spouse will realize too late that one brief incident of cheating can create heartache for a lifetime.

Warren Buffet once said, "It takes years to build a reputation and only five minutes to ruin it." The same can be said for infidelity. It takes years to build trust in a relationship, and only seconds to destroy it. The innocence and exclusivity that existed prior to a betrayal is a thing of the past. The emotional security within the relationship now becomes unstable. The marital safe haven turns into an ever-present danger. The acceptance previously felt from one's spouse is replaced by feelings of rejection. Life, as it was, changes.

Some couples never recover, and they end their relationship and try to move on. Others struggle their way through this crisis to a new normal. Those couples whose relationships remain unbroken can slowly regain a greater sense of love and mutual respect together. They can begin the painstaking journey of processing the regret, remorse, forgiveness, recommitment, the rebuilding of trust, reconnection, and reunion that often takes years to accomplish.

The 2010 National Opinion Research Center's General Social Survey indicated that approximately 15–20 percent of married men and women who were polled had been sexually unfaithful. Specifically, 21 percent of men and 14.7 percent of women admitted to infidelity. When behaviors such as inappropriate physical contact or emotional affairs were included, the percentages jumped another ten to fifteen points for both sexes. Other studies on sexual infidelity have estimated a much higher percentage, approaching 30–50 percent in men and 20–40 percent in women. Over the last thirty-plus years in my own private practice, the 20–30 percent range of sexual unfaithfulness within marriages seems more accurate. It increases another 10–15 percent when inappropriate emotional, physical, Internet, and phone contact with the opposite sex is included.

Infidelity is clearly on the rise in our culture.

A recent indicator of this occurred in August 2015 when hackers acquired and published 33 million user identities from the infidelity website AshleyMadison.com. All of these individuals had signed up with the intention of cheating on their spouse, fiancé, or significant other. Some clients in my own practice were impacted by this site. The fallout from that discovery has been catastrophic for thousands of marriages and relationships and has allegedly led to several suicides.

The website DivorceStatistics.info indicates that 17 percent of all the divorces in our country is caused by infidelity. Other sources estimate the rate of divorce from unfaithfulness at 20 percent or higher. It is impossible to know how accurate these figures truly are due to the secretive nature of infidelity. Incidentally, only about 10 percent of individuals who have affairs together ever marry. Ironically, the majority of these couples eventually end up divorced as well, according to Snyder, Baucom, and Gordon, authors of *Getting Past the Affair*. One of the biggest reasons for their splitting up is that they do not trust each other. Tragically, many unfaithful partners who end up marrying the other person have a permanently estranged relationship with their children and their grandchildren.

Fortunately, the majority of couples who experience an affair do not divorce. They remain together, initially damaged and hurting from the infidelity, but they do not give up. Their marriage is not irretrievably broken.

The 2014 movie *Unbroken* is an inspiring tale of survival based on the real-life experiences of Louis Zamperini, an American pilot held by the Japanese during World War II. His plane crashed into the Pacific Ocean, and he was adrift at sea for forty-seven days. He was brutally tortured during his capture, but he remained unbroken. He never gave up and never gave in.

Although infidelity devastates a marriage, that relationship does not have to end or be permanently broken. Couples can return from the brink of divorce and rebuild a marriage that can last—a marriage that is unbroken.

My psychology private practice has afforded me the privilege of counseling over 6,000 clients thus far during my career. Approximately 2,500 or more of those have been couples who were dating, living together, engaged, married, separated or divorced, but reconciling. Almost 600 of these couples had some form of unfaithfulness occur within their relationship.

During an initial office visit from a new client, a detailed family of origin history is always taken to determine background influences and frames of reference for events that have occurred in their lives. Almost half of my clients report knowledge of an affair that has occurred within the marriages of various family members, including parents, siblings, or other relatives. No matter how long ago the infidelity might have occurred, it is almost always reflected upon as having a devastating impact upon someone closely related to those family members. For some, the knowledge of the affair serves as a grim reminder of what pain can be inflicted indirectly upon innocent family members whose lives are often turned upside down.

For others, the infidelity is a legacy they too experience. When a close relative is unfaithful, it introduces the possibility that infidelity could be an option for them as well. The power of example has a life-changing influence.

CHAPTER 1

THE END OF INNOCENCE

"Some people create their own storms and then are surprised when it rains."
— D. Charles Williams

Some couples' lives look perfect from the outside looking in:

John and Cheryl had what most people thought was an amazing marriage, with two beautiful children and a great lifestyle. He was a rising corporate star and destined for great things in his industry. He was personable, bright, and well regarded in his church. She was a woman any man would have hoped to marry because of her inner and outer beauty. Not only was she a great mom, but she worked at the church directing the children's educational programs. No one could have known that their lives together would come crashing down when John was discovered having an affair. He had been involved with a female associate who worked for another division in a city halfway across the country that he visited every quarter. Nor did anyone suspect that Cheryl had been emotionally involved with the associate pastor at their church for nearly two years. A marriage that appeared to be so perfect to others really was not.

ARE WE ALL SUSCEPTIBLE?

"It's what you learn after you know it all that counts."
John Wooden

Most people do not believe that they *are capable of cheating on their spouse*. Yet even a great relationship can be compromised if enough factors come into play in just the right way at just the right time. My clients almost always respond confidently with "But I have never cheated and I never would!"

The fact is that *most people don't cheat*. Even when an opportunity occurs, they do not give in to that temptation. Perfect storms do sometimes happen when enough random influences converge in an individual's life and relationship at the same time. These factors can weaken anyone to the point of crossing boundaries they never intended to cross.

These influences include:
- often being out of town alone
- anonymity or being in a place where no one knows you
- going through a particularly difficult time in a marriage
- experiencing a loss of confidence and feeling negatively about one's self
- being flattered or made to feel important by the opposite sex
- loss of inhibitions due to alcohol use
- habitually surfing inappropriate websites
- regularly working late with an opposite-sex colleague
- mutual flirting with the opposite sex
- too much openness and sharing of private and personal information with the opposite sex

These influences may seem insignificant in the moment. Over time, they cause us to question what we believe, relax the limits we set for ourselves, and compromise the values we hold.

> *"Be self-controlled and alert. Your enemy the devil prowls around like a roaring lion looking for someone to devour. Resist him, standing firm in the faith, because you know that your brothers throughout the world are undergoing the same kind of sufferings."*
>
> 1 Peter 5:8–9 (NIV)

THE TEMPORARY INSANITY OF AFFAIRS

"The Nice Guy Who Finished First"

Jack and Jill had been married fourteen years and had three children. Jill had recently reentered the workforce. She was highly driven and quickly advanced in the ranks of her company. Jill insisted they seek counseling, as she felt Jack had not grown as a person or made his career a priority. When some of her issues of disrespect, harshness, and control were addressed in counseling, she quickly dropped out, maintaining she had no problems. Jill would not honestly look at herself and blamed the problems solely on Jack. Not long after, they separated, as they had "grown in different directions," so Jack agreed to move out. He continued to work on himself in counseling, be more involved with the kids, and remain open to reconciliation. Several months later, it was discovered that Jill's complaints and dissatisfaction about her marriage were the result of an affair she was having with a married colleague. She eventually realized that her new lover was not who she initially thought he was, and the relationship ended. Jill asked to work things out with her husband and he agreed to consider it. Jack had demonstrated patience, character, and faith during this trial, and Jill realized that he was really the type of man she needed. Unfortunately, Jill had severely damaged her marriage, harmed her relationship with her children, and lost credibility with her colleagues.

"Didn't you think about me before having an affair?"

Most affairs are not premeditated. They do not have the intentional purpose of hurting one's spouse, even though they always do. The reckless impulsiveness of an affair is often the culmination of a number of poor choices that gradually lead to self-induced, temporary insanity. The players in this destructive drama are caught up in the moment without regard for the inevitable tragedy that will ensue. Many individuals in an affair report a stark contrast between the emotions they feel in their marriage and those they experience in an affair. These differences can create a type of temporary insanity that compels individuals to make poor, irrational decisions and act impulsively in spite of their better judgment.

Below are some examples of the contrast between the emotions an affair elicits and those that occur in a marriage relationship.

An affair often begins with infatuation and intensity that is intoxicating and flattering. The excitement makes people feel young again. Most marriages have passed this stage of exhilaration. They may even be routine or mundane, focusing primarily on the day-to-day tasks of living.

An affair is a foray into the exciting unknown, often with someone who is new and unfamiliar, so interest and curiosity in each other is high. Conversely, a spouse is someone who has become very familiar. It seems that there is nothing else to know about them.

An affair often occurs between two people who mutually idealize one another. They see only the good and none of the bad in each other. A married couple has been together long enough to realize who their partner really is, for better and worse.

An affair is energizing and often makes people willing to try things they might not have been inclined to do before. Marriages tend to gravitate toward a mutual comfort zone, so relaxing or "chilling out" together is often preferred after a hectic week. Couple's lives may even seem a little boring and uneventful.

An affair introduces a certain element of risk because of its secretive nature. Forbidden fruit is alluring and titillating to some because of the fantasy of what it holds. Marriage, on the other hand, is a calm, secure relationship where partners know what to expect and may even take each other for granted. The element of risk and titillation is often a thing of the past.

An affair brings back the heated passion that has often been lost in the familiarity and routineness of having sex with the same person year after year. After all, new sex is good sex—or is it? In marriage, sex may or may not be satisfying. It often becomes routine and less passionate. Other things get in the way of making sex a priority, and married couples often relegate it to the last item of the day. Many times, sleep wins out.

THE UNANTICIPATED CONSEQUENCES

Doug and Sandy were a young couple who had only been married a few years. Sandy intercepted a text message from a woman on Doug's cell phone that said, "You were amazing last night!" Doug was supposed to have been working late at his job, but he was seeing another woman. When this couple came in for emergency counseling, a detailed family history was taken. It was reported that Doug's father had quite a lengthy history of cheating on Doug's mother as well.

Life does not occur in a vacuum. We may have heard the comment "Whatever happens in Vegas, stays in Vegas." This is a rationalization individuals use when trying to justify or cover up bad behavior. In reality, everything we do in life, whether in public or private, either directly or indirectly affects others.

I have had clients who never knew that one of their parents had been unfaithful until later in life. Ironically, some of these clients have ended up struggling with the same infidelity that their parents had. They never realized this family legacy would be left for them to eventually face as well.

Adults who as children or teens knew about a parent's affair when it was occurring almost always disapproved. Ironically, a significant proportion of them end up being unfaithful to their spouses when experiencing struggles in their own relationships.

David's Legacy

In the Old Testament, David is blessed by God for his courage and faith. He is a recognized warrior and "a man after God's own heart." He wins many victories for God, who eventually makes him king. David also suffers many consequences for poor decisions he makes in his personal life.

On one occasion, from his rooftop, he sees a beautiful young woman bathing. Her name is Bathsheba, and she is the wife of one of his commanders, Uriah. The longer he watches her, the more he is captivated. The more he dwells on the image of her beauty in his mind, the greater his desire for her grows. David finally pursues her; they eventually have sex, and she accidentally becomes pregnant. As a result, he concocts a plan to have her husband, Uriah, placed on the front lines in an attack on an opposing army, so that Uriah will be killed and conveniently eliminated. David can then legitimately have Bathsheba for himself. His plan succeeds, and he and Bathsheba eventually marry.

However, the consequences of their affair are devastating upon the entire family. Their children are full of jealousy, bickering, and competitiveness toward one another. One of the daughters, Tamar, is raped by her half-brother, Amnon. Another son attempts to overthrow David. His son, Absalom, kills his brother, Amnon, over the rape. Sadly, we do eventually reap what we sow in life.

WHAT LIES BENEATH? THE DANGER IN AFFAIRS

> *"An adulteress preys upon your very life. Can a man scoop fire into his lap without being burned? Can a man walk on hot coals without his feet being scorched? So is he who sleeps with another man's wife; no one who touches her will go unpunished."*
>
> Proverbs 6:26 (NIV)

What about the hurt it causes?

Infidelity always hurts someone. It hurts the partner who has been faithful and committed in the marriage because their relationship is not what they thought it was. It hurts the children who depend on their parents for protection, guidance, and an example of how to live their lives. Infidelity hurts the person who cheated, even if it somehow goes undetected. He or she carries a secret that haunts them and keeps them from being fully open and honest with their spouse or themselves.

What if your lover is jealous, retaliatory, or crazy?

When Michael Douglas's character has a one-night stand with Glenn Close's character in *Fatal Attraction*, he goes on with his life as if nothing happened. His lover, however, is not done with him, and so a series of bizarre attempts to keep him engaged with her follows. Both of their lives unravel insanely until she is killed.

It is not uncommon for individuals who venture into the world of infidelity to later discover that their lover has emotional problems, is insanely jealous, has a borderline personality disorder, or is recklessly retaliatory. The lover may stalk, call incessantly, or even contact the individual's spouse when he or she refuses to stay involved. That brief foray into bliss becomes a nightmare that is a terrifying roller-coaster ride from beginning to end. We have all read about murder-suicides that have resulted from love triangles gone bad. *A spurned lover will not go lightly into the night.*

When I was in college, I had a fraternity brother who was liked by everyone. He was a genuinely good guy, possessed a warm personality, and had absolutely no enemies. Several years after we all graduated, I heard that he had been caught in bed with the separated wife of another man. The estranged husband killed them both and then himself. This was an untimely end to a nice guy who didn't use good judgment and was in the wrong place at the wrong time with the wrong person.

> *"Jealousy arouses a husband's fury, and he will show no mercy when he takes revenge. He will not accept any compensation, he will refuse the bribe, however great it is"*
> Proverbs 6:34–5 (NIV)

What if you are never trusted again?
Everything in life is based upon our ability to trust and depend on others. In the absence of trust and integrity, hope for the future is in question. When people are betrayed, they often feel that they can never trust others again and can only depend upon themselves. They become self-sufficient, self-protective, and skeptical about life and love. Though trust in a marriage can be rebuilt after infidelity, it can never be quite the same as before the loss of innocence. Our word, our reputation, and our character are inevitably all we have to offer others in life. When these have been compromised, trust is not easily recovered.

What if the kids never forgive you?
> *"To the world you may be one person; but to one person you may be the world."*
>
> Dr. Seuss

Our kids worship us and believe we can do anything—until they become teenagers. Even then, they still want us to be their heroes. When we break the trust of our spouse, we also shatter the admiration and image our kids have of us. When infidelity in a parent is discovered, it rocks their world and causes them to lose hope that anyone can live happily ever after.

One of the reasons our young people are marrying later in life, or not at all, is because of the last two decades of divorce they have witnessed. What legacy are we leaving our children? When a parent cheats, children often think that parent is the biggest fraud there ever was. Their hurt is masked by their disdain because they feel betrayed as well. The values and expectations shared with them by that parent become just empty platitudes that signify nothing. That parent's stock, in the eyes of their child, becomes all but worthless. It is very difficult to regain their respect again, but it can be done over time with honesty, remorse, patience, and humility.

What if you get HPV, an STD, or become pregnant?

The risk of unforeseen consequences occurs when people get sexually involved outside their marriage. Many affairs begin in a fit of passion without thinking about outcomes. These impulsive actions are the cause of much sadness. The unknowing spouse is often the victim of these actions and may need medical treatment for conditions they are exposed to by their spouse. When a pregnancy occurs from an affair, there is the additional agony, shame, and expense that negatively impacts everyone for a lifetime—especially the innocent child. Former vice presidential candidate John Edwards saw his life and career derail when his mistress became pregnant.

What if it breaks up the family?

Affairs break up families. They are broken even if they do stay together. They will require a long period of healing, which can occur, but the family never fully recovers. If divorce is the result, there are long-term consequences for everyone. The relationships in the family are often not the same because of the sadness and regret. Though time may pass, the elephant is still in the room, even if it is never discussed again. It defines, in part, who that family has become. Although young adults may adjust to having several different family-member groups because of divorce and remarriage, they always long for their original family and wish they could have stayed together.

What if you are remembered as a betrayer and liar?

When marriages do not end in divorce after an affair, the cheating spouse who shows remorse can often make amends and eventually put their relationship back together again. It may take years to repair their reputation and be trusted again, but reminders of their past behavior will occasionally resurface. When marriages end in divorce after infidelity, the unfaithful spouse is always remembered in part as a betrayer. Though it may be seldom mentioned, it is never forgotten.

In those instances where the unfaithful spouse has gone on to marry the person with whom they cheated, it is rare that a close, positive relationship ever develops between the children and the new union. Sometimes, the new spouse makes it very difficult for their partner to maintain a relationship with his or her previous family.

Have you ever been to a funeral of someone whose adult children, whom no one knew existed, attended? It is not uncommon for a couple who has had an affair to move away and begin a whole new life apart from anyone they previously knew. While a parent's affair is painful to their children, being erased from that parent's life adds insult to injury.

THE LOSS OF INNOCENCE AND EXCLUSIVITY FROM AFFAIRS

"Wisdom consists of the anticipation of consequences."
Norman Cousins

When we know the true cost of something before investing our resources in it, our decisions are generally better informed. We also avoid buyer's remorse. The costs or losses associated with an affair are cataclysmic, though rarely considered beforehand.

These losses include:
- loss of commitment
- loss of trust
- loss of reputation
- loss of self-respect and the respect of others
- loss of security
- loss of sexual exclusivity
- loss of honesty and integrity
- loss of safety in the relationship
- loss of feeling special
- loss of friends and family
- loss of self-confidence
- loss of peace in our lives
- loss of character
- loss of finances
- loss of a future together

Five Things We Can't Recover
1. A stone after it's thrown
2. A word after it's said
3. An occasion after it's missed
4. Time after it's gone
5. Innocence after it's lost

PAYING NOW OR PAYING MORE LATER

> *"For there is nothing hidden that will not be disclosed, and nothing concealed that will not be known or brought out into the open."*
> Luke 8:17 (NIV)

A husband who had an affair with an old acquaintance called the office for an emergency marital appointment. His wife had discovered the affair after it had gone on for a year. They came to counseling, but he was mostly interested in putting it all behind them as quickly as possible. They attended for a few initial visits; he never called back to reschedule because he was "too busy at work." Six to eight months later, he called back wanting to get them into treatment as quickly as possible because his wife just wouldn't "let it go" or forgive his cheating on her.

This is a scenario that occurs when people try to put the past behind them too quickly, without healing the wounds or making the necessary repairs that their marriage needs. Feelings of betrayal do not go away with time, despite what people may think. It is a cancer that grows and permeates one's mind until it is treated and eradicated. It is not uncommon to see couples who are still arguing over the same feelings of hurt twenty-five years after the untreated aftermath of the affair. Those who do not deal with the affair through counseling, once it is discovered, can expect to have a more difficult time dealing with it later.

Tammy and Ray were a couple who had been married for thirty-five years. He discovered in their thirty-fifth year of marriage that she had been involved in an affair twenty-eight years earlier. She was surprised that he was so devastated over her past infidelity since it had been over for so many years. She didn't understand that, for him, it was as if it had happened yesterday. What made it worse was that he questioned how legitimate their entire thirty-five-year marriage had been. He never forgot it and never forgave her. They spent the rest of their marriage fighting over why she didn't love him enough to have never had an affair.

> *"A man who commits adultery has no sense; whoever does so destroys himself. Blows and disgrace are his lot, and his shame will never be wiped away."*
>
> Proverbs 6:32–33 (NIV)

WE ARE ONLY AS SICK AS OUR SECRETS

> *"It's really none of her business." "This might upset him if he knew this." "What she doesn't know won't hurt her." "It doesn't really matter; he'll never notice it anyway."*

I knew a family once that demonstrated the following dynamic: the wife openly urged her daughter to collude with her in keeping things from the father. The wife would not disagree with her husband in his presence, but would secretly go behind his back and do things her own way. The daughter, subsequently, grew up learning to limit what she told her significant other.

Do you ever keep secrets from your spouse?

Husbands and wives who keep secrets from each other will inevitably create trouble in their relationship. If we have to hide something from our spouse, we probably should not be engaging in the behavior in question in the first place. Rationalizing that it is not that important is only a form of lying to ourselves. We may not want to address something that might upset our spouse. We may feel we are protecting our spouse or managing a situation that might cause stress for him or her. Whatever the nature of the omission, it is a secret. It does not take much for these secrets to become little white lies, which are ultimately deceptive.

These secrets run the risk of becoming just another issue that you as a couple cannot talk about. As these secrets mount up over time, a pattern is set that creates distance and becomes an eventual emotional abyss between you.

Secrets generate trust issues within the relationship, because eventually, these omissions are discovered. Once an individual realizes her spouse is lying to her, she also wonders, "What else has he been lying about?" Once suspicion has been created in a relationship, both people go into a self-protective mode and withdraw from the other.

We all need to feel safe in our marriage and believe our partner has our back. Since our spouse is our closest confidant, they generally know everything about us: our insecurities, our fears, our past hurts, and our inadequacies. When we no longer believe our spouse has our best interests at heart, we feel vulnerable and pull back emotionally to protect ourselves. When this occurs, over time, these spouses feel that they cannot depend on each other.

This is one of the times when loneliness makes us more vulnerable to sharing our personal problems with others. Sharing personal issues with an opposite-sex confidant inevitably causes emotional bonding to occur. This relationship is often, by nature, a secretive one. When a relationship has to be a secret, we should not be in it.

One of the most important reasons to have a no-secrets policy in marriage is that it forces us to approach our spouse about potentially problematic issues. It may not be easy bringing up issues that are important to us, but we can become more adept at handling conflict together while keeping our spouse informed. Talking regularly together helps determine when it is best to talk about things and how to bring them up. In the process, a stronger bond is forged together by openly working through those difficulties.

Conflict is intended to bring us closer, not cause a rift between us. The closeness and trust that deepens by handling both the day-to-day challenges and major issues makes us the force for good together.

CHAPTER 2

WHY WE CHEAT

"Knowing is half the battle."
—G.I. Joe

TWENTY-ONE OF THE MOST COMMON REASONS PEOPLE ARE UNFAITHFUL

Why do affairs occur?
Some affairs are intentional, premeditated, and planned, but most are accidental or opportunistic. They are like getting dangerously close to a precipice for a better view and then slipping over the edge, falling into the canyon below. Maybe someone paid attention to you when your spouse didn't. Perhaps there was an unexpected attraction to someone who felt the same way, too. It can occur when individuals in close proximity spend too much time together. A common trigger is being validated or complimented by someone who seems to truly appreciate you. Maybe you liked the way he or she made you feel. A professional kinship or common interests shared together can be powerful aphrodisiacs.

The following personal factors represent influences in the lives of unfaithful individuals, problems they experience, beliefs they hold, and how they view the state of their marriage. Although *no reason ever justifies having an affair*, these are the factors that contribute to having an affair. They are intended to be used as a means for greater understanding and further discussion. The most common question betrayed spouses ask is "Why did this happen?"

These factors attempt to explain how and why infidelity occurs for some people. Sometimes, counselors do not realize how important it is for clients to understand why an affair happened. When our lives feel out of control, we instinctively try to get more information. It gives us some sense of control, even if it is just an intellectual understanding. It is also an attempt to make sense of the chaos we are feeling emotionally.

Here are some of the common contributors to cheating.

1. FEELING UNDERAPPRECIATED

"Happy marriages are a 'mutual admiration society.'"
                                                    DCW

Most of us want our spouses to believe we are the best thing that ever happened to them. Likewise, they want us to regard them in the same way. Happy marriages are mutual admiration societies. Optimally, each person wants to feel blessed to have been given the privilege of such a wonderful partner with whom to go through life.

It is easy to feel taken for granted if caring expressions and thoughtful gestures diminish in a relationship. As a result, our appreciation for each other may start to wane. What used to be a privilege to do for one another starts to feel like an expectation and an obligation. Disappointment and resentment may follow when a spouse feels like she is giving more than she is getting. Criticism and bickering begins at this point in most relationships.

This crack in the veneer provides an opportunity for someone else to show or tell your spouse what an awesome person he is or how lucky his wife is to have him in her life. If your husband or wife feels they are no longer getting acknowledgement at home, they will be flattered if someone else affirms them.

Tom and Tina's marriage had cooled off after fifteen years of marriage. They had not been able to have children, so Tina felt like a failure as a woman. Even though Tom was still in love and attracted to her, Tina was too disillusioned to be there for him emotionally or sexually. It wasn't long before he was surfing the chat rooms for exciting conversations with other women who showed interest in him. Eventually, he rendezvoused with several women who made him feel important and wanted again.

There are people in the workplace who will compliment, encourage, and validate your spouse. This attention may cause your partner to feel that others appreciate them more than you do. It may entice them into wanting to spend more time with these encouraging people and lead them to share personal issues and struggles with them. Getting too close to a coworker has been the catalyst for many affairs because of the unwitting bonds forged when this type of intimate sharing occurs.

2. OPPORTUNITY

Early in my career and marriage, I was the director of the adult and aging clinics of the local mental health center in Gainesville, Florida. We had just concluded a staff meeting that was particularly lively and participatory when a woman from one of the other clinics walked up beside me. We chatted for a moment, and before she walked away, she said, "If you ever decide to have an affair, please let me be the first to know!" Then, she walked off. I was taken aback by how forward but nonchalant she was about the offer. I was also embarrassingly flattered that she found me attractive and desirable. Almost immediately, I felt as if I might have done something to give her the wrong impression.

What is the best course of action when these types of situations present themselves?

Those who spend time contemplating the possibilities of a relationship with someone else are playing with fire. Wondering *what if*, fantasizing about a tryst together or a rendezvous, and finding ways to be in the company of the other person can lead to acting on those thoughts. Impulsively acting on an opportunity without thinking about the consequences is inevitably life changing. Yet people do this on a regular basis when they travel, meet someone at a bar, stay late at work on a project with an opposite-sex coworker, or practice with their mixed-doubles opposite-sex tennis partner without having another couple there. Opportunity is a primary factor that contributes to the incidence of one-night stands.

So what did I do with the opportunity presented to me? I thought about how I should handle it. I considered telling her, "Thanks, but no thanks." Then, I decided to pass it by a male friend at the mental health center in a different department who happened to be a mentor and a fellow Christian. He urged me to say nothing unless she approached me again. It would be my word against hers if she felt rejected and decided to retaliate. He did encourage me to be kind but firm in declining. Secondly, he urged me to share the exchange with my wife so that she would be aware of the incident in case anything else came up about it. This also set a precedent for a no-secrets arrangement with my wife for any possible future scenarios.

3. THE SEXUAL EXPERIENCE

People who complain of lackluster sex with their spouses desire to experience that passion again.

Some men admit that they primarily cheat because they are seeking a new sexual experience outside their marriage. They think that new sex is good sex. In recent years, it has also become more common for married women to have sex outside their marriages for the same reason. This occurs more frequently because the majority of our workforce is now composed of women. Workplace affairs are the most common affairs (approximately 40 percent) because of the time spent around other people, according to Snyder, Baucom, and Gordon in *Getting Past the Affair*. Many men and women complain of lackluster sex with their spouses and long to experience that passion with someone again.

In the past, men had affairs for sex and women had affairs for love. This is not necessarily the case any longer, especially for younger, recently married women. Some affairs occur within the first year when a couple is adjusting to being married. Others occur when the marriage experiences turbulence. Still others become susceptible to an affair if the marriage has cooled off and lacks passion.

4. A NEED TO BE VALIDATED

The greatest need we have is for acceptance or to be loved; however, some people never seem to receive enough. They have a deep need to be reassured often and by many other people. Early in life, they may not have received the nurturing they needed in order to believe they were acceptable just the way they were. People who are on a constant mission to prove themselves will find self-acceptance elusive. They crave reassurance from others that they are still attractive and sexually desirable. They may attempt to prove this by their sexual conquests. No matter how many people they seduce, it will never be enough to remove their insecurities since the deeper self-esteem issues reside within them.

John had cheated on every person with whom he had ever been involved. When he finally decided to get help, he was with a woman he wanted to marry. However, he had already been sexually involved with other women during their short year together. It seemed no amount of attention from other women could satisfy his deeper emotional emptiness.

5. LONELINESS AND VULNERABILITY OVER A DISAPPOINTING MARRIAGE

Desperate people take desperate measures.

Men are often criticized for pursuing women until they get them, and then ignoring them afterward in pursuit of other things like jobs, status, and accomplishments. In reality, women do the same thing to men for similar reasons, which include securing a family, status, and children. The result for both is inevitably feeling taken for granted. Eventually, the loneliness of not feeling like a priority to one's spouse leads to emotional vulnerability.

In Gary Neuman's book *The Truth about Cheating*, lack of attention and emotional connection was the number-one reason men were unfaithful. Over 90 percent of the men surveyed maintained that emotional dissatisfaction outweighed sexual dissatisfaction as the main reason they cheated.

When we are lonely and vulnerable and another person pays attention to us or thinks we are interesting, we will be flattered.

Quite often, these conversations can drift into discussions about family life and problems at home. This type of personal sharing forges a mutual bond and closeness that can lead to eventually crossing other emotional or sexual boundaries. This is the most common way many inappropriate relationships begin.

6. BOREDOM

Boredom in a relationship has been the cause of many affairs. The routines of life may begin to feel like a treadmill after being married for a few years. Normal responsibilities such as a job, a home, kids, bills, school, and managing commitments begin to feel like a burden. Time together, having fun, dating, and lovemaking are often relegated to a lower priority on our never-ending list of things to do. Day-to-day life starts to feel boring and obligatory.

Meeting an interesting person can be energizing and may make us feel alive again. It can also lead to looking negatively upon our marriage. Further discontentment in a relationship is magnified by imagining how much more fun life could be with someone new.

Why couldn't we have met this person earlier? How would our life have been different?

Boredom in one's current marriage may cause regret or the belief that we made a mistake in the choice of our current spouse. The use of selective memory can magnify marital problems by recalling only the bad times over the good. Rewriting history occurs when the things that are wrong in the relationship are emphasized over the things that are right. The contrast between the idealness of *what could be* in a new relationship and the reality of *what is* in the marriage makes one pale in comparison to the other.

Jack and Jerri were two young professionals with promising careers and two young children. Jack was very involved with his job and traveling regularly to meet with clients. Jerri was trying to balance a demanding career with two children who wanted all of her attention by the end of the day. Eventually, Jerri grew tired of the all-work-and-no-play lifestyle they were living. When a neighbor asked her to join his mixed doubles tennis team, she accepted the opportunity to get to know some other people. It wasn't long before Jerri and her new tennis partner were "working on their game" several nights a week together. Her life with Jack seemed unexciting compared to her time with her new male friend.

Almost all relationships begin with infatuation, where each person idealizes the other. They only see the best in one another and dismiss or ignore any flaws that exist. It is not until after a couple of years does day-to-day life lend perspective to the view of who a person really is. It is unreasonable and at best misguided to compare an older relationship to the potential of a new one. It lacks the validation that being with one person for several years provides. This type of boredom and disillusionment most often occurs in either the first two years of marriage or by midlife.

Individuals who jump from one established relationship into another that they think is better eventually realize that the issues the new relationship faces are similar to the issues that existed in their previous relationship. However, now they must deal with the complications that leaving one person for another causes— the aftermath of divorce and the resulting regrets when the new arrangement doesn't measure up to their expectations.

7. RETALIATION

> "Resentment within a relationship will eventually become retaliatory."
>
> DCW

We have the most conflict with those we love. In a good relationship, this conflict inevitably brings us closer. This is because we find mutual solutions, grow to understand each other, and make adjustments to meet the needs of one another. When a person fails to make those accommodations for the benefit of the relationship, the result is hurt and resentment.

What happens when the person who is supposed to love you most ignores your needs, doesn't listen, and makes you feel like you are not a priority?

You may find ways to ignore them and make them less of a priority as well. The relationship becomes conditional. "If you won't do this for me, I won't do that for you." "If you do something for me, I will do something for you." Keeping score eventually turns into resentment. Resentment in a relationship will eventually become retaliatory.

Wayne and Wanda had been married for almost ten years and had two children together. In addition to his regular job, Wayne played in a band on the weekends. Wanda used to go with him to his gigs, but after a while, it was too difficult to find sitters to watch the children. She was occasionally uncomfortable with the fan club of women that would admire and show interest in Wayne when playing at a venue. He seemed to want the attention of these random women over spending time with her. There were a couple incidents in which she questioned Wayne about how friendly he was toward certain women who came to watch him regularly. He dismissed her concerns and even got defensive. Feeling ignored and discounted, Wanda started having lunch with a male colleague without Wayne's knowledge. They eventually had a brief affair, but it ended without being discovered.

Some couples eventually give up asking for anything from their spouse because it turns into something unpleasant or disappointing. These types of individuals are prime candidates for straying. This is because others will give them the time and attention they crave without begging for it. It is not uncommon when one person discovers that their spouse is cheating to also retaliate by having an affair, too. Retaliatory affairs bring a faltering relationship dangerously close to imploding before anything can be done to repair the damage.

8. A PREVIOUS FLAME OR SOMEONE IN THE PAST

Before social media existed, individuals may have, on occasion, reflected back on previous flames with a combination of fondness and nostalgia. Today's technology enables us to find people we have lost touch with, reconnect, and even pick up where we left off with them. This is often just playing with fire. If we still have feelings for an old flame or entertain the idea of having another chance with them, these overtures could easily damage our marriage relationship. The selective memory of what might have been in the past is almost always a seriously flawed fantasy.

Sam and Monica had a marriage that seemed happy, although he avoided conflict and mostly deferred to Monica. At his thirty-fifth high school reunion, Sam reconnected with an old girlfriend who was recently widowed and lived in another state. They secretly communicated via e-mail, text, and cell phone for about six months. Unbeknownst to Monica, Sam had also visited his former sweetheart on a couple of business trips as well. It was quite a shock when he announced to Monica that he was unhappy and wanted a divorce. It didn't take long to discover that he had been having an affair with his former girlfriend and was planning to start a new life with her.

Individuals who have restarted a relationship with a person they haven't known for twenty or thirty years believe they can recapture an experience they had in their youth. Outside observers often believe that they have lost their minds. These individuals are almost always, in fact, disappointed. In most cases, this is a fantasy that creates incredible hurt and pain for their current family and rarely has a happy ending. Those previous relationships were not successful for a reason, and they generally are not successful later for the same reason.

9. DISINHIBITION

Disinhibition while under the influence is often one of the major contributing factors to affairs. A spouse who drinks excessively or uses recreational drugs may at some point do something impulsive that they regret. Boundaries crossed while under the influence have caused many spouses to be jealous or hurt by this reckless behavior. If imbibing makes a partner more outspoken, flirty, overly affectionate, or lacking in self-control, it may only be a matter of time before some impropriety occurs.

Ron was engaged to Robyn, and they were planning a wedding. One night while drinking with some of his friends at a downtown bar, he met a young, single woman. She found him cute and interesting, and after a dance or two, they ended up kissing. Robyn found out about this incident and immediately called off the engagement.

Some people use these substances to loosen up, and then blame their actions on that influence. We have all heard that a drunk man speaks a sober man's mind. It might also follow than that a drunk man acts on a sober man's mind. Whatever the case, disinhibition is a slippery slope to acting out and a frequent excuse for irresponsible behavior and infidelity.

10. IMPULSE AND EMOTION

> *"'Fast-forwarding' means asking yourself, 'Where is this going?'"*
>
> DCW

While living in the moment is important, acting without thinking can be disastrous. Many affairs begin because intense emotions are stirred and the two people involved act on impulse. That involvement can then become an entanglement from which they cannot easily extricate themselves. They may have realized it is wrong, but keep seeing one other. The other person may relentlessly pursue them and their lover cannot end it. Ironically, discovery of the affair is often a relief because they are forced to choose with whom they want to be.

The ability to "fast-forward" in these situations can mean the difference between getting involved with another person or setting appropriate boundaries with them. I use the term "fast-forward" to get my clients to ask themselves in the moment, "Where is this going?" Steven Covey in his book *The 7 Habits of Highly Successful People* notes that successful people always "begin with the end in mind." If people actually think about what is going on in the moment and where this could end, most would exit quickly. Seeing the big picture can bring about a sobering perspective.

In Genesis 39 of the Old Testament, Joseph, the servant of Potiphar is pursued by his master's wife, and he "flees" to keep anything from happening with her. She still accuses him of coming on to her in retaliation for his rejection of her.

The lesson is not to see how close we can get to the precipice without falling off the cliff, but to back away quickly while we still can.

11. A SECRET PREOCCUPATION WITH PORNOGRAPHY AND SEXUALLY EXPLICIT MATERIAL THAT FUELS LUST AND FANTASY

"What you behold, you become."
Marshall McLuhan

Almost all the research done over the last twenty years in the area of compulsive exposure to pornography and sexually explicit material has determined that it is damaging to a healthy, long-term, intimate relationship. It interferes with an individual's ability to genuinely connect emotionally or sexually with his or her spouse. It short-changes the experience of romance and hampers the feelings of closeness for one another. It also, ironically, contributes to sexual performance problems.

The themes in almost all explicit material involve forbidden fruit, secret encounters, cheating on a spouse, multiple partners, and high-intensity, sexual risk taking. These are intended to fuel the excitement of the experience. When an individual exposes himself to this type of material, his capacity to enjoy just one person for life is heavily eroded. The unfaithfulness may move from fantasy to action. The natural next step is to replace those fantasies with seeking out different people and a variety of other titillating sexual experiences. Most spouses consider this secret foray into an endless pursuit of a pleasure with Internet images as a betrayal. When it leads to face-to-face sexual encounters, many marriages end.

When Dan was in his forties, he was released from a job he had for over fifteen years due to the company downsizing. He spent a lot of time at home trying to find a job using the Internet. It wasn't long before he was looking at pornography online on a regular basis and masturbating to the videos and images. Eventually, he was contacted by instant messages and e-mails to view sites of specific women. They, in turn, invited him to meet with them. He met with several escorts over a period of time until his wife noticed he was draining their bank accounts with unexplained expenditures.

12. A SHY LATE-BLOOMER WHO FINALLY FEELS CONFIDENT

Karl was a guy who never felt that girls found him attractive in school, so he didn't date much. After he married, he finally realized he had a good personality and could be quite entertaining. He traveled with his job and started meeting women with whom he easily connected. It wasn't long before he started having one-night stands with a number of the women he met out of town.

The country singer Toby Keith had a hit song a number of years ago entitled "How Do You Like Me Now?" It is about a guy who had been ignored by a girl he wanted to impress in high school, but she never gave him the time of day.

Chubby, pimply, shy kids who grow up to be successful adults in their own right sometimes wish they could go back and relive their early years. When that wish is played out by seeking out the attention of others, it can seriously damage an otherwise good marriage. The shy late bloomer who finally feels confident is a variation on the need-to-be-validated factor. There is one thing we may not realize until later. The regrets and disappointments from our past can be the catalysts that motivate us to become the best person we can be. Don't live in the past, learn from it. We can't go back, but we can go forward!

13. "IF I DIDN'T SEE OTHER PEOPLE, MY MARRIAGE WOULD END"

This rationalization is often used by high-status individuals, politicians, or wealthy people who would have a great deal to lose if they ever got a divorce. Instead of working on their marriage and taking a hard, honest look at themselves, they blame their spouse for their problems.

Janice was a professional who had been unhappily married for twenty years to someone she cared for, but with whom she was not in love. She owned a successful company with which she was very involved. Her children no longer lived at home, so she was free to travel as regularly as her job demanded. Janice became involved with a colleague in a different state she traveled to often. This relationship helped her tolerate her coexisting marriage that she had no serious intention of leaving.

Individuals who travel often, work in different cities, or have a spouse with an alcohol or substance abuse problem avoid facing their unsatisfactory home life for years by secretly seeing other people. Sometimes they wait until the children leave or their matriarchal or patriarchal parent passes away before actually exiting the marriage to avoid their disapproval. Perhaps a better solution could have been forged had they faced the marital issues sooner, but usually one of them is unwilling. These unsatisfactory marriages are often ignored in hopes that they will eventually get better in the future, but they usually don't.

14. SERIAL CHEATERS ARE OFTEN UNTREATED SEX ADDICTS

Compulsive sex is only demonstrated loneliness.

If you are married to a person who can never have enough sex, he or she probably has a large hole in their soul that they hope sexual experiences will fill. The high that sexual variety generates only makes them less capable of connecting genuinely with anyone except their addiction.

Jim was a ladies' man—well built, charismatic, nice looking, and conversational. He could meet a woman, give her that intoxicating smile, act vulnerable, get them to talk about themselves, and be sexually involved with them in short order. He was a quick study with the social versatility that persuaded most women to drop their guards despite their better judgement. Jim prided himself on his power of perception and persuasion. The problem was that Jim was a sex addict. No amount of success with women was enough. Nothing could fill that hole in his soul. He burned through several marriages and scores of other women who just wanted him to notice them. Jim had everything, and he had nothing.

If you are married or involved with an individual who has a preoccupation with pornography, dating sites, chat rooms, strip clubs, or cheating, know that you are not the problem. You will not change them, and it isn't your fault that they are never satisfied. If you are a spouse who feels he or she can never be satisfied with one person, consider examining your discontentment and its origins. It is probably not your spouse who is responsible for your unhappiness and discontent.

15. THE BELIEF THAT MOST PEOPLE CHEAT

Show me your friends and I'll show you your future.

Some individuals have grown up in families where most of the people they know have at one time or another cheated. Their parents, siblings, aunts, uncles, friends, and acquaintances bounce from one relationship to another, sometimes marrying four to six times. The lifestyle they have observed and become accustomed to is going out on your significant other.

Jim's father was unfaithful to his mother and left her for another woman. When his mother initially discovered the affair, she retaliated with an affair of her own. Even though Jim experienced the upheaval that cheating caused, he has been unfaithful several times during his ten-year marriage.

In a study of one hundred cheating husbands cited in Neuman's *The Truth about Cheating*, it was determined that those with fathers who had cheated once were 50 percent more likely to also cheat in their marriages. Over 75 percent of the men who were unfaithful also had friends who were unfaithful. "Bad company corrupts good character" (1 Corinthians 15:33, NIV).

When times get tough, these individuals find someone else to comfort them. Their lives are chaotic, unstable, and constantly filled with drama. There is little trust or loyalty to be found among them. This pattern gets repeated from generation to generation. These individuals finally begin to settle down in mid- to later life. It is not uncommon for there to be children born from each of these relationships. This further complicates their dire economic plight because of their multiple families. It also leaves their children with a legacy they too will often imitate.

16. AN EARLY HISTORY OF SEXUAL ABUSE
Lessons unlearned are destined to be repeated.

A portion of adults who have been sexually abused as children or teens find a sense of power in their sexual prowess. Having been exposed to sexual promiscuity earlier in life than their peers, they have learned how to wield it effectively in a relationship. Instead of sex being a celebration of the love two people share together, it becomes a means of negotiating to get what one wants. Their ability to connect quickly, although superficially, belies the deeper, damaged person they really are. Their initial portrayal of confidence eventually erodes away to reveal a much more unstable person beneath. Their marriages are often fraught with inconsistencies, mistruths, and irrational volatility that leave the innocent spouse confused and dazed about how to keep this person happy.

Tammy was a twenty-nine-year-old single woman who had lived with several men over a ten-year period. In every relationship, she had eventually become bored or dissatisfied and sought the sexual attention of other men. Tammy did not know why she could not be happy with one person for very long. In counseling, she revealed that her grandfather had sexually molested her for several years as a child. The result of her earlier abuse manifested in her inability to connect emotionally with others, as well as her compulsion to sexually engage with different men for attention and comfort.

17. ENTITLEMENT, INFLUENCE, AND AFFLUENCE

"Talent is God-given. Be humble. Fame is man-given. Be grateful. Conceit is self-given. Be careful."
John Wooden

There is a group of people who have grown up feeling special, favored, and entitled. They have rarely been told no, and they are used to getting what they want. They are sometimes people of means, afforded by their family or by their own personal success. They are often refined individuals who come from prominent families, are in politics, possess high status, and are used to wielding power in their professional lives. They may even be ministers or leaders in a church who are charismatic, well thought of, and highly persuasive. Their narcissism leads them to believe they are entitled to full, unquestioned compliance from the people who work for them. They are able to rationalize having discreet, extramarital relationships. Often, their wives are busy with their own active lives and are completely unaware.

Sometimes, they both have convenient secret relationships with other people that are overlooked and ignored by each other, so as not to disturb the marital status quo. These power couples do not want to lose face or prominence by divorcing, and find it more convenient to accommodate each other's indiscretions with a covert contract. These covert contracts are mutually understood and allow each spouse to have their discretionary private lives. Both look the other way as long as the stability of the arrangement within their marriage is not threatened.

18. A DESIRE TO END THE MARRIAGE

In some unhappy marriages, neither person wants to be the bad guy and ask for a divorce. Neither one seems to know how to straighten out the problems, nor are they ready to be the one to call it quits. This impasse can lead to much volatility or passive-aggressive behavior. One devastating tactic that some spouses use is to have an affair knowing that the other spouse will ultimately discover it. This leads to the offended spouse feeling justified in pursuing a divorce. Sometimes, this is exactly what the cheating spouse had hoped for. Finally, they have something they both agree upon. This strategy is often referred to as an *exit affair*.

Rob had been married for eighteen years to Marsha, who had become child focused, matronly, and appeasing. The spark had left their marriage years ago, but neither was willing to admit it, much less do anything to change it. Rob became involved with someone who was younger, more exciting, and willing to be with an unhappily married man. Eventually, Marsha discovered evidence of his affair and confronted him. To her surprise, he admitted it outright and told her he had been unhappy for a while. He knew she had been unhappy, too. He refused to end the affair, and in her indignation, Marsha filed for divorce. Shortly after the divorce, Rob ended his other relationship, but was not interested in a reconciliation of his marriage.

19. A RIGID, JUDGMENTAL MINDSET WITH BLACK-AND-WHITE THINKING

> *"Their Achilles' heel is unmet needs. Their Waterloo is suppressed emotions denied for years."*
>
> DCW

Jim was an impressive guy—at first glance. He seemed to always be organized, have a plan, and know what he wanted. His strong personality served him well in his profession, and he appeared to be a sure success. However, he was a control freak in his relationships. He always seemed to choose women who were quiet, passive, and timid. They admired him and did whatever he wanted. Eventually, these relationships did not work out. He either got bored or they left him because he was so difficult to get along with.

We admire individuals who are decisive, have strong beliefs and convictions, and will take a stand on relevant issues. However, there are individuals who act like they know it all, have an opinion about everything, believe there are no gray areas, and think almost everything is either right or wrong. They have difficulty accepting that there can be different opinions, perspectives, and preferences that are not necessarily right or wrong. They are almost always in dominant-submissive marriages. These people live in their head and not in their heart. They judge others harshly but seem to rationalize their own actions. This lack of empathy for others keeps them from seeing their own weaknesses. Their arrogance makes them more susceptible to unfaithfulness because they don't acknowledge their limitations.

The more rigid and self-righteous they are, the more likely they are to fall prey to infidelity because their Achilles' heel is unmet needs that they have denied for years. Their Waterloo is the very emotions they have been suppressing, which eventually overtake them at a weak moment and bring about their downfall. When their actions are discovered, they either adamantly deny or demonstrate over-the-top remorse that may, in part, be sincere, but is almost always short lived. They finally redouble their efforts to try and be compulsively perfect again without ever really dealing with their core emotional flaws.

20. A LACK OF RESPECT FOR ONE'S SPOUSE

Successful marriages occur between two people who are equals and respect each other. Individuals who are in marriages with passive partners eventually lose respect for them. A passive spouse doesn't express their wants and desires. A spouse who is conflict avoidant eventually loses their voice and their vote in the marriage. Their abdication forces their husband or wife to run things on their own.

In some cases, it is a domineering spouse who wears their partner down emotionally over time to the point of withdrawing. They often conclude that it is futile to try and reason with someone who is always insistent on their way. These conflict-avoidant, parent-child relationships are eventually destined for disillusionment.

Tony has been married three times, and in each of his marriages, his wife has cheated on him. He was a nice guy, didn't ask for much, and hated any kind of conflict. He would rather go along to get along. His tendency to be easygoing, compliant, and low key had lost him the respect of each of his former wives. Although he thought he was being a good spouse, his lack of engaging in the face of differences caused his wives to lose respect. They saw him as boring. He grew up in a family with constant drama, so he decided he was not going to repeat that in his family. Unfortunately, his reluctance to weigh in on what he wanted or needed in his marriages created another type of dynamic. His former wives felt that he just didn't care that much about them, so they found someone who did.

Ironically, both of these types of partners have a high probability of straying in their marriage. The domineering spouse who loses respect for their partner may eventually find a more interesting, independent-thinking person who is closer to their equal. Similarly, the spouse who has become a doormat may meet someone who pays attention to them and makes them feel like they actually have something to offer.

21. A HISTORY OF CHEATING WHEN SINGLE

Joan had cheated on almost every boyfriend she ever had. When times were tough in a relationship, she managed to find someone else who was easier to be with and more interesting, at least initially. She wanted all the good times and none of the difficulties that all relationships inevitably had.

Individuals who have a history of cheating while dating or in committed relationships are more likely to continue that pattern into their marriages. They seem to always be looking for the next-best thing. They never seem to be satisfied with what they have, and they get bored easily with others. They do not realize that their lack of contentment is really about themselves, not others. They are much like chronic shopaholics who are on a quest for another gadget or item of clothing to make them feel better. The emotional void within is often a result of their childhood, where things were more valued than people. Who you were with was more important than who you were.

When times get tough in their relationships, they get going—in search of someone else. However, they rarely leave until they have the next-best thing lined up. Young guys and girls who always had a significant other or who could never be alone in high school and college are the typical prototype. They make others feel that they do not measure up, while the real problem is that they do not feel they measure up.

SEVEN OF THE MOST COMMON SOCIAL INFLUENCES THAT ENCOURAGE INFIDELITY

Just because everyone is doing it doesn't make it right.

On September 11, 2001, four airline jets were hijacked by terrorists, resulting in the destruction of the Twin Towers in New York City, damage to the Pentagon, and another plane crashing in Pennsylvania. In all, a total of almost three thousand people were killed. Over four hundred firefighters and policemen were casualties as well. Following this tragedy, the other local firefighters and policeman embraced and supported the families of their lost comrades. All these families gladly sacrificed to help the widows and their children cope with their horrific losses. Several years later, an unexpected outcome of these generous overtures occurred. Dozens of firefighters and policemen left their own families and married their lost comrades' widows. The trauma they had shared together had bonded them emotionally in ways that had never been anticipated. The 9/11 tragedy highlighted how powerful sociologic influences can affect our society for better and worse. This attack brought our country together, but it also tore some families apart.

Infidelity is openly disapproved of in our society. When an individual who cheats on his spouse is discovered, family, friends, and peers disagree with their behavior. Though our moral position on unfaithfulness seems very clear, certain social influences exist that serve to weaken personal convictions about fidelity. These influences present challenges to maintaining faithfulness, even though we may not see a direct correlation.

Here are some social practices and rationalizations that tend to contribute to infidelity being a greater option for some.

1. *Always Wanting More*
   "Folks are usually about as happy as they make their minds up to be."

   Abraham Lincoln

Our lack of contentment with what we have often drives us to be dissatisfied. We have become consumers with an insatiable desire to have the next-best thing. Whether it is a bigger flat-screen TV, a larger house, a faster car, or the newest computer, we seem to long for the latest and greatest.

Jake Owens, the country singer, wrote a song entitled "What We Ain't Got." It talks about wanting what we don't have.

We covet what we do not have, and our competitiveness causes us to extend ourselves in ways that jeopardize our very well-being. When the desire for more involves wanting someone who is more attractive, has greater status, is younger, or who makes us feel good about ourselves, we are tempted to risk what we have for what we don't have.

There was a man who left his wife of many years for a high school sweetheart he had not seen in years but reconnected with at a high school reunion. He moved in with his high school sweetheart, only to discover she wasn't the person he remembered her to be at eighteen. Within six months, he was regretting his decision to leave his wife and friends for what might have been.

How much money is enough? Probably just a little bit more. Finding contentment in who we are, what we have, and who we are with is a task we must each face in life. Our society would have us believe nothing is ever enough. Envy is a waste of time. The challenge is in enjoying what we already have instead of worrying about what we don't.

2. *Our Lack of Boundaries*
> *"Like a city whose walls are broken through, is a man who lacks self-control."*
>
> Proverbs 25:28 (NIV)

"It was an accident. I never meant for this to happen!" We live in a society that lacks boundaries. We do not like restraints, limits, or others telling us what we can or cannot do. So we often allow ourselves to get into situations that move us closer to the proverbial edge and then wonder how we got there.

Andy Stanley's book, *The Principle of the Path*, cites examples of individuals who were totally surprised at their circumstances and how they ended up where they were. People whose spending habits exceed their incomes can end up losing their homes or cars. People who flirt or are sexually provocative can put themselves in compromising situations that lead to actions they regret for a lifetime. Individuals who drink too much and drive under the influence may get a DUI or even harm someone else. They may be arrested, suffer lawsuits, face financial ruin, or even risk being sentenced to prison.

Samson was reportedly the strongest man who ever lived, but he would not say no to Delilah. No matter how strong a man or woman is in certain areas of their lives, they can easily lose sight of their personal boundaries and principles if their weakness is the opposite sex. No one travels down these paths expecting the worst to happen, but it can. Sometimes good people take unnecessary risks because they lack boundaries and use poor judgment in the moment.

Similarly, many affairs begin innocently by individuals who get into compromising situations that result in outcomes that change their lives forever.

3. *Our Have-It-Your-Way Society*
> *"To each his own." "Live and let live." "It's my right to choose."*

Who doesn't want their way? We all do, and we live in a society that reinforces that philosophy. Many people have grown up in families where parents have made many sacrifices for their children to have what they want and need. When these children become adults, they still act as if they should have it their way.

Most people believe that it is our individual right to do what feels good to us. We do not think anyone should dictate morality because we want to choose for ourselves. In America, we are very protective of individual rights and our right to choose the lifestyle we prefer. That privilege can, however, become our rationale to do whatever we want to do without considering the impact it has upon others.

Tim grew up the youngest son in his family. No one ever said no to him, so he was able to do whatever he wanted to do. He was irresponsible, messy, and expected others to overlook his shortcomings. Ironically, he married a very responsible wife who started complaining about his bad habits, but he laughed it off and ignored her pleas. Eventually, he grew frustrated with a wife who actually expected him to act like an adult. He found a free-spirited woman who thought he was cute and fun to be with. She didn't expect him to change. Tim's unwillingness to accept responsibility for himself led to an affair that almost cost him his marriage.

Our individual choices will naturally affect others, for better or worse, when we get married and have a family. Our individual decisions should be made jointly, as a couple, for the good of all. We have to learn to transition from *thinking like an individual* to *thinking like a couple* because of the impact our actions have upon those we love. It is most likely a good decision if the decision we make benefits everyone in our immediate life. If that decision has risks of negative consequences, a joint determination should be made.

4. The Media Has Romanticized Affairs
Marriages are made, not born.

We have all seen the movies about couples who have fallen out of love or believed they married the wrong person. As the plot unfolds, they finally find someone with whom they can truly be themselves or experience passion. These stories are effective in eliciting our sympathy for the plight of the unhappily married person who now has a chance at true love. It causes us to unwittingly collude with this person to encourage them to go find what makes them happy.

People who believe they are with the wrong person often don't take responsibility for not being the right type of person. These individuals are at a greater risk of looking outside their marriage for the answers to their problems.

"In a lawsuit the first to speak seems right, until someone comes forward and cross-examines" (Proverbs 18:17, NIV). In my experience, there is always another side that adds greater perspective and a reality check to what initially sounds like an unfortunate and unfair plight.

Everyone deserves to be happy, but the reality of relationships is that marriages are made, not born. People make their happiness by give-and-take and by mutually trying to please each other. It is not just about having the right person in our lives, it is about being the right person. Being "there" is not better than being "here" because wherever we go, *we* will still be there.

5. Technologies That Allow Us to Remain Anonymous

I often tell my clients to always conduct themselves in a manner as if they are wearing a baseball cap with a video camera and microphone attached, streaming directly to their spouse. When held accountable for everything said and done, most act differently than they would otherwise. People are prone to making decisions based upon impulse or the immediate influences they are exposed to at the moment, unless some accountability exists.

Technology has provided people with the opportunity to act remotely, independently, and anonymously so that we sometimes act without thinking. People can fly under the radar of detection with tools like cell phones that are password protected; untraceable, throwaway phones; unlimited e-mail address options; websites that allow us to create profiles and portray ourselves in any way we choose; and software programs that hide our text messages. This anonymity is more than some people can handle without making poor choices. According to a 2015 survey of the American Academy of Matrimonial Lawyers, 97 percent of the members said they had seen an increase in evidence taken from smartphones and other wireless devices during the past three years.

6. Changing Values

> *"A lie doesn't become truth, wrong doesn't become right, and evil doesn't become good just because it's accepted by the majority."*
> Rick Warren

Throughout history, there has existed societal pressure to be more broad minded and relax certain commonly held values and beliefs. Some of these values needed reforming as they were oppressive to gender equality and discriminated against different races. However, some of the changes in values that have occurred have arguably been harmful to the stability of marriage and the family.

Having the right to choose how we live our lives is one of the freedoms we cherish in America. However, some individual choices become destructive when they harm others. Everything we do has a direct or indirect impact upon someone, even if we do not see it initially. The phrase "live and let live" sounds good until we see the negative implications of allowing people to do whatever they feel like doing. This is precisely what an anarchy is: a state of disorder due to the absence of authority.

It is each person's right to divorce their spouse, have a relationship with another person while still married, or to leave one's children to embark on what appears to be a more attractive lifestyle. When a society begins moving toward these practices at an increasingly frequent rate, someone has to live with the consequences of those actions. What may initially seem appealing may eventually become more destructive than anyone intended.

7. The Ashley Madison Influence

"If you don't stand for something, you will fall for anything."
Peter Marshall

There are organizations and businesses whose purpose is to promote and financially benefit from any alternative lifestyle in which people would like to engage. They portray an acceptance of anything and everything that a consenting adult might have the desire to do under the guise of openness and broadmindedness. However, they have their own motives that serve their premeditated personal agendas. If disagreed with, one might find themselves subject to being labeled close minded, inhibited, or moralistic. In some cases, dissenters are subjected to lawsuits.

Examples of these groups include AshleyMadison.com for married people who want to cheat, swinging groups who are married but engage in spouse swapping, escort dating services that are primarily higher-class prostitutes who will spend time with a customer for a price, cougar sites that promote older women teaching younger men what real women want, and sex clubs where anyone can participate in group sex while other patrons watch. Unlimited opportunities to participate in the activity of one's choice are also offered by gentlemen's clubs (strip clubs), the porn industry, chat rooms, and gay pick-up sites for married men.

Each of these alternative lifestyles plays a part in sending a message to couples that monogamy is outdated, boring, and overrated. The result is that more and more people are exploring options that can be devastating and destructive to marriages, families, and commitment as we know it.

HOMEWORK EXERCISE

Checklist: Twenty-Eight Reasons Why We Cheat

Cheating sometimes occurs because of personal factors that exist in one's life. Sometimes, people cheat because of the social influences around them. Below are some influences that contribute to making people more vulnerable to infidelity. Check the factors that you believe contributed to your situation. When both individuals take this separately, the answers provide an interesting contrast in perceptions about why the infidelity occurred.

○ Feeling underappreciated
○ An opportunity presented itself
○ The sexual experience
○ A need to be validated
○ Loneliness and vulnerability over a disappointing marriage
○ Boredom
○ Retaliation, resentment
○ A previous flame or someone in the past
○ Disinhibition caused by drinking or other substances
○ Impulse and emotion
○ A secret preoccupation with pornography and sexually explicit material
○ A shy late-bloomer who finally feels confident
○ "If I didn't see other people, my marriage would end."
○ An untreated sexual addiction
○ A belief that most people cheat
○ An early history of sexual abuse
○ Entitlement, influence, and affluence
○ A desire to end the marriage
○ A rigid, judgmental mindset with black-and-white thinking
○ A loss of respect for my spouse
○ A history of cheating when single
○ Always wanting more
○ A lack of boundaries

○ A right to be happy
○ Fell in love
○ The temptation of technology
○ My values changed
○ A right to my own lifestyle

CHAPTER 3

WHAT KIND OF AFFAIR IS IT?

FIVE NEW PROPOSED DIAGNOSTIC CATEGORIES OF AFFAIRS

The next five chapters will present a new nomenclature for categorizing the wide variety of affairs that exists today. There are currently no models that organize these affairs into a coherent way of thinking about them. Most authors of previous books and articles on affairs will cite five or six types of affairs they have dealt with over the years.

In over thirty years of practicing, I have been able to identify twenty-eight types of affairs that are subsumed under five distinct categories of affairs. Below is a description of each category and type of affair, with clinical examples to further define each in practical detail. This is an attempt to bring to light the proliferation of infidelity in our society and how insidious an influence it really is having on the institution of marriage.

It is a growing problem with younger adults who have appeared to enter marriage with the expectation that divorce is inevitable at some point. Couples over fifty have also become a high-risk group, as their marriages tend to be unsatisfactory, coexistent, or roommate arrangements. They often have the financial means to walk away, often citing that they deserve to finally be happy in life. Affairs have become their exit strategy.

CATEGORY 1: IMPULSE AFFAIRS

"You can do something in an instant that will give you heartache for life."

Ryaj Ablando Catayas

When an affair is discovered, most people want to understand why it happened, what caused it, and how it came about. Trying to make sense of an affair by attempting to understand it only offers limited comfort. However, knowing is half the battle. It is the emotional upheaval that is so difficult to manage for most people.

Below represents an effort to add some meaning to the most common types of affairs that occur.

Impulse affairs typically refer to unplanned, spur-of-the-moment encounters that lead to sexual involvement, typically between at least one married or committed person and another individual. They are often opportunistic and occur in anonymous circumstances where their discovery would be difficult to detect. People who travel in their jobs are often susceptible to these moments of reckless abandon. Many times, alcohol has fueled the inhibition of acting on the impulse. There is usually no agenda, goal, or plan for a relationship. It is just sex for sex's sake. It may be brief or turn into something more involved, given the impulsive, passionate nature of the affair. Impulse affairs include one-night stands, retaliatory cheating, and cheating while dating or engaged.

1. One-Night Stands

Probably the most common and underreported affairs are the one-night stands. These represent chance encounters between people who often do not know each other and may never see one another again. They most often occur anonymously, in out-of-town situations where detection by others is not likely. Two people may meet at a bar, a party, trade show, on a business trip, or on vacation. They talk briefly, hit it off, drink too much, and end up in a motel room or the back of a car. Names and numbers are generally not exchanged, and they often go their separate ways. These rendezvous are usually not detected and go unnoticed because of their anonymity and brevity. They are chance hookups that no one talks about. They are impulsive, spur-of-the-moment encounters that are for the most part untraceable.

Participants in one-night affairs are often guilty, embarrassed, and ashamed because they truly do love their spouses. However, they may be bored in their marriage or vulnerable to the attention of the opposite sex, who may think they are interesting and desirable.

Jack traveled almost weekly for his sales job. He entertained clients often and enjoyed the association with new and different people. During an unexpected layover, Jack stopped in the lounge at his hotel for a nightcap. He noticed a young, attractive woman who made eye contact with him and seemed friendly. Before long, they began chatting, and one thing led to another before the evening was over. They never even exchanged numbers or last names, so there was little chance that the encounter that night would ever be discovered.

Once an individual experiences this type of affair, he or she may be likely to try it again or on occasion get back in touch with the other person for additional contact. At this point, the one-night stand can turn into a different kind of affair depending on the circumstances—for example, an exploratory affair.

When a spouse discovers that a one-night affair occurred, they are, of course, devastated. However, the recovery time is not as extended as those affairs where a relationship has developed.

2. Retaliatory Affairs

Jackie had always been uncomfortable with Don having female friends because of how much time he spent texting and talking to them. Jackie felt it was inappropriate for a married man to be as emotionally invested in other women as he seemed to be. Don would typically dismiss her concerns. When she discovered he had been cheating on her with several of these women, she felt like a fool and was enraged for having been fooled by his lies. They separated briefly, and she had her own affair with one of his best male friends during their time apart. He was incensed that she would intentionally go out on him.

Retaliatory affairs are impulsive reactions from a wronged spouse that are intended to punish their partner. Their partner may have hurt them by being emotionally unavailable or by treating the wronged spouse poorly for years. They may have been physically absent because of their workaholic tendencies, or perhaps they were unfaithful themselves.

These couples generally have one of two different styles of conflict. They are high-conflict couples who escalate their differences by trying to win at the expense of the other. Their stormy exchanges sometimes result in one cheating on the other. When the affair is discovered, the wronged partner promptly has an affair of their own.

The second style is one of conflict avoidance. They don't really openly argue, but their differences are rarely resolved. They internalize their differences, sweep things under the rug, become resentful, and gradually grow apart. Both of these partners are at high risk for finding someone else and justifying the infidelity because of the unhappiness they have had together.

Joe and Jean had only been married a couple of years when Joe discovered that Jean had been having an affair with her older, married, politically prominent boss. Joe was hurt and angered by this betrayal and reacted by going to a bar, meeting a woman there, and going home with her that night. This action and reaction set the stage for the eventual unraveling of their marriage and their subsequent divorce.

3. Cheating-While-Dating Affairs

Sue and Stan were high school sweethearts. During their early relationship together, Sue had sex with several guys who paid special attention to her. Stan would always forgive Sue and take her back because she seemed so remorseful. They eventually married. Later in their marriage, he discovered she was sleeping with an old boyfriend she had reconnected with over social media.

When one of the individuals in a committed dating relationship cheats, this triggers one of the first major crises that a couple will face together. Relationships that begin with one person cheating on the other have a more difficult time ever building trust together. If they eventually marry, the distrust interferes with the normal bonding that a committed relationship requires.

Marriages that begin with one partner cheating during the time they dated have some predictable challenges to overcome.

- Their original commitment to the relationship has already been broken at least once.
- Trust levels are not as high as a couple who has been faithful to each other from the beginning.
- Security and safety between these individuals is not as solidly established generally.
- The ability to be fully open and vulnerable with one's partner occurs at a slower pace.

Jack and Jill met and started dating while they were in college. She believed after six months of dating that their relationship was exclusive. During this time, he had a brief, clandestine encounter with another woman that Jill discovered eventually. They worked through it, stayed together, and later married. However, the first years of their marriage were fraught with insecurity, doubt, and distrust on the part of Jill, especially when Jack traveled for his job. She monitored his whereabouts, insisted on regular calls from him during the day, and had to hear from him when he returned to his hotel room, no matter what time of the night. His earlier cheating with another girl set in motion some difficult hurdles for their marriage to overcome.

When a relationship begins with cheating by one or both parties, how likely is it to succeed? It is doubtful, if the relationship was understood by both parties to be a committed and exclusive one. The central concern would be, with what personal problems is the unfaithful person dealing?

Those issues might include:
- their own personal insecurities and search for validation through attention from others
- their own fear of commitment
- their doubts about the person they are allegedly committed to

4. Engagement Affairs

Sid and Leslie had dated while in college. Sid graduated first and took a job in another city while Leslie finished her degree. It was difficult being away from each other, but they tried to see one another monthly. During her last year of college, they became engaged and were planning to get married upon graduating. On two occasions during her last semester of school, she was out with friends at a club, having wine and socializing, and ended up kissing different guys who were flirting with her.

Engagement affairs often happen with younger people in their twenties or thirties and generally represent a fear of commitment. This type of affair may reflect ambivalence and doubt about getting married or the person they are marrying. Sometimes it involves regret about the prospect of never being with another person again besides their future spouse. These affairs sometimes occur during bachelor or bachelorette weekends, or they may involve a final fling with an old ex.

On occasion, it might result from the reaction of a secret admirer who feels they have one last chance to express their unrequited love. It may also be the result of someone coveting the relationship someone else has and wanting it for themselves. This is often referred to as *partner poaching*. If the encounter is discovered, the engagement could be off. These incidents always damage the young couple's first year of marriage, whether detected or not, because of the doubt they generate within the cheating party.

Tom and Carol had dated for two years and were engaged to be married in ten months. Over the holidays, Tom went home to visit his parents and ran into an old girlfriend he had broken up with in college while out with some buddies. She had heard he was engaged, but she still had feelings for him. After a few drinks, they went to her apartment and slept together. Tom immediately regretted his actions but rationalized that it was just one final fling before he was with one person forever. After Tom's return, Carol found a text on Tom's phone from the other woman that said, "I'll never forget that night together."

CHAPTER 4

CATEGORY 2: PROXIMITY AFFAIRS

It is not uncommon to forge relationships with the people we spend the most time with. If we share common interests and enjoy the same things, it is only natural to feel inclined to seek them out. Similarities seem to always bring others together and foster admiration and fondness. People who spend a great deal of time together, but lose sight of appropriate boundaries between each other, can easily end up in potentially compromising situations. This slippery slope of attraction can go undetected until friendly feelings for one another turn into something more. These affairs are often accidental but wreak much havoc because of the number of other people who are impacted. They usually occur between friends, family, or coworkers. Proximity affairs include emotional, close-friend, celebrity, mate-poaching, and workplace affairs.

5. *Emotional Affairs*

Jill was a happily married young mother who was very involved in her neighborhood. Her husband was ambitious and spent a great deal of time building his career and reputation on his job at an advertising agency. Jill met Tony through the neighborhood association, where they served on a committee together. Tony was a nice guy and the father of two young daughters as well. He asked her to help him coach the girls' soccer team, as all their girls played competitively. Over time, Jill and Tony were together more regularly, serving on committees and neighborhood projects. They communicated often and got along very well. Jill found herself thinking of Tony more fondly and even comparing him to her husband. It wasn't long before she was looking forward to seeing Tony and finding reasons to talk to him. She became more critical of her husband, who seemed to be preoccupied with other things outside the family.

An emotional affair is when a married or committed partner gets their emotional needs met by someone outside their relationship. It usually begins slowly and innocently enough as a friendship or work relationship. However, it eventually blossoms into a strong attachment fueled by fantasy and anticipation. The irrational contrast between the fantasies of what could be causes the reality of a day-to-day, long-term marriage to pale in comparison.

Below is a typical scenario that can occur in a marriage that has previously been stable.

Ken was a happily married man with grown children. In high school, he had been infatuated with a girl named Susan with whom he was close friends but never dated. He saw Susan years later at a social function, danced with her, and immediately had strong feelings for her. At his twenty-fifth high school reunion, he saw her again, they talked, danced, and the attraction seemed mutual. Ken found her on Facebook and began following her posts. They began instant messaging each other often, and their previously close friendship was reignited. He was tempted to contact her and share his feelings for her. He also noticed that his feelings for his wife began to diminish.

If you wonder whether your feelings for another person have become too strong, take the following test to determine if you are at risk for an emotionally inappropriate relationship.

HOMEWORK EXERCISE

Inventory: Signs of an Emotional Affair

Please read the items below and circle each sign that is occurring. The greater the number of items circled, the more likely an emotional affair is present.

1. You can't stop thinking about the person.
2. You find yourself preferring the company of the person over your partner.
3. The time you spend together is increasing.
4. You find yourself sharing intimate details.
5. You hide the relationship from your partner.
6. You dress up before you see the person.
7. Intimacy with your partner decreases.
8. You discuss frustrations about your partner with your friend.
9. You really understand each other.
10. You start contacting each other outside friendship hours.
11. He or she gives you butterflies.
12. It is difficult to concentrate when he or she is around.
13. You start having fantasies or dreams about your friend.
14. You would be upset if the situation were reversed with your partner.

Total _____
(*A total of six or more may indicate a potential problem.*)
(Adapted from *14 Signs You Have Crossed into an Emotional Affair*, 9/12/15 by Goodtherapy.org Staff.)

6. Close-Friend Affairs

> *"Best-friend affairs are often the most devastating because of the sheer number of people who are adversely impacted by it."*
>
> DCW

Affairs between close friends are more of a common occurrence than most people realize. Individuals who are similar socially and personality wise, share the same interests, and are at the same socioeconomic level will naturally be drawn to one another. Affairs of these types are probably the most devastating because of the sheer number of people who are adversely impacted by them.

Imagine two sets of married best friends who do everything together, live in the same neighborhood, go on vacations with their kids together, and share holidays. What happens when an affair occurs between one of the partners in each marriage? The couples, the kids, their friends, the neighborhood, their church friends, and even their extended family members are negatively impacted. Everyone is hurt and stunned. How do their friends now relate to these families? How can their extended families make sense of this? How will this change the relationships among all of them?

Tony and Sarah had been best friends with Terry and Sandy for over ten years. Their children were close in ages, and they were regular playmates. They lived in adjoining neighborhoods and even went to the same church. Their families were accustomed to taking vacations together occasionally, as well. Tony came home early one day from the office before picking up the kids. He found Sarah and Terry in bed together. He was stunned and immediately became sick to his stomach. Their whole world fell apart in the subsequent months as both families were torn apart from the affair.

Even if the couples stay together, their lives and relationships will never be the same. Some families move out of their neighborhoods or out of town, their kids change schools, they attend different churches or not at all, and sometimes even change jobs. The situation is even more acrimonious if the two individuals involved in the affair try to start a new life together after leaving their respective spouses.

A relatively new but more frequently occurring phenomenon is one in which two married best girlfriends leave their husbands for each other. These are often young women with children who may have endured a disappointing ten-to-fifteen-year marriage. Their husbands are often preoccupied with their work, emotionally disconnected, perfectionistic, self-absorbed, rigid, and controlling.

These women have been there for each other through thick and thin and have treated one another with more consideration than their husbands ever have. Once the relationship becomes sexual, it causes them to question why they need to put up with their husbands when they have someone who meets all their needs emotionally and otherwise. The reactions of husbands, friends, family members, and children often cause these women to abort their plans and work on their marriages. In some cases, there is too much damage to the marital relationship, and divorce is inevitable even if the best-friend affair ends.

In some cases, the women or men who leave their spouses for a same-sex partner have struggled with their own sexual identity for years or have entered into a heterosexual marriage in an attempt to hide their sexual identity conflicts. These actually represent sexual identity affairs.

7. Celebrity Affairs or "Love the One You're With" Affairs

> *"Death and Destruction are never satisfied, and neither are human eyes."*
>
> Proverbs 27:20 (NIV)

What do Sharon Stone and Arnold Schwarzenegger, Jason Aldean and *American Idol* contestant Brittany Kerr, Jane Fonda and Ted Turner, Tori Spelling and Dean McDermott, LeAnn Rimes and Eddie Cibrian, Fergie and Josh Duhamel, Tiger Woods and Elin Nordegren, Sandra Bullock and Jesse James, Kristen Stewart and Robert Pattinson,

Reese Witherspoon and Ryan Phillipe, Hugh Grant and Divine Brown, and Matt LeBlanc and Melissa McKnight have in common?

At least one of the partners was allegedly in an affair while married to someone else.

How do people handle being famous and recognized wherever they go, wealthy by most people's standards, knowing other important people, traveling to exciting places, and feeling self-important? It might cause them to think more highly of themselves than they should. It could cause them to believe that standard social mores don't apply to them. A false sense of security could impair their better judgment.

Celebrity affairs are often impulsive, opportunistic, in the moment, and emotional. They have passion and intensity but often lack depth and the test of time. They serve the function of being a mutual-admiration society or a trading-up strategy.

Although celebrities have insecurities like everyone else, they lose sight of reality when inundated with attention, adoration, status, and fame. Those who succumb to their narcissistic need to be more famous may actually believe they are as great as others say they are. The opportunity to rub shoulders with other equally or more famous people proves too much of a temptation for many. It is a fast-paced life full of big egos, lavishness, and ambitious people who will do anything to promote their careers. A question often considered when trying to get established is *Who do you have to sleep with to get ahead?* Sometimes a celebrity will marry someone who themselves just wants to get ahead. They may be smitten by the image of who that celebrity is. Eventually, they discover that their celebrity spouse is just a talented entertainer with their own insecurities and faults. Their newly acquired status can be used to their advantage in seeking the company of other celebrities.

Celebrities seem to be vulnerable to affairs and multiple marriages because they often fall in love with the entertainers with whom they work. They may be star struck, or they may see this new person as a better match to help advance their career. Problems often occur when both people are climbing the ladder of success and one of their careers plateaus or fades. Since the relationship has been built on mutual admiration and making each other look good, in many cases the depth of the love that actually exists is ultimately tested and often found to be lacking.

8. Mate-Poaching or Coveting Affairs

> *"You shall not covet your neighbor's wife."*
> Deuteronomy 5:21 (NIV)

Mate poaching refers to individuals who want to be involved with someone who is already in a relationship. He or she covets that relationship and tries to hijack it for themselves. Mate poaching has traditionally occurred between an older, successful man who pursues a younger, married woman in the workplace. This type of affair often ravages newly married young couples who are struggling to adapt to each other and the challenges of being a married couple.

Another variation of mate poaching occurs when a similarly aged, single peer befriends a married individual and secretly competes with their unaware spouse for the coveted person's attention and admiration.

Tony and Cindy had been recently married. He was attending graduate school while she worked as a teacher to support them. Tony had a demanding class and study schedule that left Cindy often on her own. As a teacher, she had more time off on holidays and during the summer, and she often felt lonely. A single guy who owned his own business lived in the complex near them. He often saw Cindy out by the pool and at the gym when she exercised. It wasn't long before he engaged her in a conversation and a friendship ensued. He was in a position to not only give her his time and attention, but a more appealing lifestyle. It wasn't long before he had convinced her to separate from her husband for a more immediate relationship with him.

In recent years, it has become more common to find younger single women pursuing established, older, married men. Although these women might not want a permanent relationship, they do want the attention and accompanying fringe benefits. A married man is able to give her all she wants financially with no strings attached. These arrangements are also safer because these men generally want to preserve their existing marriage. Both parties can get what they want without the demands of a commitment.

John and Julie had been friends for years before they both met again after their divorces. They eventually married, and their children were grown. John started having problems on his job, and a female colleague was sympathetic with how unfairly he was being treated, so they began talking regularly. Before long, they were talking on the phone and meeting for lunch, and they became emotionally and sexually involved. He felt guilty and embarrassed but couldn't say no to his colleague's pursuit of him. She made him feel like he could do anything at a time when he was experiencing serious self-doubt. She never pressed him for a life together, so he went along willingly. He loved his wife, but no one had ever made him feel so confident about himself, especially during this very difficult time professionally. He tried not to think about what he would do if this relationship was discovered.

9. Workplace Affairs

> "Keeping work at work and one's personal life elsewhere is a good rule of thumb."
>
> DCW

Approximately 40 percent of affairs begin at work, according to Gary Neuman, who wrote the book *The Truth about Cheating*. This is not surprising, given that the workplace is almost equally occupied by men and women. Attachments will likely develop when people who have similar interests and talents spend eight to ten hours five days a week with each other. The mutual respect that occurs between colleagues can easily turn into a friendship. These friendships can deepen into feelings of affection and more.

The increased chance for workplace affairs occurs when certain boundaries are ignored and crossed. Opportunities to forge a more intimate relationship with others at work are most likely to happen with certain types of activities. These include lunching with an opposite-sex colleague regularly instead of in a group; going out of town together to business meetings; having adjoining hotel rooms; sharing personal calls, e-mails, and texts; making lingering eye contact; talking about problems in one's marriage; business dinners that include drinking; any type of touch besides a handshake; and correspondence that is suggestive and flirtatious.

Jeannie was a female manager in a male-dominated industry. She was very competent, but she could be impatient with subordinates and played favorites. Jeannie and another married staff member became intimately involved during a business retreat. When she fired an underperforming employee, he threatened to go to her boss and tell him about her affair at work if she didn't reinstate him. Her job was at risk as well as her marriage, so she eventually left her position and moved to another company. Her professional reputation was badly damaged through the process.

Keeping work at work and one's personal life elsewhere is a good rule of thumb. Sometimes employees welcome boundary violations because it is a way to receive special attention from those who can advance their careers. Trying to get ahead by unethical behavior may prove beneficial initially, but it is often at a great cost professionally and personally in the long run. Some employees are afraid to draw the line on certain practices for fear of falling out of favor with colleagues or even losing their jobs. They may eventually find that they are at a greater risk of losing their marriage due to an insidious workplace affair.

10. In-Law Affairs

Jim was married and had two small children when he found himself attracted to his wife's married cousin, who lived nearby with her husband. They shared similar interests in playing tennis and jogging, so they began spending more time together. Eventually, the relationship became physical, and they decided they were in love. Almost overnight, they each divorced their spouses and moved out of state to begin a new life together. They cut ties with their family and were not heard from again.

One of the most disruptive types of affairs is the in-law affair. The infidelity occurs between individuals who are related to each other by law. Examples might include a sibling who becomes intimately involved with his or her sibling's spouse, a cousin who has sex with another cousin's spouse, an aunt who becomes intimate with a niece's husband, or an uncle who is involved with a nephew's wife. The rarest cases involve a parent who becomes intimately involved with an adult child's spouse. These typically occur in dysfunctional families who lack boundaries and tolerate alcohol and substance abuse among their family members. A high frequency of divorce is not uncommon with these individuals, who may marry as many as five or six times. In more recent years, it has become more common to just live together instead of getting married.

Alice was unlucky in love and had been divorced twice after brief marriages. She decided to move closer to her older sister, Carey, and start her life over. Alice lived temporarily with Carey and her husband, Ron, while looking for a job. Ron was very helpful in finding Alice job opportunities that she would interview for, and they quickly became very close. Ron worked from home while his wife, Carey, taught school. It was not long before Ron and Alice were sharing more than an interest in her job search. When Carey discovered their affair, she was devastated that the two people she loved the most could do that to her. Alice was asked to leave, and Ron and Carey entered couples therapy.

11. *Family and Genetic Sexual-Attraction Affairs (GSA)*

The most disastrous type of infidelity is the family affair because the two people involved are biologically related to each other. Common examples of family affairs are between cousins, an uncle and his niece, and an aunt and her nephew, to name a few. These sexual relationships are often considered incestuous and are socially taboo.

Tammy was the office manager in a doctor's office in a small rural town. She was in her third unhappy marriage and was looking for a change. While attending a training conference in a nearby larger city, she ran into a cousin who was the oldest son of her father's sister. Her cousin, Tony, was not very happy in his marriage, either, so they started talking regularly by phone. Talking about their marriages actually helped them feel supported, and it bonded them together emotionally as well.

Eventually, they became sexually involved and rendezvoused together periodically for seven years while remaining unhappily married.

Biologically related family members who get intimately involved with each other create problems that affect the entire family. The animosity and divisiveness it causes splits the family into factions that may never be repaired. Furthermore, incest in a family leaves a legacy of shame and embarrassment that is never forgotten.

Rhianna had always had a crush on her Uncle Sam, who was the youngest brother of her mother. When Sam and his wife moved into Rhianna's neighborhood, everyone was excited to have family so close. Rhianna's husband traveled every week for his job, so he was gone regularly. Uncle Sam was very handy and available to help her out periodically when something around the house needed to be repaired. It wasn't long before they were seeing each other regularly, and the ten-year difference between them became insignificant. Their affair lasted for only six months, but they kept it a secret for thirty years. Every once in a while, a family member would comment on how much Rhianna's thirty-year-old son looked like Uncle Sam.

A less frequent but increasingly recognized phenomenon is the genetic sexual-attraction affair (GSA), more recently referred to as genetic attraction (GA). GSA occurs when children who have been separated at birth eventually meet a relative. This meeting may have occurred because an adopted adult has searched and found his or her biological family member. Sometimes the meeting is by chance, and the two adults do not know they are related. These two adults eventually realize that they have feelings of sexual attraction for each other. These feelings of attraction can typically occur between a mother and her son, a father and his daughter, or between opposite-sex siblings or half siblings.

One explanation for GSA is that most people select mates who are like themselves in physical appearance and mental traits. This is known as *assortative mating*. So it is not surprising that a strong attraction occurs when people who have not previously known each other meet and find that they are so similar. This type of sexual attraction rarely occurs between people raised together in early childhood due to a process referred to as *reverse sexual imprinting,* which desensitizes family members to sexual feelings toward each other.

GSA has also been known to occur when children are born through third-party reproduction methods involving sperm or egg donors. They may meet a biological relative later in life without even knowing they are related. These relationships pose incredible challenges for families to both understand and deal with. If they become sexual, the outcomes are often disastrous for the couple and the extended family.

Jack was a happily married man and the father of two teenage daughters. He had been adopted at birth and had always known this. He had a good relationship with his adopted parents and had never expressed an interest in finding out about his biological family. Eventually, his birth mother contacted him indirectly through an adoption registry to determine if Jack would be willing to meet her. He reluctantly agreed, and their initial introduction and subsequent meeting went very well. He discovered he had a sister who was married and lived nearby. He eventually met her, too. To their surprise, they were immediately emotionally and physically drawn to each other. Jack and his sister began talking and texting daily, and both felt they had known each other forever. The feelings they had for each other grew to be powerful and overwhelming. Jack and his sister eventually became inappropriately physically involved, and had their spouses not intervened, it would have developed into a sexual relationship. Counseling helped them each understand the origins of these strong feelings for each other and resolve them more appropriately.

CHAPTER 5

CATEGORY 3: AVOIDANCE AFFAIRS

Don't audit life. Show up and make the most of it now!

This category encompasses the majority of affairs because of the motivations that exist within it. Most of these affairs result because of the married couple's avoidance in dealing with significant problems within their marriage. They may ignore issues and hope they will go away, or they may have conflict that is rarely resolved. In any case, these couples are not emotionally well connected, and their avoidance gradually erodes their desire to keep trying. They may channel their energies into their children or job and ignore the emotional distance that is growing within the marriage. Sometimes couples accept the status quo because one partner is unmotivated to change or sees no need to be different. It eventually may seem simpler to find another partner who shows more interest. Avoidance affairs include exploratory, ulterior motive, dependency, conflict-avoidance, intimacy-avoidance, financial, and sexual identity affairs.

12. Exploratory Affairs
"Would it be better if I were with someone else?"
Susan married early because she and her boyfriend were pregnant. At the time they married, she was grateful he wanted to stay together because they were in love. A number of years and a couple of kids later, the reality of working, raising children, and a spouse who could be very controlling, rigid, and domineering had her feeling disillusioned about marriage. She began receiving attention from a guy at work who was thought to be a "player," but she appreciated his interest in her. Susan eventually fantasized about what it might be like with someone else.

Since he was married, too, she thought it might be a safe venture to see where these encounters might go. Their interactions did, in fact, lead to several sexual rendezvous. Soon afterward, Susan started thinking about the prospect of single life, and that's when her husband discovered the affair.

They went to counseling and addressed the state of their marriage, and each committed to making changes. Susan still occasionally had doubts when she wondered what a new life might have been like, but she also realized that the damage it would have caused for everyone would have erased any potential benefits envisioned. Their commitment to work on the marriage, change themselves, and take care of their children together has proven to be the best choice for everyone.

Couples who live separate lives or who are intimacy avoidant are much more likely to feel disillusioned in their seemingly loveless marriage and consider looking elsewhere. They feel ignored, taken for granted, unloved, and resent not being a priority to their spouse. When neither partner reaches out or initiates with the other, feelings of rejection begin to erode the love they have for each other. Feeling unimportant to their spouse makes them very vulnerable to attention from others.

Exploratory affairs occur when people are looking for something different in their marriage. They are curious to find if someone or something else might be a better option. Don-David Lusterman, who wrote the book *Infidelity: A Survival Guide* notes that exploratory affairs sometimes make people work harder on their marriage but on other occasions bring about divorce.

13. Ulterior Motive Affairs

A much deeper motivation lies in the desire to avoid taking responsibility for ending the marriage.

Ulterior motive affairs can be confusing because the reason for the infidelity is not readily apparent. The telltale signs that something is amiss are generated from the calmness demonstrated by the offending spouse over the discovery of the affair. The offending spouse may even show a pseudo-appearance of remorse. Their remorse is usually portrayed as not wanting to have purposely hurt their spouse. However, this pseudo-regret is often a veil for the guilt of using their affair as a catalyst to motivate their spouse to change or even divorce them. The element of premeditation is what makes this type of affair particularly heinous.

Emily Brown, in her book *Patterns of Infidelity and their Treatment*, refers to these as *exit affairs*. The discovery of the affair is intended to provoke the betrayed spouse into ending the marriage with the offending spouse. Therefore, both partners get what they want.

Some offending spouses have been so frustrated by their spouse not changing in specific ways that they used the ulterior motive affair to create a crisis. This last-ditch effort to force their recalcitrant spouse to change rarely works, but it highlights the desperation of the dissatisfied spouse.

Dave and Denise went to counseling on an emergency basis. Dave had been observed at an out-of-town conference slow dancing, kissing, and acting sexually provocative with another woman. He dismissed the significance of the incident, but his wife was devastated. This incident was enough to cause their coexistent marriage to be at risk. He seemed concerned for how badly his wife took the revelation, but relieved that they were discussing ending their marriage. Rather than accept responsibility for not working on their marital problems, he blamed her for how poorly the marriage had been for years. The ulterior motive was to portray himself as the victim in the eyes of others, blame his spouse, and walk away from the marriage feeling justified for leaving.

Other ulterior motive affairs are more predatory and calculated with a specific purpose in mind to exploit others for one's own benefit.

Sharon has been married three times. In each relationship, she pursued her future husband, got pregnant "accidentally," and subsequently married each man. Sharon was very calculating and used her pregnancies to trap each of her husbands. She has improved her socioeconomic status with each relationship. Her motives were not for love, but to be taken care of financially. This was guaranteed by having a child with each of these men. She left each marriage with a lump-sum settlement, child support, and another lover waiting in the wings. Sharon was dependent but predatory. The men were all clueless about her agenda until after the relationship ended.

14. Dependency or "I Can't Be Alone" Affairs

> *"Please take care of me because I don't believe I can do it myself."*
>
> DCW

This type of affair typically occurs with individuals who have always had someone to depend on in their lives. Even as early as high school, they constantly had a boyfriend or girlfriend. They were never comfortable being alone or independent.

When things start getting difficult in their primary relationship, they quickly start looking for a replacement. It is not uncommon to have the next spouse waiting in the wings until their current marriage ends. These affairs are more likely to occur with women who are unhappy and having problems in their marriage.

Sandra had a history of having one boyfriend after another throughout her life. If she had problems with one, she would either cheat with another guy or simply move on after she found a significant other. When her husband started paying more attention to his job than her, she resumed her pattern of shopping around again for another guy to be with.

This person's *modus operandi* is either establishing emotional and financial security or improving their status in life. They are generally dependent individuals who are quite resourceful. Their focus is predominantly on their current spouse. Children are often of secondary importance to their strong motivation for security. These adults, as children, were reared in these unstable family configurations and often report long-term feelings of anxiety and uncertainty. They also grew up feeling that the most current man or woman in their parent's life was more important than them.

15. Conflict-Avoidance Affairs

> *"Their conflict avoidance is like undetected high blood pressure—a silent killer."*
>
> DCW

Joe and Connie were a late-thirties couple who had been married for twelve years and were the epitome of what others might describe as happy. They were easygoing, accommodating, rarely if ever argued, and seemed to handle life well. No one would know that part of the reason for their outward success in their marriage was that they didn't face issues. They went along to get along and never made waves. Whenever a potential conflict occurred, they would drop it quickly. Their love life had cooled down as well. Their conflict avoidance was like undetected high blood pressure—a silent killer. One day out of the blue, Connie discovered that Joe had been soliciting women online. He admitted to having several trysts with random partners he had met on various Internet sites, just for the excitement of it all.

Conflict-avoidance couples are like the science class experiment of a frog in a pan of water. The temperature is incrementally turned up, but the frog does not detect the increase in temperature and ends up boiling to death. These couples place a premium on being peacemakers. They often came from families where there was high conflict on one extreme or no conflict on the other. They are fundamentally afraid that facing problems will turn out badly, so they act like it is no big deal.

Eventually, one of them meets someone who makes them feel alive again or who embodies excitement to them. They realize how boring their life has been up to now and jump ship. Since they are so ill equipped to handle someone like they have found, these relationships often do not work out, either, and they find themselves alone. If they do go back, it is often out of obligation or guilt for having hurt their spouse. When reconciliation occurs, there is deep hurt and resentment that is difficult to express. This couple will need to look at what they each need to change to face their problems, embrace life, and love more intentionally.

16. Intimacy-Avoidance Affairs

"Intimacy-avoidant couples use conflict to keep a safe distance from each other."

DCW

Ken and Kay were two professionals who had a sickly son whom Kay spent a great deal of time caring for. Ken traveled often and was away during the week. Kay became very focused on keeping their son well, and Ken worked harder to pay for the expensive treatment he received. Most of their time and energy was invested elsewhere. Problems between the couple resulted in curt exchanges and both parties feeling unappreciated and misunderstood. Ken felt ignored by his wife because she numbed herself with alcohol. Her discovery of his involvement with another woman prompted immediate indignation on her part, followed by a bitter divorce.

Intimacy-avoidance couples have the same difficulty connecting emotionally as the conflict-avoidance couples, but their interactions together are just the opposite. They use conflict to keep a safe distance from each other. They crave closeness but are afraid of the vulnerability required for it to occur. Therefore, they settle for the next-best thing—intensity generated by arguments and their differences. The intensity they experience together isn't as validating as genuine closeness, but it does keep them engaged. They are equally terrified of being alone and of being too close.

Intimacy-avoidance couples may keep themselves so busy with their educations or careers, raising children, caring for a sick family member or child, or doing good elsewhere that they have no real time for each other. They often craft lifestyles that require them to spend time apart from each other because of their jobs or other obligations. Their marriage relationship is on life support, and they don't even acknowledge that they are in ICU.

Individuals in these marriages often come from families where high conflict has occurred, including divorce; emotional, verbal, physical abuse; alcohol or substance abuse; parental neglect; and chaotic lifestyles.

Donna was a forty-eight-year-old woman who had an affair with the same man during most of her twenty-five-year marriage. Her husband died unexpectedly of a heart attack. Shortly thereafter, her lover expressed a desire to have a permanent relationship with her. She, however, did not want this, and their relationship ended as well. Donna's best friend, who had been her confidant during the twenty-five-year affair, urged her to get some grief counseling to look at her issues. Donna ended their relationship as well, even though her best friend was only trying to help. Donna used people for her own purposes, but did not want closeness or intimacy with anyone.

Sometimes, intimacy-avoidance affairs occur because they are finally able to temporarily drop their guard with someone else with whom they work closely or have no history. The lack of attention and lack of sex in their marriage leave them vulnerable to someone who might actively pursue them. When the betrayed spouse discovers the affair, they are either terrified of abandonment or enraged and want revenge.

Jack and Jill were both reared in dysfunctional families. Jack's parents had multiple divorces, and their kids were emotionally neglected. Jill's parents split up because of infidelity, and Jill felt she could never please them. Jack and Jill had a hostile, dependent marriage in that they could not live with or without each other and regularly bickered with one other. Their love life was erratic and unsatisfactory because of the existing atmosphere of emotional conflict. When Jack had an affair, she was devastated and worked very hard to make things better between them. He became angry that it took so long for her to finally work on the marriage. Jack didn't acknowledge that he damaged the relationship over the years because of his hostility as well. They both eventually recognized through counseling how each of them avoided emotional intimacy by their constant bickering.

17. Financial Affairs

> *"Men are more likely to have a hidden credit card, while women are three times more likely to have a hidden savings account."*
>
> CreditCards.com

Jim is an entrepreneur who has started several small companies that have been both successful and unsuccessful. He started one business in which he agreed to cosign on a $75,000 loan with a partner, but never told his wife about it. When the company failed and he had to pay back the loan, his wife became aware of his omission. She felt betrayed that he had risked their financial well-being without ever consulting her. She was a businessperson herself, so she could have added valuable input to what, in hindsight, was such a poor decision.

Financial infidelity occurs when one partner hides money without their spouse's knowledge; does not disclose significant debt before marriage; engages in clandestine, excessive spending; accrues unreported gambling debt; acquires secret loans; gives money to family members or friends without their spouse's consent; or takes on significant business debt that could negatively impact the financial stability of the family without disclosing it.

One in five Americans has spent $500 or more without their spouse's knowledge, according to CreditCards.com. This represents 7.2 million Americans, with 4.4 million being men and 2.8 million being women. Men are more likely to have a hidden credit card, while women are three times more likely to have a hidden savings account. These results were determined by a random survey that occurred in January 2015 by Princeton Survey Research Associates.

The number-one issue couples have conflicts around is money. Money is recognized as a source of power. Whoever controls the money is often said to control the relationship. The manner in which an individual handles money reflects how he or she operates within a relationship.

A 2012 Kansas State University study involving more than 4,500 couples found that arguments over money were the top predictor of divorce.

In an August 2013 survey of 191 certified divorce financial analysts, money was cited as the third cause of divorce behind incompatibility and infidelity, according to the Institute for Divorce Financial Analyst's website.

Secrecy over one's use of money is indicative of much larger problems within a relationship.

- The marriage is not an equal partnership where both parties have a say-so in how their resources are utilized.
- There is a lack of trust and confidence in how the money is managed.
- One partner believes he or she is entitled to spend as they choose.
- Money is used to fund other secret behaviors that exist.

Successful relationships require transitioning from thinking like an individual to thinking like a team. Secrets sabotage that goal. Happy relationships are about making personal changes and finding outcomes that are best for both parties.

18. Sexual Identity Affairs

There is a segment of our society that is married with children, living a secret but undisclosed lifestyle. They are men and women who do not wish to openly acknowledge being homosexual or lesbian. Often conflicted, they have embraced a heterosexual marriage and a family as a way to deal with their deeper, sexual-identity issues. They generally use chat rooms, gay dating sites, and online technology to contact same-sex individuals with whom to engage. They may be in professions that allow them to travel and have rendezvous that maintain their anonymity.

These split-self affairs reflect the conflict they have within but are unwilling to address. Their double life is the middle ground they have adopted to help them cope with their ambivalence. The deceit, shame, and guilt they live with creates an inner agony that constantly plagues them. Their spouses have adjusted to their intimacy avoidance by busying themselves with other things in their lives, like their jobs or the children. Denial and minimization characterize their lives.

Tom was a young, up-and-coming music minister at a large, popular church. He had a sweet, loving wife with three small children. Every Sunday, he would direct the choir, play in the praise band, and sing beautiful solos. When he was discovered to be involved in a sexual relationship with one of the married men in his choir, the entire congregation was shocked. His wife was stunned and had no idea that he was really gay and living in a heterosexual marriage to hide his sexual orientation.

When an unsuspecting spouse discovers that their spouse is having an affair, they are, of course, devastated. When it is someone of the same sex, they are in shock and disoriented. While heterosexual affairs are traumatic enough, homosexual affairs seem impossible to know just how to deal with them. How does a heterosexual spouse compete with their spouse's desire for a same-sex partner? How will their families react and view them? What should the children be told? Is there any hope for reconciliation? Does the spouse want to come out now that their secret is known? How does the injured spouse deal with feeling like the entire relationship has been a lie?

CHAPTER 6

CATEGORY 4: ADDICTION AFFAIRS

Self-destructive behavior takes away our self-respect, even if no one else knows about it.

These individuals almost always have a hole in their soul. Their emptiness and loneliness is obscured by their relentless search to be validated through their most current sexual relationships. They have perfected the art of charming others for their own personal pleasure. If ever questioned about their reckless behavior, they will have a well-developed rationale for their actions that may include a high sex drive, a special appreciation for the opposite sex, or that they are just enjoying life. They are generally narcissistic and self-absorbed, but they often feel inadequate and are searching for significance at another's expense. This category almost always involves some level of sexual addiction and fantasy that is facilitated by the active utilization of technology for the purposes of multiple hookups. Addiction affairs include cyber, fantasy, serial, swinging, and sex-with-yourself affairs.

19. Cyber Affairs

As marijuana is a gateway drug to trying other chemical substances, so is pornography a gateway to participating in cybersex. Pornography is laced with fantasy and promises ultimate entertainment. It is a slippery slope that, once engaged in, can lead to curiosity about other types of sexually explicit venues. The desire to explore what else is available becomes not only enticing, but addictive.

Technology has enabled us to have sex without even being physically present with the other person, but often in real time. Chat rooms, instant messaging, sexting, webcams, and video conferencing allow people to engage in all types of flirtatious, solicitous, and erotic exchanges in the privacy of their own homes, or over their personal communications devices, wherever they are.

Some people try to maintain that these types of exchanges do not constitute an affair, primarily because there is no face-to-face physical contact. Most of their spouses would beg to differ that sending naked pictures, sharing explicit sexual words and phrases, and engaging in cybersex (mutual masturbation) with all the accompanying sights and sounds associated with it does constitute, at best, a betrayal and, more likely, a sexual affair. The pain and hurt that spouses experience upon detection of these encounters by their significant other is as devastating as if sexual intercourse had actually occurred.

Jeff and Cindy had been married twelve years and had three small children. He was busy with his job as well as with a part-time, entrepreneurial endeavor. Cindy was working, very involved with her children, and struggling with some health issues. Eventually life and other competing factors got in the way, and they didn't make time for each other. Jeff began surfing the web, looking at pornography, and frequenting bored-spouses chat rooms. He eventually was introduced to cybersex, where two online parties share pictures, talk sexually to each other, and mutually masturbate together. After about two years, Cindy discovered he had been doing this and withdrew from him sexually. In her frustration with his ignoring her, she had a brief, retaliatory affair with a coworker, which only made their marital situation worse.

A 2008 article in the *Journal of Marital and Family Therapy* by Katherine Hertlein reviewed eight studies of Internet affairs and documented the negative effects from cybersex that included less interest in sex with one's committed relationship, neglect of work, and neglect of children. Two-thirds of the participants in the study had met with and had sex with their Internet partners.

There are three levels of cyber affairs that represent a progression from an observational mode into actual contact and, finally, sexual involvement.

Level-one cyber affairs primarily involve the use of pornography. They may include regular viewing or collecting pictures and videos of adult nudity or graphic sex via the Internet. This type of voyeurism is accompanied by masturbation approximately 80 percent of the time. Discovery of level-one cyber affairs is a primary reason many women initiate couples counseling, because they feel betrayed by their spouse's secret life.

Level-two cyber affairs involve remote interaction with others via the Internet or phone that is accompanied by some form of cybersex. The remote contact may begin in a chat room, on a dating site, a sex website, or by calling an 800 number. It may include the exchange of nude pictures, the use of live webcams, or explicit sex talk that involves graphic sexual conversation and mutual masturbation. It is a convenient way to have sex without ever having to meet the other person.

Level-three cyber affairs represent a progression to actual contact with another person that initially began via the Internet or phone. The purpose is purely sexual, although some personal relationships do actually begin this way. It may just involve sex for money, but it often is the vehicle used by sex addicts to act out with others.

20. Fantasy Affairs

> *"There is always an element of delusion in fantasy affairs."*
> DCW

Smokey Robinson and the Miracles wrote a song entitled "Just My Imagination" in which the singer describes a relationship he has with a woman who walks past his house every morning that is merely imaginary. Fantasy affairs have a similar flavor of both fact and fiction associated with them. What the beholder of the relationship believes about this idealized lover is not always what is actually occurring, though. The other person does not necessarily view the relationship from the same romantic perspective. Though similar to emotional affairs where both people are smitten with each other, fantasy affairs primarily involve one individual who believes this person will eventually return their love. The other person is often oblivious to their affections and almost always reacts with surprise and shock when they find out.

Jason was a forty-year-old married man who took an unusual interest in another married woman with whom he served on a church committee. He began sending her e-mails, seeking her out in fellowship, and following her on Facebook. She was friendly at first and then felt uncomfortable with his persistence and avoided him. Eventually, her husband spoke to him, but he ignored his requests. He continued to pursue her friendship, despite having been told to back off and stop his overtures. In the end, he felt he had been wronged and still wanted a chance to be friends and associate together. Months later, he was still unclear why they couldn't be good friends.

The following scenario is an example of a fantasy affair with elements of an emotional, workplace, and an exploratory affair.

Joe was a midfifties guy who had been married for over twenty-five years. He loved, but was no longer "in love," with his wife. They had a good life together and shared grown children and grandchildren. Joe met a much younger, divorced woman at work who was a single parent. They worked and traveled together and became good friends. Joe had even met her kids and spent time at her house visiting. He helped her repair things that she needed assistance with. Joe had on many occasions imagined them together, although she seemed to regard him as more of a father figure. Their frequent phone conversations caused a problem for Joe's wife, who was concerned this was more than just a friendship. His wife tried harder to improve their marriage, but Joe seemed oblivious to her efforts. When Joe finally gathered up the courage to express his feelings for his much younger colleague, she was taken aback and surprised he felt that way for her. She had never had a father and was flattered Joe was willing to take such a personal interest in her life. Her interest in Joe was not romantic, even though she was fond of him. She clearly had been naïve toward his deeper feelings for her.

Here is another example of another fantasy affair in the making:

Steve was a retired school teacher who had been married for many years, though the relationship was coexistent. He had always given special attention to his students and kept up with some of them after graduation. He interacted with them over social media and through phone calls, texts, and e-mails. Some of these exchanges were very personal. There were several young women he had helped out financially on occasion. He had also gotten involved with their problematic relationships, and helped them get jobs. His family was concerned he was too close and using poor judgment in how he related to these women. Though he would never admit to feeling romantic affection for them, it was clear his curiosity about their day-to-day lives and willingness to get more involved was quite excessive. Most of these young women took advantage of him, but he didn't seem to see it that way.

"Foolish old men" who get immersed in similar fantasies are accidents waiting to happen. They often hide and compartmentalize this area of their lives, are able to rationalize their motives, and thereby justify their actions. The boundary violations that are apparent to others are ignored by these individuals because of their loneliness and deep need for validation. They live in a world of *what could be* instead of *what is*. They often get taken advantage of, risk their reputations and careers, wreak havoc in their marriages, and sometimes have legal action taken against them for harassment and stalking.

21. Serial Affairs

"Serial cheaters operate from a fill-me-up-I'm-empty frame of reference."

DCW

June had been married for thirty years when she finally decided that her husband's constant cheating was no longer tolerable to her. Over the years, she would discover evidence that he was involved with other women. She rationalized that their kids needed a stable influence in their lives, and she couldn't consider leaving. Later, she found out that he had fathered a child with another woman. She was so embarrassed and humiliated; she just became emotionally numb to it all. June had very little education and practical job experience, so she couldn't financially support herself. Eventually, she went to technical school for some training and started saving money to prepare for her divorce. She went to counseling to become emotionally stronger in preparation for her exit from a spouse who had cheated on her most of their marriage.

Womanizers, players, philanderers, and sex addicts never get enough sex. They are on a constant mission to find someone with whom to sexually engage. They love the chase and the conquest. Having perfected the ability to read who is a potential partner, their technique is disarming. The ability to meet and connect with the opposite sex is impressive, to say the least, because they are masters of the subtle nuance.

These are both men and women who know how to get the attention of others and cultivate an exchange that often leads to something more. Unless a person's boundaries are very clear, they will charm and disarm with the greatest of ease, leaving the object of their desire wanting more of their attention. This group is predominantly composed of narcissists who require the constant validation of a new and different person who will make them feel they still have it. They operate from a "fill me up, I'm empty" frame of reference. No one is ever enough because *they* are not enough. They are often "daddy's girls" and "mama's boys" who need to feel favored and special. Their compulsive sexual behavior only momentarily distracts them from the depth of their emptiness by their latest efforts at conquest. All form and no content characterizes them.

John had only been married eight years, but he had already had six affairs. He was supposedly bored with his marriage and angry that his wife wasn't very interested in having sex. He admitted that he drank too much, smoked pot to relax, and used pain pills for an old football injury. As a child, he witnessed various scenarios where his mother cheated on each of her multiple husbands. When he was older, he began using sex and drugs to ease his emotional pain. His affairs were his attempts to feel some excitement and acceptance in his life, although they only made him feel empty and discontent. When his wife discovered his secret life, she asked him to leave and get some help while she decided how to proceed with her own life.

The *Two and a Half Men* character played by Charlie Sheen is a classic example of someone who can be entertaining, but his motives are always the same: self-serving. Serial cheaters are emotional-intimacy avoiders with poor impulse control who lack a real sense of themselves. Some feel deep shame and embarrassment about constantly using people, while others seem to show little evidence of regret about the people they hurt.

Bill Clinton has been portrayed as a serial cheater. He was clearly the quintessential pied piper of oration. Women were easily taken in by him, even though they knew he was married. He most clearly represents a public figure who never grew up emotionally nor demonstrated any genuine regret over his actions. His charm was disarming. His rhetoric was so convincing that even though people knew they were being lied to, they sat mesmerized and enjoyed how he made them feel. His marriage appears to have remained functionally intact, perhaps primarily for political purposes. Many couples involved in politics remain together for the sake of image and appearances, though privately, their relationships are empty shells. The marriages of most serial cheaters are also *all form, but no content.*

22. Swinging Affairs

Swinging affairs occur when couples switch partners and have sex with someone else's spouse in twosomes, threesomes, foursomes, or in group sex. Sometimes one spouse watches while his or her spouse has sex with someone else.

Though couples who "swing" would not likely consider their sexual excursions with other couples an affair, it is a fundamental betrayal of the commitment in their relationship. "It's not cheating if we both agree to do it!" Even if both parties have willingly agreed to experience sex with someone else, they are opening their marriage to many risks. Most of these couples will talk about how they are primarily committed to their spouse, and the sexual encounters with others only enrich the appreciation they have for each other. A closer look into their relationship usually indicates otherwise. There are usually a number of other problems that exist between them.

In many of these couples, there is one more-dominant partner who is advocating "swinging" while the other, passive partner goes along. This allows him to cheat with his spouse's full knowledge and cooperation. The accommodating spouse is curious, to say the least, but primarily accommodating their spouse. Alcohol and drugs are often used to facilitate the uninhibitedness and receptiveness to the experience. Once this lifestyle begins, it does add excitement that has been perhaps missing in less-than-fulfilling marriages. These are generally intimacy-avoiding relationships that use sex with other people to fill the void. They would adamantly deny that they are anything other than committed partners who are more broad-minded than most.

Tim and Lynn were a middle-aged couple who were both employed and had two children. They considered themselves progressive, broad-minded individuals whose marriage was only enriched by new, unconventional experiences. Tim introduced the idea of getting with other couples socially, and slowly seeing what might happen sexually with the assistance of a little alcohol, fun, and frolicking. Lynn was at first reluctant, but after they had some initial sexual experiences with other spouses, she was willing to continue. At first, they would find couples who were unsuspecting but willing to try new things. Later, they sought out couples who identified themselves as "swingers." Lynn was dissatisfied with Tim's work ethic, irresponsibility, and insensitivity toward her. Getting with other couples sexually in this manner offered a distraction that made their difficulties tolerable. Tim primarily liked the idea of having sex with other women with no strings attached. Lynn went along and could hardly protest since she had agreed to participate as well. She would have preferred to have a more emotionally intimate relationship with Tim.

23. Sex-with-Yourself Affairs (SWY)

The ever-widening world of technology has contributed to a relatively new form of narcissistic affair that involves exclusive sex with oneself. These individuals typically have a spouse or partner, but may no longer have much of a shared sex life together. They have either grown weary of each other sexually, or their infrequency belies other problems they each have with emotional and sexual intimacy. These are generally distant but dependent relationships where an entrenched pattern of separate lives has been established. Neither wants to be alone, and each may secretly believe that they would not be able to find another relationship should this one end.

In many cases, pornography fuels an active fantasy life that involves frequent masturbation. It has become simpler and more convenient for the individual to isolate and have sex with themselves rather than to initiate a sexual interaction with their partner. Some unintentionally celibate spouses will occasionally ask their partner if they are ever going to have sex together again. Some sexually ignored spouses are relieved that this part of their life is a thing of the past. However, most spouses feel hurt and angry if their partner is ignoring them and resorting to pleasuring themselves only. They feel emotionally abandoned and sexually betrayed that their spouse is sexually taking care of themselves and neglecting their needs.

Sexaholics Anonymous Twelve-Step groups view sex with oneself as detrimental to recovery and therefore counter to resolving the problems of sexual addiction. SA recommends that their members agree to not self-stimulate in order to establish and maintain their sobriety from acting out sexually. The intention is to learn how to relate to others in healthy, emotionally intimate ways by being open, honest, respectful, and considerate, instead of being self-absorbed or exploitive. The inability to bond with others and connect emotionally is at the core of most sexual problems, including sex with yourself.

Jim and Tina had been married for fourteen years, and it was the second marriage for both. They had no children together and were heavily involved in their jobs. Their sex life had never been great, and over the years, it became less and less of a priority. Jim and Tina were the proverbial ships that passed in the night. They did not share many interests together but were happy to have someone to come home to. She loved to read and watch old movies, and he enjoyed computer games. Tina was unaware that Jim's computer-game playing was really an addiction to pornography and daily, compulsive masturbation. She was hurt when she discovered he was more interested in having sex with himself than with her. She admitted she had been relieved earlier in the marriage that Jim wasn't pestering her to have sex regularly. She had not expected that sex would eventually disappear from their relationship altogether.

CHAPTER 7

CATEGORY 5: STAGE-OF-LIFE AFFAIRS

"It takes years to build up trust, and only seconds to destroy it."

—Unknown

Stage-of-life affairs often occur during a transitional period in life where an individual comes to the realization that certain personal dissatisfactions exist. They may feel disillusioned with their life and the need for a change to occur. Life seems to be passing them by, and they had expected more from it. Sometimes they will meet a person who gives them a different perspective on life regarding who they could be or what else life might offer them. They may feel they deserve something better than what they previously have had. These individuals may finally have the resources to experience things that they could not afford before. Sometimes it is an attempt to feel relevant, important, or young again.

On occasion, an individual may make a dramatic change in life after a parent who represented strong moral values or who was the moral compass of the family passes away. This category can encompass couples who have been married for a long time, but have settled into a status quo resulting in a comfortable coexistence. They may lack passion together, and so they might discretely seek it elsewhere. Stage-of-life affairs include midlife, empty-nest, tripod, entitlement, and sweetheart or old-flame affairs.

24. Midlife Affairs

The affairs most popularized over the years in the movies and in the media are midlife affairs. They generally involve a married male approaching his forties who discovers how dissatisfied he is with this stage of his life compared to where he thought he should be. Midlife women realize they are not as young, cute, firm, trim, or supple as they once were. They are often not very happy with their home lives, either. Midlife men and women may feel they have made great personal sacrifices in the roles they have chosen and do not feel it has been satisfying or aptly rewarded. These "middle-age crazies" usually appear completely irrational to outsiders who can see what a great life they actually have and do not understand why they risk jeopardizing it all.

These men and women may try to regain their youthfulness by working out; buying stylish clothing; changing or coloring their hair; associating with single, younger, or divorced people; participating in extreme sports or activities; and buying the proverbial sportier car. Men are almost always drawn to much younger women who admire them and make them feel young and virile again. Women often find someone who shows interest in them and is willing to spend time having fun together.

Having found a new zest for life and possessing the financial means to do these things makes them a magnet for the attention they want and crave. Their new friends and social lives often don't include their spouses. This desire to reinvent themselves makes them susceptible to crossing boundaries that lead to affairs. Their new lifestyle often fuels the need for significance and self-importance. It also creates a great deal of tension and strife at home. Their spouses do not initially understand what is happening, especially when they are being portrayed as boring and not the same person their middle-aged spouse first married. It is not too difficult for a concerned spouse to eventually discern what is going on since this phenomenon has received so much media attention.

Jane was an attractive, fortyish-age mother who had it all. Her husband owned a successful business. She had a job she could work at her leisure, she had plenty of time for herself, and her children were almost grown. Unfortunately, she had become bored and thought there had to be more. Eventually, she met a married guy who was interesting, funny, and lived in the neighborhood. They would see each other at social functions and rendezvous secretly when everyone else was at work or school. To everyone's surprise, both of them divorced their spouses and eventually moved in together.

Younger women in their mid- to late thirties are a recent addition to this category because many feel underappreciated and bored at home. They have busy husbands who work long hours and take them for granted by forgetting birthdays, anniversaries, or special occasions. These moms are often busy at home, dealing with preteens or teenagers. They miss having someone pay attention to them, appreciate them, and enjoy their company. They sometimes engage guys who are serial cheaters because they are easy to recognize and are always looking for an opportunity to act out. It may only begin as a one-night stand, but it sometimes turns into periodic rendezvous that go on for years. "Hubby" is often completely oblivious because he is in his own world.

25. Empty-Nest Affairs

Couples ranging from the late forties to the early sixties are most likely to experience an empty-nest affair. Their youngest child is getting ready or has recently left the family home for college. The marriage has a history of being preempted by work, kid's activities, job demands, the needs of aging parents, etc., and no longer seems to be a priority. Often, the relationship has more of a roommate quality to it. Both individuals have admittedly drifted apart.

Emily Brown, who wrote *Patterns of Infidelity and Their Treatment*, describes these affairs as split-self affairs. These men or women have always done the right thing and denied themselves for the good of others but have underdeveloped emotional lives. Their personal needs have been sublimated, the individuals live separate lives, and the marriage is empty.

Men experience what Frank Pittman describes in *Private Lies* as "reaching the summit," where they have accomplished a great deal professionally but are dissatisfied in their personal lives, especially their marriages. Women in their fifties have seen the kids leave and do not look forward to feeling ignored by an unappreciative, inattentive, or absent spouse. They may have their own successful career as well. The couple has amassed enough assets that they could afford to consider other options.

John had been a "big man on campus" when he and his future wife met in college. After they were married, they each had busy jobs and two children to raise. Their marriage went well until the kids left home and he lost his job due to his company downsizing. He struggled to recover professionally and drifted from one unfulfilling job situation to another. Simultaneously, his wife's career had continued an upward trend, and she was carrying them financially. During this time, he was feeling unimportant and experiencing a crisis of confidence. Then, he met a middle-aged, professional woman who thought he was the greatest. She was willing to spend time just as friends together, helping him get back into his industry. Eventually, they became sexually involved. John subsequently left his wife for this new person because she made him feel alive and confident again.

One of the partners may introduce the idea of having been unhappy and dissatisfied with the marriage for years, assuming their spouse has felt the same way. The disenchanted partner might suggest a separation to "think," "get some space," or reflect on their future. This proposal often means he already has another potential person that he has met and would like to continue to see. It is not uncommon that one of the spouses has had a well-hidden, private affair that has gone on for quite a long time. The other spouse is almost always surprised, assuming they were busy with other parts of their lives by mutual agreement. These partners often are distraught, apologetic, and ready to do whatever is needed to repair the marriage. The exiting spouse may feel guilty and concerned how this will all affect his or her image, especially with family members.

Counseling is often too little too late, as the betrayed spouse is in survival mode while the exiting spouse has come at the other's request. The offending spouse has either come to counseling in order to at least say he or she tried or to leave their partner in the hands of a therapist while they leave the relationship.

Sometimes the spouse who thinks the grass is greener elsewhere discovers how much he is leaving behind in his loyal spouse, his children, grandchildren, and the history they have shared. He may even realize after leaving that the person he was running to was not who they portrayed themselves to be. The painful journey into a fearless, personal assessment of themselves and making amends begins.

26. Tripod Affairs

Don-David Lusterman, PhD, who wrote *Infidelity: A Survival Guide*, describes people who stay in unhappy marriages indefinitely for reasons that include economic concerns, status in the community, fear of hurting the kids, or receiving disapproval from family members. The unhappy spouse finds a third person to prop up the unstable marriage that would fall apart, from their point of view, without this outlet.

There is generally a great deal of rationalization and denial going on by all three parties. The cheating spouse believes the affair is necessary to maintain the marriage. The injured spouse on some level knows something is amiss, but does not bother to seriously question their problems or their spouse's inconsistencies. The outside individual often acts like they have no expectations, but becomes very distraught if the relationship ends or never progresses to something more substantial.

June is a middle-aged woman who owns her own business and works all the time. Her husband has been under- or unemployed in recent years and goes through the motions of reestablishing himself. She is a high-energy, ambitious person who easily attracts the attention of other men.

Her husband is suspicious but has only circumstantial evidence that she plays around, which she denies adamantly. They do care for each other, but she has little respect for him. They will probably never directly address his sandbagging and her forays into the other side until she is caught red handed. The possible outcomes will be a crisis finally faced in their marriage, her leaving him for someone else, or a nasty divorce.

27. Entitlement Affairs

Entitlement affairs may have the same self-important, narcissistic quality of celebrity affairs, but the purpose is different. It is not status driven, nor is the function to improve one's standing personally or professionally. In some cases, it is purely for sex and enjoyment with no strings attached. In other instances, it is about trying to compensate for the loneliness that exists in one's current, traditional marriage. In both cases, the married individuals believe they are due a little happiness in their lives because of who they are, what they have, and what they do.

There is nothing about these trysts that is intended to be permanent, but they are often long term. The marriage is often a high-status one, but their relationship has cooled based upon their ages, levels of responsibility, and the long-term neglect it has endured. The affairs are discreet and sometimes even represent a covert contract, where there is knowledge of a "special friend," but it is never discussed. In some relationships, both spouses have a significant other.

Entitlement affairs are more commonly accepted in certain cultures and countries where double standards between men and women exist. In these cultures, men are known to have their mistresses, but nothing is said about it as long as they are financially responsible to their original families.

While married to Princess Diana, Prince Charles is said to have had a long-term affair with his mistress, whom he later married. This relationship was known by many but ignored as long it remained discreet. A well-known television tycoon in the Atlanta area was rumored to have multiple mistresses around the country that he financially supported and visited for services. High-profile politicians are also exposed periodically by the media for having arranged relationships with younger women. These women's lifestyles are often maintained in exchange for their time, attention, and favors. When the media discovers these arrangements, the careers of these high-profile individuals are often badly damaged. Governor Mark Sanford, President Bill Clinton, former vice presidential candidate John Edwards, and New York Governor Eliot Spitzer are just a few who suffered a crisis of credibility when their stories of impropriety were made public.

28. Sweetheart or Old-Flame Affairs

Technology has ushered in a new era of connecting with old friends and lovers from times past. This has also given rise to a new trend of affairs that were previously relegated to memories of what might have been. While stories of reconnecting at high school reunions are not uncommon, social media has given people the option of searching for certain people who might have been a part of their lives in the past.

This type of affair has now become a common occurrence that may innocently begin with e-mails, Facebook communication, texts, or the exchange of pictures. It sometimes gravitates into spending an inordinate amount of time chatting or talking over the phone. Eventually, an unsuspecting spouse will stumble upon the same telephone number multiple times on the phone bill or some other evidence of contact with an unknown person, leading to a marital crisis.

Don and Donna had been married for twenty-seven years. Their children were all grown and gone, so they were empty nesters. It was a time for them to do some things that they previously did not have the opportunity or the resources to enjoy. Donna was shocked one day when out of the blue, Don told her he didn't love her anymore and needed to time to think and reflect upon his life. At first, she thought he was having a late-life crisis and gave him space to try and work it out in her effort to be understanding. She later discovered some e-mail communication between Don and an old girlfriend from college. Don had been talking with her for months, and they had even discussed how they might move forward in their lives together. Donna had no idea that Don had been unhappy or was longing for more excitement in his life.

In worst-case scenarios, a secret rendezvous occurs, and the emotional affair turns sexual. The unsuspecting spouse is often shocked to hear that their partner isn't happy with the marriage and hasn't been for a long time. They have been oblivious to an old-flame affair that has been reignited and burns hotter than ever. This crisis brings many couples into therapy to determine if the marriage can be salvaged. Once family and friends weigh in on their disapproval of the affair, many of these illicit relationships are quickly snuffed out.

Jim and Cathy had been together for twenty years and had their ups and downs in the marriage. Cathy discovered through his phone that he had been in touch with his old college girlfriend, who was also now married. Apparently, they had been talking, texting, and e-mailing for several months and had even met for lunch. He admitted that he was reflecting back on his younger years and yearned for the excitement he had with her back then. Even though the relationship had not become sexual, it was very emotionally intense.

More chronically coexistent marriages often do not survive this opportunity for love again, and they end. Rarely do old-flame reunions work out, because neither party is the same person they knew many years before. These impulse affairs are often over within six months of finally moving in together. Unfortunately, they have burned the bridges back to their previous lives and are left with no one. In some cases, the betrayed spouse reluctantly takes their wayward partner back. Sometimes they can work it out, but often the damage can never be completely repaired.

HOMEWORK EXERCISE

What Type of Affair Are You Dealing with?

(Please circle the appropriate item or items that best represent the type of affair you believe you are dealing with)

1. One-Night Stand
2. Retaliatory Affairs
3. Cheating-While-Dating Affairs
4. Engagement Affairs
5. Emotional Affairs
6. Close-Friend Affairs
7. Celebrity or "Love the One You're With" Affairs
8. Mate-Poaching or Coveting Affairs
9. Workplace Affairs
10. In-Law Affairs
11. Family and Genetic Sexual-Attraction Affairs
12. Exploratory Affairs
13. Ulterior Motive Affairs
14. Dependency or "I Can't Be Alone" Affairs
15. Conflict-Avoidance Affairs
16. Intimacy-Avoidance Affairs
17. Financial Affairs
18. Sexual Identity Affairs
19. Cyber Affairs
20. Fantasy Affairs
21. Serial Affairs
22. Swinging Affairs
23. Sex-with-Yourself Affairs (SWY)
24. Midlife Affairs
25. Empty-Nest Affairs
26. Tripod Affairs
27. Entitlement Affairs
28. Sweetheart or Old-Flame Affairs

CHAPTER 8

TRAUMATIC RESPONSES TO DISCOVERING INFIDELITY

The worst kind of hurt is betrayal because it means someone was willing hurt you just to make themselves feel better.

Everyone who discovers that their spouse has had an affair will be emotionally hurt, angered, and wounded. The trust between them is shattered. Uncertainty about the future of the marriage is foremost in their minds. Their world as they have known it unravels before their eyes. The emotions experienced are intense and gut wrenching. The discovery of infidelity for those individuals who have grown up in dysfunctional families or have different types of trauma in their past will experience even more severe reactions. Richard Blankenship in *Spouses of Sex Addicts: Hope for the Journey*, describes in detail how a history of emotional, verbal, sexual, and spiritual abuse, neglect, and abandonment can magnify the reactions the betrayed spouse encounters with the discovery of infidelity. Barbara Steffens in *Your Sexually Addicted Spouse* describes the discovery of infidelity as traumatic with the occurrence of symptoms including anxiety, nightmares, sleeplessness, hyperarousal, reliving the event, intrusive images, flashbacks, rage, depression, and panic attacks.

1. SHOCK, DEVASTATION, AND DEPRESSION

The most intense, tearful calls that I receive from clients are when they have just discovered that their spouse has been unfaithful. They can barely utter the words without gasping because the pain is so overwhelming. The person they relied on, believed in, and would never in a hundred years expect to do something like this has rocked their world. The betrayal has changed their fairy tale existence into a nightmare that doesn't dissipate once they have awakened.

When the offending spouse makes the initial call to request counseling, their mood is as if someone had died at their own hand. The regret and shame they seem to feel is unlike anything they ever anticipated could happen. The disturbance in their universe is earth shattering, and everything comes to a screeching halt in order to deal with this catastrophe. Their world has forever changed and the marriage may not survive. The next two to four weeks of their lives may determine whether their marriage together can be repaired or if it is over. Perhaps only the loss of one's child could be more painful and depressing.

When David's wife asked for a separation, he was totally caught off guard that she had been unhappy in their marriage. After she moved out to "take some time to think," he found out she had been seeing another guy from her workplace. David was so devastated he could not eat, sleep, work, or otherwise function. Within weeks of this revelation and her decision to pursue divorce, he tried to take his own life with an overdose of pills.

2. DENIAL AND DISBELIEF

When an affair is discovered, most people will say they never expected it could occur in their relationship. Conversely, some people refuse to believe that it has occurred and choose to find alternative explanations. *"We love each other. It could never happen to us!" "I don't believe it." "The other woman must have taken advantage of him."*

Some individuals ignore the indicators of an affair and find ways to dismiss the possibility that anything illegitimate is occurring. They accept their spouse's excuses readily and do not want to even examine obvious inconsistencies. This "head in the sand" approach can go on for years in some marriages, even when everyone else around them knows what is going on. There are some long-term marriages in which there has been a pattern of extramarital relationships that have occurred. They have an understanding that is a covert contract of "don't ask, don't tell" and to look the other way.

Women tend to be in the majority of spouses who take this posture in reaction to these unwanted revelations, because they are protecting and preserving the stable life they believe they have. Men who assume a position of denial about their wives' cheating are often so dependent upon their spouses that they do not want to risk the possibility of losing them. These unfaithful spouses are already gone emotionally.

Connie and Bill were in a second marriage together. She owned her business and he was underemployed for the level of his education and talents. There was some strong circumstantial evidence that Connie had been involved with some previously inappropriate relationships with other male colleagues, but she denied them. Bill responded to these situations by becoming more controlling and monitoring Connie more closely. Although he seemed generally hostile toward her, he was emotionally and financially dependent upon Connie as well. At the risk of ending their relationship, he tried to just get past the incidents and redouble his efforts to keep her in line.

When the evidence becomes impossible to ignore, the reactions are often surprisingly minimal. There is disappointment and hurt, but they quickly move on to making sure the tryst is over. The normal devastation and anger typically betrayed spouses experience seems to be absent or repressed. The betrayed spouse may even blame the person their spouse was cheating with, laying the majority of the fault with them. These conflict-avoiding couples sweep it under the rug and continue on with business as usual. These couples are rarely seen in marital counseling even though they need it badly.

3. ANGER AND RETALIATION

> "Heaven has no rage like love to hatred turned. Hell hath no fury like a woman scorned."
>
> William Congreve

Some of the most intense exchanges witnessed in my office have occurred between couples who have recently discovered an affair on the part of one spouse. Even meek, demure women who are soft spoken and the epitome of social appropriateness can turn into "rage-a-holics" when confronted with betrayal. The hurt and anger seems to come from deep within their soul and can be quite intimidating to observe. Although I normally do not let couples get out of control emotionally at each other in my office, this is one exception. The injured spouse often needs to have an opportunity to fully express their anger if they are to ever move past this affront to the marriage. I personally prefer that they do this in the privacy of their own home, but it has on occasion erupted in my office. If the catharsis is brief and controlled, it can generally be helpful.

Sue and Dick had a perfect relationship prior to Dick's affair, according to Sue. Even though they both had horrible first marriages, they had finally gotten it right in this marriage. When Sue became aware of his brief affair with a coworker, she was initially overwhelmed with grief. Not long afterward, however, she was so angry that she took every opportunity to verbally berate Dick for his actions. Although Dick was legitimately remorseful and expressed his regret often, it was not enough for Sue. It was eventually apparent that her pain was not only caused by her husband's betrayal but by previous betrayals she had experienced in her early family life. As a young child, her mother would use her as a confidante to talk about all her father's affairs. She had even taken Sue with her on a number of occasions to find her father when he was with other women.

Couples who remain in this mode of regularly taking out their anger on the guilty spouse will eventually do more damage than good if their ultimate goal is to repair their marriage. Anger's purpose is to motivate us to solve a present problem or protect us from impending danger. When it is used solely for the purpose of punishing someone else, it becomes counterproductive.

Retaliation is one form of anger that only adds insult to injury. One destructive form of retaliation is to tell everyone in the couple's life that their spouse has cheated, including friends, parents, children, coworkers, or even the spouse's boss. Unfortunately, the negative tide of rejection can end up backfiring and doing the relationship more damage than good. This is especially true if the couple decides to work out their marriage. Those who have chosen sides then wonder why the betrayed spouse would consider going back or trying to work it out since they initially portrayed their straying spouse in such an egregious manner.

Spouses who respond by having a retaliatory affair of their own demonstrate another form of insult to injury. *Hurt people hurt people*. When this type of "eye for an eye" behavior occurs in a marriage, no one wins. These relationships generally have a history of mutually punitive reactions to marital problems. Often the "affair for an affair" is enough to end the marriage. This type of demonstrated resentment is like *drinking poison hoping one's spouse will die*.

4. PANIC, ANXIETY, AND DESPERATION

When Kathy discovered that Fred was having an affair, she had a panic attack. She hyperventilated, her heart raced, and she could not calm herself down. She knew that their sex life was unsatisfactory to him, but she never imagined he would turn to another woman. Kathy grew up feeling neglected and ignored by her parents. Her father was very successful in his business and always busy doing things for others. Her mother worked and was never around. They later discovered she had a long-term affair with another man. Even though Fred's affair ended and they began working on their marriage, Kathy was obsessed with the other woman. What did this woman have that she didn't have? Why did Fred want her instead of Kathy? How could she be assured this would never happen again? Kathy even began having sex with Fred every other day to make sure he would never stray again.

Sometimes people will not do anything to keep a marriage from breaking, but they will do anything to repair it after it is broken. The panic they feel is legitimate because often the offending spouse has given up on the idea that their marriage can be saved. Though inexcusable, it is not surprising that the unhappy spouse will find someone else who will show interest in them.

Another reaction betrayed spouses sometimes have is wholesale panic and desperately pleading for the unfaithful partner not to leave them. All vestiges of self-respect are abandoned for the purpose of staying together at any cost. Sometimes these marriages can be saved if there is still some substance to the relationship. Many times this reaction is a reflection of a marriage that has been over for quite some time.

Danez and Sam were high school sweethearts who married while still in college. Danez became pregnant as a student and discontinued her education to take care of their child. She never went back to finish her degree and continued having children. She was a very child-focused parent who lost interest in having sex and had gained a lot of weight. When Sam came home one day unexpectedly and told Danez he was no longer in love with her and moving out, she was terrified. What would she do with three children, limited education, and no work experience? Danez begged and pleaded for Sam to stay and work it out. He felt guilty and ashamed, but it eventually came out that he had become involved with another woman. Danez was willing to forgive and move on if he would just give their marriage another chance.

The affair is sometimes the final death blow in a destructive attempt to exit the relationship. This ulterior motive affair is intended to make the offended spouse so indignant that they will give up and concede. It is not uncommon that the cheating spouse has a lover waiting for them to get a divorce. Revealing the affair often causes the wounded spouse to cling even tighter to a failing marriage that slowly dies despite the pleas for reconciliation. This scenario is extremely painful to witness in a counseling setting. Sometimes the threat or likelihood of suicide is high for the wounded spouse. They are often abandoned and left with the counselor to try and recover the pieces of their shattered life.

When a betrayed spouse has a history of other traumatic events that have occurred in their past, the infidelity usually triggers these memories of the past and magnifies these emotional injuries in the present.

5. FEELING PARALYZED

Martin Seligman coined the phrase "learned helplessness" to describe a state of resignation to the inevitable. Spouses who have been subject to a relationship in which they feel powerless to change their circumstances sometimes give up. They do not believe that anything they do will change the outcome, so they do nothing. They focus on the kids or household responsibilities and try their best to ignore their slowly deteriorating marriage. Denial, panic, and surrender can lead to dissociating, used to escape the painful reality of what is actually happening. It is like the person in hell that says to himself, *"I'm not here and it's not hot."* It does not change what is happening, but it alters their reality. The trauma of infidelity can cause a person to feel so helpless, that they believe nothing they do will make a difference. So they continue forward feeling resigned to their lot in life. Their learned helplessness renders them powerless to make a difference. They are broken and defeated.

Jean was married to a man who had cheated multiple times on his previous wives. Although Jean knew about his past, she was devastated when another affair was discovered. Her initial reaction caused him to end the other relationship. His feigned remorse became evident when she expected him to become more accountable and keep her informed about his whereabouts. Though Jean made threats, she never took action. She did not want to lose him, their lifestyle, and the imaginary security she had. It wasn't long before he was back to doing whatever he wanted to do.

6. THE FINAL STRAW: ENDING THE MARRIAGE

In contrast to the panic and pleading reaction is the spouse who, upon discovering infidelity, promptly ends the marriage. Unbeknownst to others, this affair may represent the last straw in a long list of affronts that have occurred in the marriage. There is often nothing left to fight for in this relationship, and it is time for the wounded spouse to cut their losses. While ending the marriage so abruptly may seem premature to the casual onlooker, the history of gradual deterioration has been occurring for years.

Dan was the CEO of a midsized company that had been quite successful with him at the helm. His marriage, however, had not been so successful, as he had allowed himself to have two brief affairs within a five-year period. His wife had patiently worked through the discovery of these betrayals for the sake of their children, the family, and his reputation. When she discovered yet another affair by using the services of a private investigator, she was finished with his philandering and promptly acquired the services of a divorce attorney. She filed for divorce, obtained custody of the children, negotiated alimony along with rehabilitative alimony to upgrade her professional skills, and never looked back. This was the final straw for her.

On occasion, taking this no-nonsense posture elicits a complete turnaround on the part of the offending spouse. Perhaps for the first time, he or she commits to making changes that should have occurred long ago. If the wounded spouse is willing, sometimes this last-ditch effort is worth the risk and the marriage can be saved. Of course, the proof is in the pudding, and it will be a long road to rebuilding trust and credibility. This often represents the first time the spouse who has been cheated on has gained equal power in this relationship. Letting something go may bring it back, but sometimes it is too little too late.

HOMEWORK EXERCISE

Which of These Traumatic Reactions Best Fits You?

After reading the most common reactions to discovering an affair, review the examples below and circle one that seems most relevant to you.

1. Shock, devastation, and depression. *"I can't believe the pain!"*
2. Denial and disbelief. *"I don't believe it." "There must be some other explanation." "My spouse wouldn't do this."*
3. Anger and retaliation. *"You will be sorry for hurting me!"*
4. Panic and pleading for reconciliation. *"Please don't leave me. I'll do anything." "Why wasn't I enough?"*
5. Feeling paralyzed. *"I'm at a loss as to what to do."*
6. Ending the marriage. *"This is the last straw. It is over for me."*

CHAPTER 9

FOUR INFIDELITY RECOVERY STAGES:
A TWELVE-ACTION-STEP PROCESS

"Look for three things in a person—intelligence, energy, and integrity. If they don't have the last, don't bother with the first two."

—Warren Buffet

One of the most painful and destructive incidents to occur within a marriage or a committed relationship is the emotional or sexual involvement of one of the partners with another person. The havoc reaped upon the couple is unlike any grief or loss one can endure and is often described as "gut wrenching." It is like seeing the end of a dream that turns into one's worst nightmare. The betrayal, feelings of abandonment, and disillusionment cause an individual to question everything he or she has ever known or believed in. Some people's worlds are so turned upside down that they never recover. It is not uncommon to hear, "How can I ever trust you or anyone else again?"

When couples courageously decide to face the crisis of this betrayal together, they have the best chance for recovery and repair within their relationship. It is a long and difficult road. They can come out with many aspects of this agonizing dilemma understood, repaired, and ultimately resolved if traveled with patience, courage, and forgiveness. Many times the relationship can become stronger than it ever was.

If the relationship cannot be salvaged, going through this process can help either partner understand more fully what happened, heal, and move on with his or her life.

Here are the progressive stages and steps that most couples and individuals in my experience must take for resolution over the affair.

STAGE 1—DISCOVERY: "THE REALITY CHECK"

1. Action Step One: Recognition
When in doubt, just take the next small step.

When You Have Suspicions

The discovery of a past or present affair is a day and time that will be etched in the memory of the betrayed spouse forever. Most unknowing partners accidently find an e-mail, text message, picture, receipt, or some other evidence leading them to further explore the inconsistency. They often have had a gut feeling or vague sense that something has been amiss for a while, but did not want to believe it. Others are caught totally off guard and have been oblivious to what was going on with their wayward partner.

Sometimes an anonymous person, friend, or family member relays concerns or observations they have had regarding the activities of one's spouse. Even questions from the children can be a relevant clue to clandestine behavior that could be occurring. No one wants to believe that their spouse could be cheating on them. Most likely telltale signs have been ignored or denied for quite a while.

The betrayed spouse rarely wants to believe the evidence. They hope for a reasonable explanation for the information they have discovered.

The unfaithful spouse will most likely deny the evidence or have a reasonable explanation for it.

Lies, Vagueness, Inconsistencies, and Deceit

Ignore words, believe actions.

One of the most telltale signs that something has changed with your spouse is the gradual occurrence of white lies. These are small omissions or even commissions that seem irrelevant but become a pattern of avoiding accountability. Examples of changes that occur are not mentioning a lunch out with a certain person, tardiness, failing to answer the phone or return calls promptly, unexplained cash withdrawals, a new password on their phone, or new, unfamiliar friends.

Common routines previously followed change with no explanation, and when questioned, excuses follow. There is a noticeable decrease in sharing about their day, and periods of silence or preoccupation with technology occur more often. The distance is apparent to the concerned partner but denied by their spouse. Interest wanes toward activities done as a couple, and mutual friends do not seem as important as they once were. When inquiries are made about the reasons for their behavior, irritability and impatience may be shown. Job pressures are often the excuse given for these gradual changes.

The betrayed spouse will gradually start to question his or her own sanity. He or she will begin to doubt themselves and seem confused in spite of overwhelming evidence to the contrary. The unfaithful spouse will become adept at eliciting sympathy for what they are going through or becoming immediately incensed at being questioned.

What If I Suspect That My Spouse Is Cheating?

It is no easy task to be patient in the midst of feeling overwhelmingly insecure. It is essential, however, to step back and get the big picture. Take a deep breath and give yourself some time to take stock of the situation. Our first impulse is to question, confront, and ask what is going on. The problem with this approach is that it alerts the unfaithful spouse of your awareness that something is wrong. Most people will redouble their efforts to cover their tracks if some clandestine behavior is actually occurring.

Don't tip your hand. Just observe and take note of what is happening. Gather evidence as it is revealed to you and document it. When you decide to have a heart-to-heart conversation with your spouse, you have evidence to back up your concerns. If he or she launches into a diatribe or tries to make you feel like you are crazy, the hard evidence acquired will strengthen your resolve to hold your ground over the issues.

HOMEWORK EXERCISE

The purpose of this exercise is to take a methodical approach to gathering information instead of reacting impulsively by prematurely confronting your spouse. It is less likely that denial will create self-doubt or weaken your resolve by gathering, documenting, and organizing information.

Gathering the Evidence

If you have legitimate concerns about the actions of your spouse, do not immediately get upset, accuse, assume the worst, or search through his or her phone, computer, or credit card receipts.

- *Just step back, keep your doubts to yourself, and observe calmly for a while if possible.*
- *Begin a **journal** of your observations, impressions, and concerns. Include situations, dates, specific statements made, and inconsistencies discovered.*
- *Begin a **file** of any evidence to document and support your suspicions and keep it in a secure place or with a friend.*

HOMEWORK EXERCISE

Below is a checklist of behaviors you may have observed in your spouse but did not place any significance upon.

Inventory: Infidelity and Cheating: Thirty Signs to Look for

Please circle all items that apply to your situation and total them at the bottom.

1. Previous rituals of affection before saying goodbye end.
2. The cell phone is hidden or kept on their person at all times.
3. Preoccupation with the phone occurs.
4. Texts are received at all times of the day or night.
5. You don't know the passwords to their electronic accounts any longer.
6. A sudden tendency to be secretive occurs.
7. They complain often about small issues and become negative.
8. A sudden change in attention to looks, clothes, weight, and working out occurs.
9. May not seem to be as "into you" as before.
10. Cannot look you directly in the eyes easily.
11. Sex drops off or increases suddenly.
12. Guilt purchases or offerings occur.
13. Trips are taken with friends, coworkers, or others, and you are not invited.
14. Your fidelity or trustworthiness is questioned.
15. Fights and arguments about insignificant things seem to occur more often.
16. Routines or schedule changes to working later begin.
17. Inconsistencies, white lies, and vague explanations become more frequent.

18. He or she hangs out with single and divorced friends, or others who have a history of infidelity or cheating.
19. You rarely do anything alone together anymore.
20. There may be a change in sexual routines or practices.
21. He or she may have more friends of the opposite sex.
22. Someone's name keeps coming up at work in their conversation.
23. You have that gut feeling that something is not right despite assurances that things are fine.
24. They have cheated before on someone else or earlier in the relationship with you.
25. They deny everything even if you can document it, have proof, or saw the evidence yourself.
26. Spends more time away from home.
27. An avoidance of contact with you occurs around conversations, calls, texts, or time together.
28. There are frequent examples of circumstantial evidence that cause you doubts.
29. Your spouse is dismissive of your insecurities or feelings and seems annoyed.
30. He or she has a quick explanation for everything, but you do not feel reassured.

Total _____

(A score of ten or more is a cause for concern and may warrant further inquiry.)

2. Action Step Two: Typical Reactions of the Offending Spouse

"The integrity of the upright guides them but the unfaithful are destroyed by their duplicity."
Proverbs 11:3 (NIV)

Denial as the First Line of Defense

"Sin is not ended by multiplying words, but the prudent hold their tongues."
Proverbs 10:19 (NIV)

Once the injured spouse has enough evidence to move forward to face the situation, the hardest part begins. The unfaithful spouse typically resorts to rationalizations, denials, minimizations, blame shifting, and stonewalling in order to dismiss the accusations presented. Their emotions often range from a calm but detached dismissal to rage-filled indignation at the accusations.

Most straying spouses will outright deny the charges in the face of overwhelming evidence, in hopes to shake the resolve of their partner. Others will lie quite convincingly and have a number of reasonable explanations that would probably convince a jury.

During my years as an executive coach and management consultant, I had many opportunities to meet and work with CEOs and the executive officers of various companies. I remember vividly a conversation that occurred during a break at a presentation I was doing for a group of CEOs. One of them asked about a colleague who was not attending the meeting that morning. Another CEO responded, *"Oh, he made the mistake of being honest with his wife about an affair he was having, and now she is divorcing him."* His mistake was in having an affair, not being honest about it. If his spouse reacted that quickly to divorce him, there was more wrong within this relationship than just the affair.

Denial seems to be the first response an unfaithful spouse offers when discovered. The more adamant and indignant the denial, the more likely it is to cause the questioning spouse to doubt themselves. We want to be wrong about our suspicions.

"I did not have sexual intercourse with that woman." When we heard President Clinton state that on national television, *were we not all tempted to believe him?* He was so convincing that it initially shook our resolve. This is what lying with a straight face does to most of us.

Defensive Anger, Blaming the Victim, and the Trickle-Out Approach

> *"Blame shifting puts most of us on the defensive."*
> DCW

The unfaithful spouse will often get angry at the accusations and turn them back on the questioning party for invading their privacy. We all know a good offense is the best defense. The offending partner may take a minor issue such as looking at their cell phone, and turn it into a major infraction in order to shift the attention away from their deceit.

The betrayed spouse will often find themselves on the defensive and start to question whether they have made a mistake. It is important to hold the line here because your spouse is hoping to weaken your resolve.

Refrain from showing them the evidence prematurely. Give them a chance to tell you about what has happened. It is important to give the accused an opportunity to come clean on their own in order to demonstrate a willingness to accept responsibility for their actions. You may let them know you have irrefutable evidence to support your claims, but that you want them to voluntarily admit to what they have been doing. You might give them partial information about what you know, in order to give them a chance to explain the details without revealing all your evidence.

Some offending spouses will use the trickle-out approach to disclosing their involvement with someone else. When denial fails and they realize that they must offer some explanation, they will admit to a small but limited involvement. This is intended to appease their spouse with hopes that they will accept a minimized or edited version of what really happened. It also gives them more of a confirmation of how the betrayed spouse will react to knowing the truth. Rarely does this satisfy a betrayed spouse, and they will increase their efforts to find out what else may have occurred.

Gradually more details are acknowledged by the offending spouse until hopefully the entire truth is out. The problem is that the betrayed spouse at this point still believes there is more about which they do not know. The offending spouse, in trying to protect themselves, has proven to be an astute liar, and they no longer have any credibility with their spouse.

When Tina discovered that her husband, Rob, had been receiving texts and calls from an unknown woman, she was suspicious and asked him about it. He dismissed her concerns and attributed their exchanges to work-related issues. Later she discovered sexually oriented e-mails from the same woman and asked Rob again what was going on. Again, he minimized the interaction and said he had not encouraged her overtures. When Tina discovered a nude picture of the other woman on his phone, she was livid and demanded to know what was happening between them. Rob admitted they were sexting but that nothing physical had occurred between them. At this point, Tina believed nothing that Rob was telling her, and she redoubled her efforts to find out what else was happening.

Other unfaithful spouses will quickly admit to the affair and show willingness to make amends or acknowledge what has been going on. Those spouses who show immediate remorse are more likely to genuinely work on repairing the marriage. Their open admission provides the wronged spouse with the option to address what they expect next regarding the future of the relationship.

HOMEWORK EXERCISE

Hurt and anger go hand in hand when a spouse has been betrayed. Below is a compilation of comments and feelings injured spouses have relayed. See which ones you can relate to in the exercise below.

Checklist: The Invalidating Effects of an Affair on the Betrayed Spouse or Partner

Below are actual statements made by betrayed spouses. Please **circle** *the number next to the feelings and thoughts you have had since discovering the infidelity. When you have finished, show it to your spouse so that he or she might better understand what you are experiencing.*

1. I'm such a fool.
2. My whole world is unraveling.
3. Why didn't I see it?
4. How could he/she do this to me and our family?
5. I'll never trust him/her again.
6. What did I do to deserve this?
7. Our life as it was is over.
8. What will my future hold?
9. My family will never forgive him/her.
10. Will this pain ever go away?
11. I feel so humiliated.
12. No one is ever going to hurt me this way again.
13. I'm staying for now but just until the kids grow up.
14. I gave the best years of my life, and this is what I get in return?
15. I'm so numb, I don't know what I feel.
16. I can't work, I can't eat, I can't sleep.
17. It was like I was punched in the stomach.
18. I want to make him/her hurt the way I hurt.
19. This is over for me.
20. I'm walking around in a fog.

21. *I don't want him/her to touch me.*
22. *I don't know this person anymore.*
23. *I want you gone.*
24. *What am I going to do on my own?*
25. *Our friends are not going to want to have anything to do with us.*
26. *You have ruined my life.*
27. *Every time I think about them being together, I just feel sick.*
28. *I feel like a failure as a partner.*
29. *What will others think of me as a wife/husband?*
30. *I must not have been enough for him/her.*
31. *I am so embarrassed; I don't want anyone to know.*
32. *I don't feel safe with you any longer.*
33. *I have turned into someone I don't like.*
34. *I don't feel attractive or appealing any longer.*
35. *You gave what we had away to someone else.*

HOMEWORK EXERCISE

As the betrayed spouse, you must understand all the ways you are angry and to document those in detail. By identifying how you specifically feel, you can begin working through this injury and begin the process of repair.

The Anger List

Go off by yourself and take at least thirty minutes to journal about all the things causing you anger about:

- *about the affair*
- *your marriage*
- *about your spouse*
- *about yourself*
- *how you feel you have been treated*
- *what has happened to you*
- *regrets you have*
- *missed opportunities in your relationship*
- *things you have imagined doing as a result of this revelation*

(Be honest, thorough, and frank about your feelings.)

CHAPTER 10

ACTION STEP THREE: TAKING RESPONSIBILITY

"Wisdom is knowing the right path. Integrity is taking it!"
—M. H. McKee

Ladies! Do you want to marry a man or a boy?

BOYS AND MEN
Boys play house, men build homes.
Boys shack up, men get married.
Boys make babies, men raise children.
A boy won't raise his own children, a man will raise someone else's.
Boys invent excuses for failure, men produce strategies for success.
Boys look for somebody to take care of them, men look for someone to take care of.
Boys seek popularity, men command respect.
Boys forget, men remember.
Boys put it off, men follow through.
Boys blame someone else, men take responsibility.

TOTAL DISCLOSURE
If you lie to yourself, you lose.

The person who accepts responsibility for his or her problem is the person who will overcome it. In order for the stages to progress toward some possible resolution, the unfaithful spouse or partner must begin to acknowledge and disclose the details of the affair, otherwise an impasse occurs. Even at this point, it is rare that total disclosure occurs immediately. Rather, it trickles out slowly in painful stages as the wounded but unrelenting spouse continues to discover more secrets.

What occurs next is the "sixty to ninety days of obsessing" as the betrayed partner tries to understand the who, what, when, and where of the affair. Endless questioning occurs at this point, sometimes to the detriment of the relationship. Further conflicts often erupt as more information is revealed. If the offending party does not fully discuss the specifics of the other relationship, however, reconciliation may be indefinitely postponed.

Healing (repairing trust) cannot occur without total disclosure, and any progress forward is often forfeited upon the discovery of omitted information. When vital information is withheld, the initial progress in rebuilding trust is also short circuited, and the repair process goes back to square one.

Most cheating spouses are reluctant to disclose everything for fear that their partner will end the marriage if they do. Sometimes, the relationship does end when total disclosure occurs. If the marriage can be saved, it will not move forward unless the whole truth is revealed.

John Kador wrote *Effective Apology: Mending Fences, Building Bridges, and Restoring Trust*. He found in a study of eight thousand customers that people who are more willing to say "I'm sorry" make more money than people who rarely or never apologize. People earning over $100,000 a year were almost twice as likely to apologize after an argument or mistake as those earning $25,000 or less. Their apologies were an indicator of their confidence, strong people skills, and security in themselves.

> "God opposes the proud but gives grace to the humble."
> James 4:6 (ESV)

Infidelity recovery cannot begin until the wronged spouse feels relatively certain that he or she knows about all the improprieties that have occurred on the part of their spouse. There is always the risk that total disclosure could end the marriage, but there is a higher risk of divorce if total disclosure is not provided. The repair process cannot start until the full extent of the damage is known and the injured party believes they have the whole story.

CONSEQUENCES OF NOT DISCLOSING

- It postpones the repair process.
- It prolongs the pain suffered by the wronged spouse.
- It exacerbates their hurt and anger.
- It reduces the offending partner's credibility.
- It destroys the possibility of rebuilding trust.
- It increases the likelihood of divorce.

HOMEWORK EXERCISE

Ending-the-Affair Agreement

The affair must end if the marriage is to be saved. If the betrayed spouse is willing to consider saving the marriage, the first order of business is to determine if his or her spouse is willing to stop the affair.

Have your spouse read this document and sign and date it as an acknowledgment of acceptance.

- Agree that the affair will be ended.
- Determine how that relationship will be ended.
- Define how that ending will be verified (letter, e-mail, or mutual phone call).
- Accept that there will be no friendship with the other person hereafter.
- "Burn the ships." Eliminate all means of communication with the other person and establish a no-contact policy.
- Any attempts by the other party to contact the offending spouse will be immediately reported (within twenty-four hours) to the spouse, along with the intact message sent.
- All calls from one's spouse must be answered immediately.
- The offending spouse is compelled to provide open access to all means of communication (phone, computer, e-mails, Facebook, etc.) to the spouse.
- Close friendships with the opposite sex must be approved of by the spouse.
- Tardiness or changes in schedule merit a call to one's spouse.
- No meetings, travel, lunches, etc., with the opposite sex without the approval of the spouse.

- No secrets.
- Questionable circumstances that could be misconstrued if discovered must be disclosed proactively.
- If the affair was with a colleague, a change of job, working arrangements, department, or company may need to occur.

_____

Signature   Date

HOMEWORK EXERCISE

This is an exercise for the betraying partner to provide to his or her spouse.

Full Disclosure

Write out in detail the history of the relationships that have occurred outside your marriage or exclusive relationship.

Include:

- How and when you met
- How the relationship began
- How long it has been going on
- What is the nature of the relationship?
- How you feel about this other person
- When did the sexual activity begin?
- What kind of sexual activities occurred?
- How many times?
- Where did you meet?
- What did you feel you were getting in this relationship that you didn't receive with your spouse?
- Did you consider being together with this other person permanently?
- What other relationships or encounters have you had in addition to this one?

Share this with your spouse or significant other, and be prepared to spend time elaborating on additional questions asked. Sometimes, it is more productive for couples to meet with their therapist during the disclosure exercise to mitigate the extreme reactions that can occur.

HOMEWORK EXERCISE

The injured spouse often needs to balance his or her demands for control with being respectful toward their spouse. The following represents ways to encourage greater cooperation toward repairing their relationship.

Post-Traumatic Stress Disorder (PTSD) and Managing Triggers over the Affair

- Keep a journal.
- Write down your feelings so that you will not be so likely to replay them over and over in your head.
- Make a list of questions and issues you would like to discuss as they occur to you.
- Refrain from peppering your spouse with endless questions.
- Have set times to talk through what is on your mind.
- Limit those times to an hour or less.
- Listen to what your spouse has to say. If you trump his or her response with "but you are the one who cheated," nothing will move forward.
- Refrain from using your spouse as a whipping post, verbally or physically.
- Take the negatives that have occurred between you and determine how to make something constructive out of it that will rebuild your marriage.

Best Times Not to Talk

The betrayed spouse will want to talk about all aspects of the affair over and over until they believe they have all the relevant information, an understanding of why it occurred, and reassurance it will not reoccur. Sometimes, couples will talk for hours daily or into the night. It is not always productive to do this and may make your situation worse.

There are times when it is best not to talk. Forcing interaction will only make things worse, and it could escalate into something ugly and hurtful.

Here are a few of those times.

- First thing in the morning before you are awake and coherent
- Over the phone when one or both of you are in the middle of working
- When one of you is dealing with parenting issues
- When one of you first walks in the door from work or out of town
- When you are angry and worked up
- Before, in the middle of, or after lovemaking
- After 9:00 p.m.
- When one or both of you have been drinking
- When you are tired and exhausted
- When you are hungry and irritated
- In the presence of your children, family, or friends
- In the car during rush-hour traffic
- When you are sick and do not feel well
- After a bad day at work
- On the way to church
- When you are overwhelmed and flooded by other things that are going wrong
- During the loss of a family member or friend

What's Done in the Dark

HOMEWORK EXERCISE

Partners who have betrayed their spouses have reasons and rationalizations that they have privately thought or even repeated to their spouse about why the affair occurred. The following comments are actual statements made by spouses or partners who were unfaithful.

Checklist: My Rationalizations for the Affair

Please circle each of the thoughts, feelings, reasons, or rationalizations you have had at one time or another before and during the affair process. Then, show this list to your spouse, and discuss in depth why you felt that way at the time.

1. He or she was just a friend.
2. There is nothing wrong with having a close friend of the opposite sex.
3. We had drifted apart and were more like roommates.
4. We hadn't had regular sex in months.
5. I never felt like a priority.
6. He/she understood me more than my spouse.
7. I just needed someone to talk to.
8. I could never measure up to your expectations.
9. All we did was argue and fight.
10. I was attracted to him/her, but I thought I could handle it.
11. Your job seemed more important than me.
12. You put the kids ahead of me.
13. Sharing personal things with him/her helped me not resent you as much.
14. I was always last on his/her list.
15. We weren't close in our marriage and I needed more.
16. My spouse didn't understand me and he/she did.
17. Sex was unimportant to him/her.

18. I rarely felt listened to.
19. This relationship helped me feel less dissatisfied at home.
20. Other people actually found me interesting.
21. I received more attention from others than my spouse.
22. If I hadn't had an affair, I might have gotten a divorce.
23. It was just sex. The other person didn't mean anything to me.
24. It just happened. I couldn't stop it.
25. I felt constantly criticized.
26. The other person thought I was great and my own spouse didn't.
27. My spouse wasn't meeting certain needs I had.
28. My spouse didn't seem to be interested in me anymore.
29. It is discouraging living with someone who is always right.
30. My opinions didn't seem to matter.
31. The other person made me feel alive again.
32. I gave up trying.
33. I thought our relationship was not going to change.
34. Being talked down to made me feel worthless.

WHAT IF MY SPOUSE WON'T STOP THE AFFAIR?

Staying Together

If you discover your spouse is having an affair and he or she will not agree to end it, you may decide to give them more time while you try to talk it out. Keeping them close by to help them see what you both have together can be effective. Even though it is very painful to live with someone who you know is involved with someone else, it can be a powerful influence to just love them anyway.

If you are dependent upon a spouse because of children or finances, it will be important to consider what could happen if he eventually leaves anyway. Women who do not have a job, an education, or any marketable skills are most at risk for being treated like a doormat. Sometimes, biding your time while the situation plays itself out, but also coming up with a plan to improve your options, can be a good strategy.

Many marriages are turned around because a woman decided to complete her degree or find a job and enter the workforce. This decision immediately improves her self-esteem, empowers her as an individual, and eventually impacts her economic future.

In the meantime, a wayward spouse may realize how capable and valuable their partner is and come to their senses. It could be invaluable to seek individual or couples counseling utilizing a third party to both look at your options and help you anticipate your future.

Jackie was a middle-aged woman with three children married to a guy who recklessly had several illicit relationships with his female employees. She felt trapped and powerless in the marriage because of their financial burdens, young children, and lack of education and marketable skills. She entered individual counseling, closely evaluating her options. She was a woman of faith who did not want a divorce, yet did not want to be mistreated any longer. During counseling, she was able to regain some confidence in herself, look at college options, and determine that she could begin working part time while finishing her degree.

Eventually, she felt strong enough to influence her husband to get counseling to look at his problems with the idea that they would ultimately see a marital therapist together. If he had not seen the writing on the wall, she would have eventually been strong enough to leave him.

Separating

Separation for the sake of "time apart," for having time to "think," or "just needing space" is rarely helpful. Sometimes, an agreed-upon separation that has defined objectives can provide a way to work through things while determining whether the marriage can be saved. For instance, in highly conflictual marriages, a time apart can keep a marriage from eroding beyond repair if it includes maximizing the positive times when together and having the option to stop the interaction and retreat to separate residences when unproductive conflict occurs. Establishing rules of engagement, or conditions around which you will have contact together beforehand, can make this transition smoother. Examples might be setting up a regular time to meet weekly, calling before coming over, and scheduling times to see the children, to name a few.

Separating when one spouse will not end their involvement with the other person is a way to (1) protect oneself, (2) set a limit on the cheating spouse going back and forth between home and lover, (3) disempower the enticement of the forbidden-fruit dynamic (when an affair is no longer a secret, it loses its excitement), and (4) give the undecided spouse a chance to decide what they want without the benefits of having full access to their spouse.

Letting Go

In most cases, the spouse who has been cheated on has to decide if they can live with someone who is lying, duplicitous, and won't genuinely give the marriage a chance. James Dobson, a Christian psychologist who wrote *Love Must Be Tough,* recommends letting the straying spouse go so he can make his mind up. Of course, the stipulation is that there are no guarantees that he will be able to come back. Letting them go redistributes the unequal power balance and removes a certain amount of the enticement that a forbidden-fruit relationship creates.

Cheating Is Cheating Is Cheating

How much cheating is too much to handle?

Kissing, fondling, nude pictures, phone sex, mutual masturbation, oral sex, intercourse, multiple partners, or prostitutes?

When couples are in the throes of discovery, the truth often only trickles out in stages. Then, the quest begins for "how far did it go?"

Some maintain they will only stay in the marriage if no intercourse occurred with the other person. Others can tolerate a sexual tryst as long as their partner wasn't in love with the other person. Still others are willing to stay together if the affair is ended immediately and reconciliation begins.

Though the degree of cheating is relevant, it is still cheating. A betrayal has occurred. The exclusivity of the relationship has been given away. The trust has been broken. Why argue over the extent of the infidelity? The commitment in your relationship has been compromised.

The real question is, can you accept the past and move on or not?

Total disclosure, genuine regret, remorse with restitution, and recommitment are necessary, but can you forgive? Forgiving is not forgetting. It is not acting as if the past does not matter. Forgiveness is a very difficult but necessary stage. If the aforementioned processes do not all occur, you have to decide if you can heal without the total truth. If you can, get to work on the process of forgiving and looking at what needs to change within you both. If you can't forgive and reconcile, move on and begin rebuilding your life on your own.

HOMEWORK EXERCISE

Taking Care of Yourself

- Contact the person your spouse is cheating with and let them know who you are and what this affair is doing to your family.
- Take measures to protect yourself financially.
- Consider consulting an attorney to know your rights.
- Get family-and-friend support selectively. Can they be objective and not just take your side? Will they be confidential?
- Do not be retaliatory toward your spouse.
- If your children are old enough, discreetly let them know you are having marital problems. Say only what is necessary. Don't make them your confidants. Do not try to turn them against the other parent. It is all right to let them know you want this to work out even if your spouse is unsure.
- Do not use sex to try and compete against the other person.
- Establish a reasonable time limit for going through this.
- Establish rules for engagement regarding seeing the children, finances, calling before coming over, and other reasonable boundaries.
- Take care of yourself first.

WHY MARRIAGE TO A LOVER AFTER AN AFFAIR DOESN'T LAST

There are several studies that have concluded that marriage to a partner with whom one has had an affair do not last. One study suggests that only 3 percent of men who have had an affair divorced their wife and married their lover. Another study revealed that 75 percent of marriages with former affair partners ended in divorce. In yet another study, it was discovered that only 10 percent of marriages that began with an affair lasted (Snyder, Baucom, and Gordon).

Why marriages to a lover after an affair don't last:

The excitement and infatuation intensified by the element of forbidden fruit is often short lived. It all feels different once it is discovered and exposed. This fairy-tale romance looks very different when the realization of all the damage done becomes apparent. What seemed irresistible in the dark may look less inviting in the light.

The idealization stage of a relationship always ends. No matter how wonderful we may think a person is at first, their flaws will eventually emerge. No one is perfect. We all have our faults and shortcomings. What is left of a relationship when the *new wears off and the old shines through?* While distance lends enchantment to the view initially, the grass is not always greener on the other side.

Marriages are made, not born. They require constantly working together to forge a solid and lasting bond. Relationships that begin in a fantasy of fun and excitement have a poor foundation to build upon and often cannot handle the weight of life. Day-to-day responsibilities add a dose of reality and eventually test the viability of any relationship.

The loss of respect, disapproval from others, and diminished status in the eyes of loved ones reduces the chances that this could ever be a viable relationship. Actions taken impulsively, out of sheer emotion or under the influence, often lack good judgment, even though they may have seemed like a good idea at the time. Unprincipled decisions that ignore our value systems almost always turn out badly. Many regret what has transpired and long for their old life.

Getting a divorce is always costly. Getting a divorce because of an affair is even more costly. Whatever lifestyle a cheating couple thought they might have together is often marred by the reality of child support, alimony, division of marital assets, and attorney's fees. The financial burdens created by the affair, a divorce, and the remarriage to a lover are often costs that have not been realistically considered.

It is often surprising for a couple who has cheated together to end up not trusting each other. Perhaps they believed that their relationship was different, unique, and the exception because they were meant to be together. It is always ironic, however, when they come into counseling, bickering and accusing each other of the very problems they experienced in their previous marriages. These problems are significantly magnified by their mutual mistrust of one another. These marriages always have some element of doubt about the fidelity of one another.

CHAPTER 11

ACTION STEP FOUR: RELAPSE PREVENTION

"Knowing your weaknesses is a strength."
—G. Bastiste

TEN WAYS TO ENSURE THE AFFAIR WILL NOT REOCCUR

The greatest fear of a betrayed spouse is that their partner will resume the relationship they previously had with the other person. Relapse prevention is designed to reduce that likelihood by establishing a mutually agreed-upon plan of action.

The suggestions below represent the best strategy for protecting your relationship from further damage.

1. Mutually Agree That He or She Will Stop the Affair Immediately

If your spouse is unwilling or unable to do this, you may either give them more time as defined by you, separate to protect yourself, or see an attorney about ending the marriage.

2. End All Contact

Ending the affair can be done by e-mail, letter, voice mail, or a phone call. Most injured spouses prefer to listen to their spouse officially end the relationship by phone so both sides of the conversations are heard. A prearranged script of points to be made is generally preferred with the following included:
- "I am calling to end this relationship."
- "My spouse knows everything."
- "I do not want to lose my marriage."
- "There is no hope for this to continue."

- "Please do not try to contact me again through any medium."
- "I regret that this ever happened; it was the biggest mistake of my life."
- "Do you understand me?"

3. "Burn the Ships" (No Way Back)

When the straying partner voluntarily agrees to give access to all personal devices, accounts, and communication mediums, along with their passwords, there is a higher likelihood for the successful retreat from the affair. If arguments over invasion of privacy or protests over control tactics occur, chances are a lack of commitment toward recovery exists. Those spouses who willingly embrace this accountability are demonstrating an attitude of openness toward change.

4. Defining Limits and Setting Boundaries

The limits and boundaries established are often specific to how the affair has occurred. These are some common ones set by most injured spouses.
- Answer all questions asked of you by spouse.
- No texting, calling, e-mails, or social media contact with the opposite sex unless previously agreed upon together.
- No friendships with the opposite sex without the consent of one's spouse.
- No conversations or discussions with the opposite sex about their personal life or relationships.
- No time alone with the opposite sex unless agreed upon by one's spouse.
- No traveling with the opposite sex unless agreed upon by one's spouse.
- Call if you are going to be more than fifteen minutes late.
- Return calls by spouse immediately.
- Call at regularly scheduled times during the day as agreed upon by spouse when traveling.

- Inform spouse immediately of any form of communication that occurs from the other party. Leave the message in its original form with no deletions or alterations.

5. *Make an Individual Commitment to Personal Improvement*

Each person should take responsibility for his own personal development. It is never healthy for a spouse to "parent" his or her partner. It builds resentment on the part of both people. The more responsible spouse feels they have to constantly monitor the behavior of the other. The less responsible spouse feels treated like a child. Eventually, a loss of respect and equality occurs, and stubbornness fuels a struggle for who is right.

6. *Agree to Regular, Voluntary Accountability with Another Same-Sex Married Friend*

It is best to find a same-sex friend to help with accountability. It doesn't help the marriage for a spouse to have to monitor their partner's behavior. That is the job of the individual, and this can be facilitated by a good friend who is willing to tell them the truth. Using a coach or mentor to help accomplish goals in a particular area is common today, but a close friend can be just as helpful in our personal lives.

7. *No Secrets*

Alcoholics Anonymous maintains that *"We are only as sick as our secrets."*

If we cannot share something about ourselves with the person we love the most, then we are living with shame. Shame causes us not to accept ourselves and to believe others wouldn't accept us, either. What we hide about ourselves makes us feel like an imposter in life and magnifies our feelings of being a failure.

Sharing our secrets allows us to experience acceptance in spite of our faults. It is freeing to know someone knows the good, bad, and the ugly about us and loves us anyway.

8. If Drinking Causes Problems, Stop Drinking!

Drinking is an inhibition-lowering action that can facilitate risky social interactions. Alcohol can also blur boundaries and impair sound judgment. When drinking is a contributing factor in making poor decisions, it needs to be eliminated. The consequences are simply not worth it. Alcohol always makes it harder to say no to something we are trying to overcome. It lessens our resolve and makes us more impulsive. Many people have reconnected with the "other person" in a weak moment when under the influence. This relapse often is the beginning of another round of secrecy and lies that will take its toll on a marriage.

9. No Porn

The Porn Trap by Maltz and Maltz does a thorough job of reviewing all the latest research on the damage done to an individual and to a relationship by using pornography. Pornography interferes with an individual's ability to fully give themselves to another person emotionally. It also robs them of their ability to feel sexually satisfied with their spouse. Although pornography can cause immediate arousal, it short-circuits a person's emotional connection with their spouse. Our emotional connection is the strongest and most powerful source of continued arousal and sexual satisfaction. Pornography erodes long-term, real-life satisfaction for a short-term, fantasy high.

10. Align Your Values or Move On

Everyone deserves a second chance and maybe more. However, if dishonesty, lies, secrecy, and an unwillingness to change exist, it will eventually be time to let go and move on. We cannot change another person, but we can influence them by being the right kind of person. It is not our job to save them from themselves if they do not want to be committed. Even God lets go of individuals who are intent on self-destructiveness in hopes that the consequences of their choices will return them to Him (Romans 1:24–25).

HOMEWORK EXERCISE

Most injured spouses will temporarily need a great deal of reassurance that the affair is not continuing and is truly over. This checklist assists in accomplishing the means toward that end. If the offending spouse refuses to agree to the trust-rebuilding item, discuss his or her reasons and attempt to negotiate a workable compromise. If you discover an overall lack of cooperation between each other, consult a therapist to mediate the differences.

Checklist: What I Need to Rebuild Trust

First, in **Column A***, check the items (that are not already occurring) that you need your significant other to agree to do in order to rebuild trust.*

Next, in **Column B***, your significant other should then check the items (that he or she is not already doing) that he or she is willing to do on behalf of rebuilding trust in the relationship.*

A B
- ☐ ☐ Total disclosure: Tell me everything that happened.
- ☐ ☐ Give me the name(s) of the other person (people) involved.
- ☐ ☐ Provide a written apology.
- ☐ ☐ Open Access: Give me the passwords to your e-mail accounts, voice mail, social media accounts (Facebook), etc.
- ☐ ☐ Give me Internet access to your cell phone records and credit card purchases.
- ☐ ☐ If he or she calls, texts, e-mails, or voice mails you, do not delete the message, and inform me immediately.
- ☐ ☐ Terminate the relationship or any contact with the other person immediately.
- ☐ ☐ Allow me to see, observe, or hear evidence of your ending the other relationship.
- ☐ ☐ Answer all my questions, no matter how many different ways I ask you.

- ☐ ☐ Get an STD or HIV test if I request it and provide the results.
- ☐ ☐ Place a GPS tracker on your cell phone or car if I request it.
- ☐ ☐ No more secrets. If any other secrets exist, disclose them immediately.
- ☐ ☐ Be completely truthful. Do not omit or hide certain aspects of the truth.
- ☐ ☐ Answer my call immediately.
- ☐ ☐ Apologize and show genuine remorse with actions, amends, and repair attempts.
- ☐ ☐ Do what you say you are going to do. No excuses or rationalizations.
- ☐ ☐ Take responsibility for your mistakes. Do not blame me for what you did.
- ☐ ☐ Keep your word. Be accountable. If circumstances change, let me know why.
- ☐ ☐ No surprises. Keep me informed.
- ☐ ☐ Keep appropriate boundaries with opposite-sex friends, and be willing to define what this specifically means.
- ☐ ☐ Distance yourself from or even eliminate bad influences in your life and work.
- ☐ ☐ Be willing to renegotiate or redefine certain rules, limits, or boundaries.
- ☐ ☐ Be willing to change your place of employment if I require you to get away from the person with whom you were involved.
- ☐ ☐ Call when you say you will call.
- ☐ ☐ Be home within fifteen minutes of when you agreed upon or call.
- ☐ ☐ Keep your promises to me or discuss them immediately if something unforeseen occurs.
- ☐ ☐ Handle your behavior when away from me as if I were with you.
- ☐ ☐ Do not expect me to "just get over it" soon.
- ☐ ☐ Spend time with me when I need it.
- ☐ ☐ Listen, don't explain or defend.
- ☐ ☐ Be patient and supportive while I work through my pain and anger.
- ☐ ☐ Ask how I am doing when I get quiet.

- ☐ ☐ Make me feel that I am your number-one priority.
- ☐ ☐ Place me before your job, friends, activities, and family.
- ☐ ☐ Commit to deepening your emotional and spiritual life.
- ☐ ☐ Show gratitude for another chance.
- ☐ ☐ Revitalize common interests together as a couple.
- ☐ ☐ Be willing to change long-standing problems that have not improved.
- ☐ ☐ Show affection, appreciation, and attention daily.
- ☐ ☐ Go to counseling with me and for you as deemed warranted.

ACTION STEP FIVE: EXPERIENCING REMORSE

"Remorse begets reform."
William Cowper

"I Had an Affair!"

I had an affair . . . at least, in a dream. I don't know who she was or even what occurred. All I know is we were together, and as I was leaving, I realized I had just cheated on my wife. It was so disturbing; it woke me up out of a deep sleep. I realized immediately that I had just placed my entire marriage at risk.

As I lay there in semiconsciousness, I thought about how hurt my wife would be. I thought about how devastated she would be that I had so easily shared what we had with another woman. I imagined her crying over allowing someone else to take her place. She would feel that, somehow, she didn't measure up.

I also thought about what I would lose from her that I valued so much: her admiration, her generosity, her playfulness, the thoughtful things she does for me, her hugs, our cuddling in the mornings, her believing in me, her trust, her willingness to work hard and sacrifice for us, undressing in front of me, taking showers together, and our private jokes that only we can appreciate.

I was dreading how angry she would be as well. I wasn't looking forward to her withdrawing and refusing to allow me into her life. I thought about how my cheating would alter her optimism about life to a bleaker, more pessimistic outlook. I knew I would have to tell her because I would not be able to hide it or live with myself for being a liar and a cheater.

Fortunately, as I woke up, I realized it never really happened at all. What a relief I felt! Over coffee that morning, I said, "I had an affair!" She laughed and said, "With whom, your book?" I laughed, too!

Maybe she was right . . .

Sorry or Remorseful?

Most cheating spouses never expect that their actions will be discovered. They rationalize that they will eventually be able to get out of the other relationship undetected and no one will be the wiser. They do not anticipate the complexities that lying and deceit create. When their actions are discovered, the awareness of all the pain they have caused to countless people suddenly is revealed to them.

If they do not deflect, justify, or minimize their responsibility for the infidelity, they can begin to feel the devastation, hurt, anger, betrayal, and agony that their loved ones feel.

There is a difference between feeling sorry for everyone who has been hurt after getting caught and actually feeling remorseful. A cheating spouse often feels guilty and ashamed for what he has done, but he may not be truly remorseful. Remorse occurs when he regrets his previous actions and wishes they had never occurred. Genuine remorse involves the element of repentance, which is the demonstration of repairing the damage done whatever it costs.

Both spouses feel deep hurt, anger, and regret at this stage of the process for different reasons. The betrayed partner experiences deep, emotional grieving over the loss of the dream of who they used to be as a couple. The offending spouse begins to realize how much damage he or she has inflicted upon their marriage. Both people begin to painfully realize the lost exclusivity within their relationship, especially if there is a genuine desire to repair the bond.

Bo and Donna had been married for fifteen years with four children before they divorced because of his repeated affairs. Bo placed undue pressure on Donna to reunite. He had also convinced their fourteen-year-old son that it was his mother's fault the family could no longer be together. As a result, her son was very angry toward her. Bo minimized the affairs, told the kids that Donna wouldn't forgive him, and that he had changed. Donna actually had forgiven him, but his lack of contrition each time he cheated convinced her he had not really changed and could not be trusted.

Why doesn't she feel he is truly remorseful?
1. *Bo was sorry but never stopped having affairs.*
2. *He blamed his wife for their current family problems.*
3. *He minimized his behavior to his children by saying it was all in the past.*

4. *Bo was using his fourteen-year-old son as a pawn to manipulate his ex to reunite.*

What Is True Remorse?

- Recognizing and acknowledging the devastating effects of the affair
- Taking responsibility without justifying one's actions or blaming others
- Feeling genuine sorrow, grief, and regret
- Agreeing to change in very specific ways
- Asking for forgiveness from the affected people
- Making amends and repairing the damage done
- Learning from the mistake without repeating it

HOMEWORK EXERCISE

This is an exercise for the wayward spouse to complete. After writing a detailed response, give it to your partner to read and discuss together.

Remorse over the Affair

1. Make a list of everything you feel remorseful for: (for instance . . .)

    - the lies you have told
    - the disappointments you have caused
    - the betrayal to your commitment
    - the money you have spent
    - the risk of STDs
    - the risk of pregnancy
    - the humiliation to your family
    - the embarrassment to your children
    - the loss of credibility to your friends
    - the shame brought upon your extended family
    - the person you have become
    - the trust that has been lost
    - the damage to your reputation
    - the problems caused in your job

2. Rank order each item from worst to least in your estimation of harm caused.

3. Under each of these items, elaborate on:

"How has each of these emotionally affected my spouse?"

HOMEWORK EXERCISE

This is for each individual within the relationship to complete separately. Compare the results afterward and discuss what was most important to you.

What Is Worth Saving about Our Marriage/Relationship?

Take some time to reflect on the history of your relationship together.

- How you met
- What attracted you to each other?
- When did you first fall in love?
- What did you admire about one another?
- What good times do you remember?
- What kind of life have you built together?
- How were your values and beliefs similar?
- What goals you share
- What you have accomplished together

Then, write down all the reasons you can think of that makes your relationship worth saving.

1.

2.

3.

4.

5.

6.

7.

8.

9.

10.

CHAPTER 12

STAGE 2— WHAT IS? WHAT ISN'T?

ACTION STEP SIX: REALIZING THE "WHYS"

WHY DID THIS AFFAIR OCCUR?

Answering this question will not make things better. Nor will it offer an acceptable excuse. However, our minds often need explanations to make sense of the contributing factors.

Processing the meaning of the affair requires examining all the variables inside and outside the marriage that contributed to the betrayal in order to come to terms with it. The variables inside a marriage refer to problems that exist between the spouses. Problems outside the marriage refer to external factors such as jobs, in-laws, friends, stresses, and finances.

First, it should be noted that there is never a justifiable reason to cheat on one's partner. When cheating occurs, the offender is fully responsible for their actions. In some situations, the offended partner has had nothing directly to do with the actions of the other's straying.

Secondly, however, there are many occasions where the marital bond has become so weakened that it did not take much enticement for the cheating partner to go elsewhere. It is important for both people to fearlessly look within themselves to determine anything that could have legitimately impacted the relationship. If we are not honest with ourselves and our part in contributing to this, we will not be capable of honesty with others.

Sara and John had been married thirteen years and had one son. Several years before, Sara had delivered a daughter who was stillborn.

She had never recovered from the pain and grief she experienced over this. They were unsuccessful in getting pregnant after that first year. John took a second job to make ends meet and was gone a lot. Their sex life stopped because Sara had lost interest, much to John's chagrin. When she discovered John had been having brief affairs, she became severely depressed and even more withdrawn. He admitted that he felt Sara had given up on their marriage years ago. In his rejection, he had sought the attention of other women but admitted it had been an unfulfilling experience.

As much as a couple may hate to admit it, there are things both people in a relationship could have done differently to make the marriage better before an affair. Do some honest soul searching, and look at what you personally could have done to contribute to where your marriage is right now.

HOMEWORK EXERCISE

What Weakened Our Marriage?

Each partner should answer these questions independently in writing and then share their opinions with each other to compare what they each believe.

- What did I do to weaken the bond in our relationship?
- What did I not do to strengthen the bond in our relationship?
- What do I believe you did to weaken the bond in our relationship?
- What do I believe you did not do to strengthen the bond in our relationship?
- What other things could have contributed to the proverbial "crack in the veneer" that preceded the straying?
- How was that issue addressed within the relationship?
- What could I have done differently to acknowledge our problems?
- What could you have done differently to acknowledge our problems?
- Do I love you enough to want to work on the marriage?

Some honest soul-searching is required at this point. The sooner each partner can examine and take responsibility for the ways each has contributed to the breakdown in the relationship, the sooner the repair work can begin. It is generally harder for the injured spouse to see that he or she had anything to do with the infidelity. However, this is usually the exception and not the rule.

It is human nature to initially look outside ourselves for what has caused problems in our lives. However, blaming others for what has happened, when we have had a part in it, only disempowers our efforts to make it better. We are typically our own worst enemy, not others.

HOW CORE ISSUES AFFECT THE VIEW WE HAVE OF OURSELVES AND OUR SPOUSE

> *"Until you heal the wounds of the past, you will continue to bleed in to the future."*
>
> Izyanla Vanzant

Core issues are the specific insecurities each of us has about ourselves that we don't like to admit or want others to know about. The causes of our core issues are directly related to how we feel about ourselves, influences from our family of origin, and how we were treated by various people in our past or present. Our insecurities are often a reflection of the insecurities other people had who were so central to our development. It's not who we are that holds us back, but who we think we are not.

It doesn't matter whether they actually mistreated us or we were just reared in an environment that exposed us to doubts and insecurities. We take these on as if they are our own. In effect, we carry on the legacy of other people's unfinished business, adopt it, and internalize it.

- For instance, if we had a parent who constantly criticized us or expected perfection, we will often feel nothing we do is good enough.
- If we were reared by helicopter parents who constantly did things for us, pampered us, or bailed us out of problems, we will feel entitled or that we are a special case. However, we will also be secretly afraid to take risks or try things on our own.
- Hurt people hurt people. If we were bullied or made fun of by a sibling or peers when younger, we may be distrustful of others as well as self-conscious and negative about ourselves. These insecurities and fears become our core issues.

Being in a close relationship makes us feel vulnerable and exposed emotionally. We often fear that if someone truly knew us, they would not accept us. When we have a conflict with our spouse, it sometimes triggers deep-seated insecurities in both of us. These strong reactions may have little to do with what our partner truly meant, but how we filtered and translated their actions through the lens of our personal core issues. *We don't see people as they are, but as we are* (according to Anais Nin).

We may believe our spouse purposely pointed out a flaw or an inadequacy we possess in order to prove a point, get their way, or demonstrate their superiority. We sometimes treat others poorly because we feel badly about ourselves.

The intensity of our response toward them over feeling exposed or attacked elicits an equally defensive reaction back from our spouse, especially if they feel we have misjudged their intentions. They may feel we have assumed the worst of them and made them out to be the enemy when they were just trying to be helpful. The resulting escalation of conflict often makes matters much worse than the original issue warranted.

Judy and Sam had been married almost ten years when she discovered his involvement with another woman at work. He admitted to two other brief affairs and decided he needed to understand why he was sabotaging his marriage. He sought out individual counseling to better understand himself. His father had left when he was an infant, and they never had a relationship together. His mother had been married several times, but had cheated on each of her husbands when the relationship encountered difficult times. Similarly, Judy's parents fought constantly during her childhood, and violence and physical abuse had occurred often. She tried to be a good child and not cause any problems.

Sam ran to the comfort of other women when perceived problems occurred in his marriage as a defense against being rejected. Judy had reacted to her parents' high-conflict relationship by determining never to talk about problems in her marriage for fear of it ending. Sam interpreted her avoidance and distance as rejection of him and sought comfort in others like his mother did. Judy believed that conflict would only destroy a relationship instead of bringing them closer, so she avoided it. The result was that their core issues ended up almost destroying their marriage. They eventually learned how to approach each other, talk about issues they had, and craft mutual ways to solve their concerns. In the end, their conflicts brought them closer together.

This irrational exchange is not really about who our spouse is. It is about who we think they are making us out to be. It is about our worst insecurities, fears, and feelings about ourselves. It is how we secretly feel about ourselves, based upon our past or how we believe we were made to feel. It is about our core issues.

When emotional reactions to our core issues become a catalyst that accesses our spouse's core issues, repetitive patterns of dysfunctional interactions occur. These dysfunctional interactions include:

- Pursuer-distancer
- Attack-withdraw
- Blame-counterblame
- Withdraw-withdraw

Each of these dysfunctional interactions ends in defeat, confusion, hurt, discouragement, and avoidance. They contribute to couples feeling misunderstood, hurt, and alone. When this occurs, we are often vulnerable to someone else who may show kindness and interest toward us.

MEN AND WOMEN WHO ARE CHEATED ON OFTEN

> *"Living with integrity means not settling for less than what you know you deserve in your relationships."*
> Barbara DeAngelis

Men and women who have had two or more instances of significant others or a spouse cheating on them seem to have certain characteristics in common.

The most common characteristic is a mild, deferential temperament that does not engender a sense of respect from others. These guys and gals lack confidence in themselves and are insecure about many things. They often go along to get along, and rarely offer their preferences or opinions without being prompted. Even then, they are so tentative, it is difficult to take them seriously. They inadvertently inform others about how to treat them by how poorly they treat themselves. They may seem depressive and have a negative outlook much of the time.

The men and women they gravitate toward are often stronger personalities and feel forced to take the lead. Their spouses or significant others may be more comfortable just handling things, but they eventually feel too responsible for their partner. The relationship lacks energy and it becomes boring after a while. The synergy typically generated by two emotionally engaged people is sorely missing between them. The result is that they drift further apart. The more active partner becomes very dissatisfied and may find themselves noticing others who are more engaging.

Another variation on this temperament is an individual who is more of a loner and is oblivious to the needs of his or her spouse.

They are more preoccupied with their immediate life (work or children) and seem to forget that their spouse requires their attention, too. When criticized for being distant, they do not realize that they seem unavailable and feel unfairly chastised. While they may redouble their efforts to be engaged for a while, they almost always gravitate back to being self-absorbed. Their emotionally starved spouse becomes very vulnerable to someone who pays more attention to them.

In other instances, a person chooses individuals who are interesting and exciting, but who lack character and commitment. They are fun and maybe even hard to get, but they are also unwilling to be loyal. These partners are always looking for the next-best thing. They are often charismatic but narcissistic and need a great deal of external validation by others. A low-energy, sedate spouse is usually not enough to keep them interested for very long.

Jeanie was a thirty-two-year-old single female who very much wanted to get married and have a family. She was a nice but naïve person, and she wanted others to like her, so she was not very assertive. She had two previous boyfriends who had cheated on her or had left her for another girl. She was now living with a divorced guy who was personable, charismatic, and worked with a variety of women. He had many female friends, and couldn't understand why that made Jeanie uncomfortable. He also got mad at her when she questioned him about his whereabouts on occasion. Jeanie was so ready to be married, she did not scrutinize whether her choices in men were fundamentally flawed. She was settling for someone who would not commit and who couldn't be trusted.

We are all naturally drawn to certain types of people during our dating life. Even though we may not know why at the time, we can better understand it in retrospect. Our failures in relationships are just as important as our successful ones, though it may not feel that way at the time. What can we learn about ourselves by examining the types of relationships we have had?

HOMEWORK EXERCISE

Relationships we have had in the past show us the types of people we are drawn to and how we behave toward them. By detailing the following information, look for patterns and trends that could help you see the role you play in a relationship with others.

History of Previous Relationships

List in order of occurrence every significant romantic relationship you have had.

Please elaborate on these questions:

- How and when did it start?
- How long were you involved?
- What kind of person was he or she?
- What was the relationship like?
- How did they treat you?
- How did you treat them?
- What problems existed?
- How and when did it end?

By looking at the big picture of the history of a marriage, it is easier to see what and where the tough times were, how issues were resolved, what we learned, and how the relationship has evolved.

HOMEWORK EXERCISE

Our Relationship and Marital Life Timeline

Make a relationship and marital timeline beginning with when and how you met. Include highlights and lows in the history of your lives together in two-to-five-year increments or less per line. You may need to copy this page to include everything.

POSITIVE

_____

NEGATIVE

POSITIVE

_____

NEGATIVE

POSITIVE

_____

NEGATIVE

POSITIVE

_____

NEGATIVE

POSITIVE

_____

NEGATIVE

HOMEWORK EXERCISE

Inside and Outside Negative Influences

Our relationship is not an island unto itself. It is influenced by many things: our past, our previous relationships, how we treat others, how we spend our time, our view of the world, our feelings about ourselves, our friends, our emotions, etc.

In your opinion, what are the outside and inside variables that have negatively affected our relationship?

<u>Outside Variables</u>: (friends, family, work, extracurricular activities, negative influences, etc.)

1.

2.

3.

4.

5.

6.

<u>Inside Variables</u>: (the past, personal problems, unresolved personal issues, conflict patterns, feeling ignored, etc.)

1.

2.

3.

4.

5.

6.

HOMEWORK EXERCISE

"Some defense systems are part of the problem and some are part of the solution. And what we need to ask is this: Is ours defending us from hurts or keeping us from what we need? Are we inside the prison of our defenses, or are we outside walking on the wall looking out to sea?"
Merle Shain from Hearts That We Broke Long Ago (1987, 67)

Barriers within Me

What are the barriers within me that keep me from getting close to you?

Elaborate in detail about what these barriers could be and why you believe they exist.

Examples of these barriers could be:

- Fear of rejection
- Not wanting to look foolish
- Belief that if you really knew me, you wouldn't like me
- Painful rejection in past relationships
- Feeling like I'm not good enough
- Secrets that would hurt you
- Fear of disapproval
- Embarrassment
- My own insecurities

CHAPTER 13

ACTION STEP SEVEN: REOCCURRING FORGIVENESS

"The best way to heal a broken heart is to give God all the pieces."
—Unknown

THE SILENT TREATMENT

A man and his wife were having some problems at home and were giving each other the silent treatment. Suddenly the man realized that the next day, he would need his wife to wake him at 5:00 a.m. for an early business flight.

Not wanting to be the first to break the silence (and lose), he wrote on a piece of paper, "Please wake me at 5:00 a.m." He left it where he knew she would find it.

The next morning, the man woke up—only to discover it was 9:00 a.m. and he had missed his flight. Furious, he was about to go and see why his wife hadn't wakened him, when he noticed a piece of paper by the bed.

The paper said, "It is 5:00 a.m. Wake up."

Men are not equipped for these kinds of contests.

FORGIVENESS IS THE MOST IMPORTANT STEP

Allowing bitterness to remain within us is like drinking poison and expecting someone else to die!

Forgiveness is the most important step in restoring your marriage after an affair. Nothing good can come from the situation if forgiveness does not occur. Without forgiveness, bitterness is inevitable.

In *Getting Past the Affair*, Snyder, Baucon, and Gordon found that 60–75 percent of couples who experienced an affair stayed together and 50 percent of them reported having a stronger relationship than before.

How did they accomplish this?
A 2014 study about outcomes after infidelity by Marin, Christensen, and Atkins was published in the March 2014 *Couple and Family Psychology: Research and Practice Journal*. They found that when infidelity occurred in relationships, forgiveness played the largest role in overcoming the pain and hurt associated with the cheating. Those who were able to forgive their partners experienced the most progress after the affair.

Merle Shain, who wrote *Hearts That We Broke Long Ago* (1987, 90), describes forgiveness this way:

Until one forgives, life is governed by an endless cycle of resentments and retaliations, and we spend our days scratching at the scabs on the wounds that we sustained long ago instead of letting them dry up and disappear.

There is no way to hate another that does not cost the hater, no way to remain unforgiving without maiming yourself, because undissolved anger shutters through the body of the person who can't forgive, short circuiting it and overloading it, and hatred makes gray days of ones that have sun.

"Hating people is like burning down your own house to get rid of a rat," Harry Emerson Fosdick said a long time ago, and it can't be put better today because the person who harbors a hatred for another immolates himself in his own fire. When you don't learn from the past, you are doomed to repeat it, and until you forgive, you continue to impale yourself on your pain.

WHY DON'T WE FORGIVE?

"Life becomes easier when you learn to accept an apology you never got."

Robert Brault

If the betrayal of infidelity has ravaged your life, it is likely that you will be so hurt that you believe your life has been ruined. No one deserves to be cheated on, no matter what kind of challenges existed in your relationship. Sometimes, the hurt and anger is more than bearable. How can forgiveness be offered after being so mistreated?

Betrayed spouses often do not forgive because the other person hasn't changed yet. Forgiveness is viewed as being conditional upon the offender taking responsibility and showing genuine remorse. We may equate forgiving with forgetting, and refuse to make ourselves vulnerable again.

Most people are afraid to offer forgiveness because it could make them look foolish to others who are supporting them through this. Others are reluctant to open themselves to the possibility of being hurt again. Why be vulnerable again to someone who has cared so little about us? No one wants to appear naïve or gullible.

Why let a betraying spouse off the hook so easily if he or she hasn't suffered enough yet? Perhaps he hasn't fully learned his lesson and could cheat again. After all, what he or she has done has changed the relationship forever!

Sometimes, the unfaithful spouse is unforgiving. Their affair may have been fueled by the resentment felt toward his or her partner for a long time. The unfaithful partner may believe he or she has experienced mistreatment by their spouse, causing them to act out as they have. The unfaithful spouse has his or her own issues of forgiveness; they must acknowledge if repair can occur within the marriage. Their lack of forgiveness can interfere with genuinely feeling remorseful for their infidelity.

Bernie and Beth were an elderly couple who had been married more than forty years. Their marriage had been one of mediocrity and coexistence at best. When Beth learned that Bernie had an extended affair that ended thirty years ago, she was shocked. Even though many years had passed, she reacted as traumatically as if it had occurred yesterday. After months of trying to get past the hurt and anger, she was still asking, "Why did you do it?" "Did you love her?" She would not forgive him or consider looking at how she might have contributed to his looking to someone else for significance.

HOW WILL FORGIVENESS HELP ME?

When it all seems to be falling apart, it may just be falling into place.

Forgiveness is a process that can begin to free someone from the deep anger and resentment that possesses them. Forgiveness protects us from becoming a hateful, bitter person. Ongoing resentments occupy time, thoughts, and energy that could be better used toward healthy, personal growth.

If we can let go of our desire for revenge on another person, we can begin to redirect that energy toward taking better care of ourselves. It is like opening the door to hope again, believing that good could actually happen for us. It offers us the gifts of understanding and compassion.

Forgiveness is as much for us as it is for the other person. It frees us from being a hostage to hate. It does not excuse them for their actions, but it is also not conditional upon their willingness to change.

It begins by being willing to let God handle it.

In Matthew 18:21, Peter asks Jesus how many times he should forgive his brother if he sins against him. Jesus tells him to forgive him seventy-seven times (some translations say seventy times seven). The explanation suggests that if a person is truly remorseful, he deserves forgiveness. It goes on to remind us that God forgave us, so we should forgive others. Of course, this does not suggest we should continue to let ourselves be taken advantage of or exploited just because someone has asked for forgiveness. Forgiveness is our way of letting go of their problem. It is their responsibility for what they do to make the necessary changes.

"Do not repay anyone evil for evil. Be careful to do what is right in the sight of everybody. If it is possible, as far as it depends on you, live at peace with everyone. Do not take revenge, my friends, but leave room for God's wrath, for it is written: 'It is mine to avenge, I will repay,' says the Lord. On the contrary: 'If your enemy is hungry, feed him; if he is thirsty, give him something to drink. In doing this, you will heap burning coals on his head.' Do not be overcome by evil, but overcome evil with good."

Romans 12:17–21 (NIV)

WHAT IS FORGIVENESS?

Life is too short to wake up in the morning with regrets. So love the people who treat you right, forgive the ones who don't, and believe everything happens for a reason.

Forgiveness is letting go of our perceived right to retaliate for being wronged by another person. It is releasing eye-for-an-eye thinking that would justify our mistreatment of someone who has harmed us. It is doing the right thing even though someone we loved did not do the right thing toward us.

It is not justice: giving them what they deserve, e.g., punishment.

It is mercy: not giving them what they deserve, e.g., understanding.

It is grace: giving them what they don't deserve, e.g., acceptance.

If your spouse responds to this forgiveness by deciding to change their lives, show remorse, apologize, and make amends, it is possible that the relationship might have another chance. It is possible that you could begin to let go of your hurt and pain. Perhaps trust could be rebuilt again, one step at a time.

If your spouse does not choose to change, you have, at a minimum, begun to free yourself from the embitterment that could ruin your future if allowed to fester. You can learn from your past, instead of being defined by it and impaled upon your pain.

You can't get past what you can't get over.

When you can forgive, you can move on. When you are able to move on, you can change. When you are ready to change, you are to ready to welcome the new and improved into your life.

Sometimes what appears to be the end is really only the beginning!

Jon and Cindy have been married eighteen years and have two children. Jon is very independent and works hard, but can be self-absorbed. He operates from a whatever-she-doesn't-know-won't-hurt-her philosophy and sometimes even lies about little things to keep the peace. Cindy is willful and stubborn. She loves Jon but can be curt and critical at times. He confessed to a brief affair out of self-defense to Cindy because he was afraid after ending the affair, the other woman would tell his wife first. Since then, they have been at an impasse where she won't forgive him and he feels she really doesn't love him anymore. Before the affair, he resented her constant criticism of him and believed he no longer loved her. Now, he realizes he does. He felt she didn't care about him before the affair, and now she doesn't believe he cares about her because of the affair.

Each partner has resentments that were not successfully addressed in the marriage that contributed to his affair. Now, they both have things about the other that need to be forgiven before their impasse can be resolved if their marriage is to be saved.

TRUE FORGIVENESS CHANGES LIVES

> "Meet anger with sympathy, contempt with compassion, cruelty with kindness. Greet grimaces with smiles. Forgive and forget about finding fault. Love is the weapon of the future."
>
> Yehuda Berg

It is difficult to forgive someone when you have been betrayed by them. This is especially true when the person who is supposed to love you the most treats you even worse than an enemy would. It makes you want them to hurt like you hurt. Without forgiveness, *hurt people only hurt people*. Retaliation runs the risk of passing on that pain from one generation to the next.

Jesus is set up for a no-win confrontation with the Pharisees over a woman caught in the act of adultery (John 8:2–11). The law at the time mandated that a woman caught in the act of adultery must be stoned to death. Jesus is asked by these "teachers of the law" what he will do. If he agrees with keeping the law, he will be consenting to her death and accused of showing no mercy. If he agrees to showing her mercy, he will be accused of not keeping the law. Either answer will discredit him. So when posed with this question, Jesus kneels down, remains silent, and scribbles in the dirt, getting everyone's undivided attention before answering them.

In his inimitable fashion, he says, "He who is without sin should cast the first stone." One by one, each of his accusers leave. When only he and the woman remain, he asks, "Where are they? Has no one condemned you?" "No one, sir," she says. "Then neither do I condemn you," Jesus declares. "Go now and leave your life of sin."

Jesus is able to change a group of self-righteous, unforgiving men and enable them to see themselves for who they are. He is also able to provide the ultimate motivation of forgiveness to encourage the woman caught in adultery to change her life as well.

Forgiving a spouse who has betrayed, cheated, and hurt you is godly and spiritual. It enables you to avoid becoming bitter and retaliatory. Forgiveness shows love and grace when your first impulse is to exact justice upon them, to make them hurt like you hurt. There is no more spiritual act you can do than to forgive someone who doesn't deserve it. It will change your life and the life of the person you forgive.

HOMEWORK EXERCISE

Below is an exercise that can help you list resentments and determine what you need in order to consider letting go of them in order to move on in your relationship.

Relationship Recovery

What are my resentments around this situation between us? List each of them.

What do I need from you to let go of and get past this resentment?

Resentment

1.

2.

3.

4.

5.

What I need

1.

2.

3.

4.

5.

HOMEWORK EXERCISE

This exercise can change the way you regard your spouse if you do it every day for thirty days.

A Daily Prayer of Appreciation

This exercise can change the way you regard each other if you practice it on a daily basis. Start your day by recalling all the good things your significant other has added to your life. Review the unique qualities he or she has that have enriched your life. List the strengths they possess that complement your weaknesses. Pray for their day and that it is an encouragement to you both.

D. Charles Williams, PhD

HOMEWORK EXERCISE

The only person we can change is ourselves. When one partner leads the way toward identifying shortcomings within themselves and making a commitment to change, a sincerely committed spouse will also begin working on their issues. *Lead, follow, or get out of the way,* but do not wait until your spouse agrees to change.

Marital and Relational Forgiveness

No one is a perfect spouse or partner. Each person in a marriage or relationship contributes to the problems that exist and commits infractions against the other. There are also things that each person could do to make the relationship better.

Answer in written form:

1. *"How have I specifically injured our relationship?"*

    a.

    b.

    c.

    d.

    e.

2. *"How could I have done things better within our relationship?"*

    a.

    b.

    c.

    d.

    e.

HOMEWORK EXERCISE

Nothing can get better in a relationship unless some type of repair attempts are made. These are efforts to rebuild the marriage by overtures of reaching out, connection, making amends, and apologies. Sometimes, a written letter of apology helps say everything that needs to be said at one time.

Letter of Apology

1. **Make a list** of how you personally have harmed the relationship over time.

2. Next, **rank in order** each hurtful item from worst to least as you see it.

3. Then, **write a letter of apology** to your spouse or partner, starting with the worst items to the least, addressing **how this has hurt the relationship**.

4. Address **how you feel about the damage you have done**.

5. **Read these to each other** when you are finished.

CHAPTER 14

STAGE 3—WHERE ARE WE GOING FROM HERE?

ACTION STEP EIGHT: REEVALUATING EXPECTATIONS OF EACH OTHER

"There is only one thing more painful than learning from experience, and that is not learning from experience."
Archibald Macleish

The objective of this step is to determine where the relationship is going from here. The focus is upon what you both want to keep about the way you are together and what needs to change. Getting past the affair without honestly evaluating what has been going on in your marriage is like putting a new coat of paint over rotting wood. If you don't identify what needs to be remodeled or replaced, you could find yourself back in the same state of disrepair in the future. Get real with each other and yourself, because this is the best chance for you both to get what you really want from a relationship.

Don and Carly were married for twenty-one years when he reconnected with an old high school sweetheart online and began a six-month affair. He subsequently ended the affair because she wasn't the person he remembered her to be. She responded by threatening to tell his wife, so he confessed preventatively to his wife about the affair. His wife kept him emotionally and sexually at a distance for over nine months while determining if they would stay married. They eventually negotiated what expectations they had of each other if they remained together.

She wanted him to:
- Treat her with kindness and consideration
- Be truthful and honest about everything
- Do thoughtful things for her
- Give her attention without expecting something in return
- Allow her to make occasional accountability checks on his phone and computer
- Listen to her concerns without "yes, but"-ing her
- Demonstrate consistency in his words and actions

He wanted her to:
- Refrain from criticizing and "sniping" at him
- Stop reminding him that he cheated on her
- Drop her emotional guard and open up to him again
- Allow affection and playfulness to resume
- Talk about the future with him
- Not bring up the negative past on a regular basis
- Show him she cared

HOMEWORK EXERCISE

What Are My Fears about Our Relationship?

This is an exercise to do as a couple. Sit down and ask yourselves and each other these questions. Discuss what you are willing to do, as an individual and a couple, to make things better in your relationship.

What are my fears about our relationship?

- Can we make the necessary changes to stay together?
- What if it is too little too late?
- What if I mess up again?
- Can we move past the past?
- Can I meet your needs?

What is positive about us?

- What do I love about this relationship?
- What are the inherently good things about how we are together?
- What common interests do we still share?
- Can we still have fun together?
- Do we still like each other?
- Are we still interested in one another?
- Are we still attracted to each other?

What needs to change?

- What do I need from you that I have not been getting?
- What have I not been giving?
- Are there any *covert contracts* in our relationship that I have gone along with? (Covert contracts are covertly but mutually agreed-upon areas of avoidance in our lives that we do not talk about,

e.g., "I won't say anything about your drinking if you don't say anything about my weight.")
- What have I been tolerating that I am not willing to live with in the future?
- How do I need to change to be a more relationship-focused partner?
- What are my true deal breakers if we moved forward together?
- Where do we go from here?

CHANGING YOUR SPOUSE

Great changes may not happen right away, but with effort, even the difficult may become easy.

How many of us have had the frustrating experience of trying to change our spouse? Probably all married individuals have at some time or another assumed the challenge of trying to force their partner to be *who we think they should be*. Trying to change our spouse is the first roadblock encountered on the road to an improved marriage. It often locks couples into a tug-of-war, intensifies their resentment toward each other, and, most importantly, rarely works.

So what can you do if you aren't happy with your spouse?

- Identify one negative behavior within yourself and commit to improving it daily.
- Treat your partner the way you want to be treated, regardless of their response.
- Focus on what they do right and catch them doing it often.
- Admire the differences between you both because those keep you interested in each other.
- Choose to be happy and together, rather than alone and right.
- Refusing to change guarantees change for the worst.
- Criticizing, blaming, and throwing dirt only cause you to lose ground.
- There is no future in living in the past. Forgive, learn from the past, and move on.

Many times, we don't make changes ourselves first because we believe our spouse caused the problem and should be the first to take action to remedy it. We may even feel that is not fair for us to start that process of change, since they were most at fault. We are also often afraid that if we take action first, they will not follow suit and do their part.

Our fears often cause us to behave in offensive or defensive ways in our marriage. These fears are based on deeper insecurities we possess but do not like to admit. As long as we do not face our own fears or ask for what we need from our spouse, we will see them as the problem instead of ourselves.

FROZEN IN THE PAIN OF THE PAST: "HOW DO I KNOW IT WON'T HAPPEN AGAIN?"

In the beginning, all betrayed spouses who are hoping to work out their marriage agonize, worry, and obsess about the affair. They wonder what caused it, what really happened, and if their spouse will eventually go back to the other person. In many cases, the wounded spouse is able to move forward, relatively assured that the worst is over and no more secrets exist.

However, for some spouses, doubt and uncertainty about the future of the relationship continue for six to twelve months or more. These spouses return regularly to the scene of the crime in their minds, questioning whether there is more they should know or have not discovered yet. Their obsessive fears cause them to ask questions that have already been answered multiple times by their unfaithful spouses. Revisited conversations often escalate into angry arguments and knockdown, drag-out exchanges that take the relationship to the brink of insanity for both parties.

Tammy believed she and Russ had the perfect marriage. They were compatible, rarely argued, and had never had a difficult time in the relationship. Even when Russ struggled in his job, she was very supportive of him. When Tammy discovered he was having a workplace affair, she was devastated. She never saw it coming and couldn't believe he would ever do something like sleep with another woman. As her world unraveled, she tried to make sense out of how this could have happened. In couples counseling, they discussed how both sets of parents had infidelity in their pasts. Her previous fiancé had also left her for her best friend a number of years prior to meeting Russ. During couples counseling, Tammy kept asking the same questions over and over again and was not able to move past the affair.

The constant scrutinizing of the betrayed spouse's past actions is really an anxiety-provoked ritual of reassurance. It is intended to elicit a guarantee that things will work out between them. The compulsive exhuming of the corpse of the past affair is a maddening attempt to make sure nothing is going on again. It also serves as a brief reassurance that their relationship is still viable. The emotional torture created between the couple, however, ends up eroding the very repair it is attempting bring about.

There are generally two reasons why the betrayed spouse has not been able to move forward in accepting restitution for the affair.

The most common reason is that the unfaithful spouse has been less than honest about their total disclosure regarding the details of the affair. If they have denied the extent of the involvement with the other person, or if they have rushed through the therapy process in a perfunctory or obligatory manner, their spouse will not feel resolution has legitimately occurred. It will feel somehow incomplete.

The second reason the betrayed spouse has not been able to move on is often because of the wounded spouse's personal insecurities caused by their past. These are often a reflection of core issues from their family of origin. Their incessant, compulsive questioning is an indication of their own deeper inadequacies or feelings of unworthiness. They may secretly feel they do not measure up to his or her previous lover, and worry their spouse will eventually prefer that relationship over them. Then, they will be abandoned again.

Core issues from one's family of origin are often a result of infidelity within that family. When there has been a history of cheating by a parent or by a previous spouse, it is very difficult for a betrayed spouse to believe that it will not occur again in their current marriage. These spouses can never be sure that their relationship will ever be safe and secure again. Their control and monitoring tactics belie the belief that if they do not stay vigilant, something worse could happen. Almost no amount of reassurance can allay their anxieties indefinitely. Couples who go to counseling together trying to repair their marriage may experience the wounded partner repeatedly circling back around to the reasons the affair ever started in the first place. This may be an indication that the betrayed spouse needs some individual counseling to deal with the earlier, family-of-origin infidelity that still affects them on a deeper level.

What's Done in the Dark

HOMEWORK EXERCISE

Recognizing personal themes that reoccur in our lives can help us separate what our insecurities are from what our spouses may do to access those feelings.

Identifying My Greatest Fears and Needs

Read each of these statements under the My Greatest Fears Inventory and **circle** the fears that you sometimes have when you and your spouse have unresolved conflicts in your relationship. Next, take the My Greatest Needs Inventory.

My Greatest Fears Inventory

When we have unresolved conflicts, I sometimes feel that:

1. I'm not important enough to you.
2. I am not valued by you.
3. You will ignore me.
4. You don't care about me.
5. I don't measure up.
6. I will get hurt.
7. You don't need me.
8. My problems are too much for you.
9. You will control me.
10. You will see me as incompetent.
11. You will leave me.
12. You don't approve of me.
13. You'll never approve of me.
14. You'll never be satisfied with me.
15. I can't make it better.
16. Nothing I do matters.
17. I will end up alone.
18. No one will want me.

19. I'm the problem.
20. I'll be a failure at this relationship.
21. You'll never trust me again.
22. I am not a priority to you.
23. Things will never be the same between us.

Read each of these statements and **circle only three** that mean the most to you as well.

Then take both lists of Fears and My Greatest Needs and talk together about how these feelings and needs affect your relationship.

My Greatest Needs Inventory (Choose only three)

1. to feel loved by you
2. to be accepted by you
3. to be forgiven by you
4. to be important to you
5. to have value in your eyes
6. to have your attention
7. to measure up to your expectations
8. to be seen as competent and capable
9. to be approved of by you
10. to be with you
11. to be close to you
12. to be a success in your eyes
13. to be trusted by you
14. to be believed in by you
15. to be admired by you
16. to be a priority to you
17. to be significant to you
18. to be desired by you
19. to be secure with you
20. to be wanted by you

HOMEWORK EXERCISE

Reevaluating Expectations

Each individual in the relationship should answer these questions in detail. Then, exchange answers and talk about it.

1. What do I love about our relationship?
    a.

    b.

    c.

    d.

2. What have I **not** been giving?
    a.

    b.

    c.

    d.

3. What do I need that I have **not** been getting?
    a.

    b.

    c.

    d.

4. What have I been tolerating in our relationship that I **cannot** live with any longer?
   a.

   b.

   c.

   d.

HOMEWORK EXERCISE

Sometimes, we each have to make specific commitments to change things about ourselves before we can ever expect to be healthy in a relationship. If we have character flaws, bad habits, irrational ways of thinking, and destructive behavior, our marriage will be adversely affected by these personal faults. Self-awareness and knowledge is half the battle.

Character Self-Assessment

This is a fearless, personal inventory of character defects that interfere with becoming the best possible person you can be. Please take the time to honestly list all of the individual challenges that you can identify within yourself.

What are the shortcomings, limitations, weaknesses, and flaws in the area of my:

Emotions:
1.

2.

3.

Thoughts:
1.

2.

3.

Actions:
1.

2.

3.

Attitudes:
1.

2.

3.

Treatment of Others:
1.

2.

3.

Treatment of Myself:
1.

2.

3.

HOMEWORK EXERCISE

Intentionally defining the type of person we want to become is essential if we are to make changes that have purpose. Healthy people want to grow and be better than they have been in the past. It is normal to want to improve in our job, our habits, in our health, and in our relationships.

The Kind of Person I Want to Become

Begin this exercise by taking a separate piece of paper and listing:

- Qualities of the person you want to become
- What kind of character would you aspire to?
- How do you want to treat other people?
- What are you committing to do differently from this day forward?
- How will you treat your spouse and children?
- What will they see differently in you by next year?

Then, write a detailed narrative on what that person will be and what you are committed to become.

ACTION STEP NINE: REPAIR AND RESTITUTION OF THE RELATIONSHIP

"Sometimes the bad things that happen in our lives put us directly on the path to the best things that will ever happen to us."

Nicole Reed

Personal Changes

This stage involves making repair attempts and restitution to a significant other. Making repair attempts offers the opportunity to heal what is broken by making amends in words and actions to someone whom we have wronged. It involves feeling grateful for having another chance and taking the initiative to make things right. This attitude facilitates the process of forgiveness and the willingness to be vulnerable again.

Making restitution is the act of giving back to one's partner even more than is owed as a show of good faith toward restoring the relationship. It involves looking for opportunities to make a difference by putting them before ourselves or inconveniencing ourselves on behalf of our significant other. This may be a one-sided effort on the part of the betrayer without much, if any, response for a period of time, while the wounded partner tries to determine the sincerity and genuineness of the overtures.

Remember the things you did initially to make your spouse feel like he or she was the most important person in the world to you? Giving your time and attention and being available to them cultivated a greater desire on their part to be with you. Thoughtful overtures and remembering what was important to them enhanced your value in their eyes.

The process of rebuilding what was lost is a slow, arduous task that is not always initially welcomed by a hurt and angry spouse or partner. The ultimate test of sincerity for the offending spouse is how persistent he or she is in reestablishing the relationship, despite the lack of encouragement received.

Some examples of personal changes might include:
- Being open and honest about everything, regardless of your spouse's reactions
- Doing what you say you are going to do, when you say you are going to do it
- Being more flexible and open to learning new experiences
- Becoming more spiritually oriented or seeking God's purpose for your life
- Realigning your values together as a couple
- Consciously becoming more interested and curious about looking honestly at your life, making changes for the better, getting rid of negative behaviors, and embracing a healthy life
- Reducing and eliminating bad habits that annoy or upset your spouse
- A renewed appreciation and attention to what is important to your significant other
- Managing attitudes and moods that offend and alienate others
- Making your spouse's happiness more of a priority
- Complimenting more and criticizing less
- Striving to be less self-absorbed, more selfless, and grateful for others

Ben and Suzie were a young couple with two small children. When Suzie discovered that Ben had been having affairs with women he met at bars and conferences, she was devastated. She immediately sought help and decided to take a strong stand over his serial cheating by asking him to move out. During their separation, they each sought counseling and eventually began working together on restoring their marriage from his betrayals. Ben was grateful to have a chance to earn his marriage and family back. He was highly motivated to gain a deeper understanding of his insatiable need for the attention and affection of other women. They spent a year working on themselves and their marriage and were able reset expectations and repair the relationship. He worked on a wide range of personal changes, made restitution to his wife, and realized what and who was really important to him.

The Power of an Apology

If you have never been the kind of person who apologizes first, or even at all, this is a time to begin changing that fatal flaw. The unwillingness or inability to say, "I am sorry," or "I was wrong," is fundamentally a character flaw. It represents stubbornness, pride, and a lack of vulnerability. When we do not take responsibility for our actions, we show weakness, not strength. Expecting others to "get over it" will never help them heal from the hurt. Small overtures or just acting like nothing is wrong does not make it right. Sweeping things under the rug is only a prescription for deep resentment and the eventual emotional erosion of trust and closeness.

Research indicates that the person who apologizes first is actually the stronger person. They are viewed by others as more genuine and credible because while not being perfect, they are able to learn from their mistakes. They are also more easily forgiven, which allows trust to be rebuilt within the relationship sooner.

HOMEWORK EXERCISE

Take your time to thoroughly write your wishes and desires to repair your relationship with your spouse. Even if you have said these things in person, it is important for them to see it in written words that are heartfelt and well thought through. It may take several sittings to say exactly what you want him or her to understand about your feelings. Read it over several times to make sure it conveys what you really intend for it to.

Amends Letter

1. Describe how important the relationship is to you and how you feel about him or her.

2. Describe how you would like the relationship between you both to be.

3. Take responsibility for your part of the differences between you, and make amends by acknowledging your regrets for the problem.

4. Request an opportunity to make improvements to the current state of the relationship, and ask for a meeting to see what he or she might be willing to do.

5. Close by reiterating how much a new start could positively change things and how you would welcome the opportunity to talk about it.

HOMEWORK EXERCISE

This exercise is for those who are determined to win back their spouse and show them in word, thought, and actions just how much they care. Even if your relationship seems over, this forty-day exercise has been known to turn around a spouse who feels hopeless about your future together. Watch the movie Fireproof *first, and see how this couple who was at the brink of divorce came back to save their marriage.*

Daily Love Dare: Forty Days of Giving

Get the *Love Dare* book by Stephen and Alex Kendrick and do the exercises described for forty days to repair your relationship and to give back to your spouse.

HOMEWORK EXERCISE

This written exercise answers the question of "Why do you still want to be with me?" When a betrayal occurs, most people feel that they weren't enough to keep their spouse happy and satisfied. Ironically, sometimes affairs have the opposite effect. They cause you to realize just how much you actually had together as a couple. Answer each statement in detail with well-thought-out reasons. Avoid short responses or trite clichés that may not reflect the uniqueness of the person to whom you are writing.

Relationship Validation

1. Why I fell in love with you:

2. How you complete me and make me a better person:

3. Why I need/want you in my life:

4. What I admire/love most about you:

ACTION STEP TEN: RECONCILING AND RECOMMITTING

Changing Interactional Patterns

After a period of repair attempts, amends, and efforts toward restitution, many couples experience hope that the relationship can be saved. They make a mutual decision to move forward with the marriage. It is at this point that many couples drop out of counseling, feeling that their marriage is on track for success. However, discontinuing treatment at this time is at best premature and could stall progress toward genuine reconciliation and recommitment.

Reconciling is a mutual decision to stay in the marriage and move forward. Recommitment is the decision to become a couple again and leave the past in the past. It involves making up, deciding to move forward, coming back together, and resuming the relationship.

For the injured spouse who was emotionally on the fence, it is time to agree to get off the fence and resume the relationship. If the couple has been separated, it may be the right time to physically reconcile and move back in together. It requires both individuals to commit to working on the relationship without resorting to accusations or attacks about past transgressions.

Reconciling and recommitting will mean:

- Considering yourselves a team and being "all in" again
- Reassuring and reaffirming each other again
- Once again becoming each other's advocate
- Resolving to remove all barriers that previously existed between you
- Continued forgiveness
- Looking forward, not back
- Believing in each other again

Attempting to put the marriage back together in a slow, gradual manner while addressing and resolving previous disconnections that existed is a fine line to walk. It requires taking individual responsibility for damaging the relationship while tactfully but openly identifying any unmet needs that each may have experienced. There are risks that this exercise could turn into a blame exchange. The intent, however, is for each person to realize what was missing for them individually and begin asking for what they want from each other. Chances are, their individual core problems are no surprise to the couple, and they can talk about them more freely. The issues are not new, but perhaps they have never been either adequately addressed or completely resolved when they occurred in the past. Covert contracts must now be identified and the avoided issues faced. Now is the time to take each other seriously, or the relationship may drift back to whatever mediocrity that used to exist.

It is also the time to express and show gratitude for each other in a consistent manner. Feeling appreciated by a spouse builds connection and represents emotional deposits in the marriage's love bank. Noticing and acknowledging the little things done on each other's behalf strengthen feelings of commitment.

A 2015 research study done at the University of Georgia in the College of Family and Consumer Sciences by Dr. Ted Futris discovered that feeling appreciated and believing that your spouse valued you directly positively influenced how one felt about their marriage. It improved commitment and caused couples to believe the marriage would last. Higher levels of spousal expressions of gratitude reduced men and women's proneness to divorce.

HOMEWORK EXERCISE

Reconciling and recommitting involves intentionally making improvements to ourselves personally and evaluating what we can do better in our marriage. It is a decision to move forward by making changes that benefit the relationship and having expectations about the future together.

Relationship Self-Assessment

Please answer these questions based on how you currently feel about your relationship. Take time to elaborate on your answers.

What two things do I <u>currently do well</u> in our relationship?

1. _____
_____
_____
_____

2. _____
_____
_____
_____

What two things do I believe I have <u>not done well</u> in our relationship?

1. _____
_____
_____
_____

2. _____
_____
_____
_____

What two things <u>could I do better</u> in our relationship?
1. _____
_____
_____
_____

2. _____
_____
_____
_____

What two things do I fear most about the future of our relationship?
1. _____
_____
_____
_____

2. _____
_____
_____
_____

Where would I like to see our relationship by this time next year?
1. _____
_____
_____
_____

2. _____
_____
_____
_____

HOMEWORK EXERCISE

Most couples want to meet the needs of their spouse. Sometimes, the things we do for our spouse do not elicit the outcomes we had hoped for. This occurs mostly because we tend to give in the ways we want to be given to, not in ways they want to be given to. We will make our partners more satisfied, grateful, and responsive by determining what their most important needs are and taking actions to meet them.

So how do we determine just what particular needs our spouse wants met?

Love Language Inventory

Get a copy of The Five Love Languages *by Gary Chapman, or go online at www.5lovelanguages.com and take the Love Language Inventory together to determine each of your highest needs. Discuss specifically how you would like those needs to be filled.*

The five categories of needs include:

1. Words of affirmation
2. Acts of service
3. Physical touch
4. Quality time
5. Gifts

HOMEWORK EXERCISE

If you want to positively influence the way your spouse feels about the marriage, express and show gratitude. It will cause your partner to believe that the relationship will last, and you will both feel a deeper commitment to each other. If you want to reduce the possibility of divorce in your marriage, do this exercise.

Gratitude Love Letter

This is an opportunity to reflect on what you appreciate about your partner. Write a love letter that lets him or her know just how important your relationship is to you. When you have finished, give it to your spouse and talk about what you have written.

- How you are thankful for your spouse
- Qualities you admire in them
- What you love about them
- How you appreciate them
- How you feel supported by him or her
- What you enjoy about being together
- How he or she makes you feel special

CHAPTER 15

STAGE 4—DEEPENING EMOTIONAL INTIMACY TOGETHER

ACTION STEP ELEVEN: REBUILDING TRUST AND RECONNECTING

> *"Trust is the ultimate human currency."*
> — Bill McDermott

Rebuilding trust in a marriage once it has been broken is a process that can take years. Couples have to conscientiously eliminate criticisms, blaming and fault-finding, and begin asking for what they want from each other. The risk of rejection associated with this type of vulnerability is more difficult than one might imagine. It begins with understanding what one's own needs are and moves toward discovering the true emotional needs of one's partner. All of this must occur under the protective umbrella of reestablishing commitment and exclusivity in the relationship. Identifying and reinforcing clear boundaries around the relationship while setting mutual expectations for each other ensures the long process of ***rebuilding the trust*** that has been shattered. While frequent and in-depth communication is absolutely essential here, consistency in actions will speak louder than words.

CREATING A SAFE PLACE IN YOUR MARRIAGE

"Love comes to those who still hope after disappointment, still believe after betrayal, and still love after they've been hurt."
Anonymous

Trust builds our feelings of safety. Safety deepens our sense of security. Marriages need to be a safe place where we feel accepted and we can be ourselves. We have all known people with whom we did not feel safe. Our guards went up in their presence, and we felt defensive and uncomfortable while around them. We may have even felt a need to protect ourselves from them.

Marriages that are rebuilding trust within them have some specific requirements if they are to become safe havens again.

Agree to Tell the Truth

Be honest no matter what. It may seem easier just to not rock the boat. You may be trying not to upset your significant other over that e-mail or text message you received from the "other person." Even though you agreed to inform your spouse if you ever heard from them again, you don't want to risk their reliving the past. The problem is that your spouse will eventually ask if you have heard from this other person, and if you say no, two problems have been created. First, you know you have lied, and he or she might sense that, too. Secondly, when it is finally discovered, you will lose the trust that you have rebuilt since the affair ended. Be proactive and tell the truth about being contacted by the other person. Your spouse may be upset at first, but you will regain credibility in the trust department.

Keep Your Word and Be Consistent

If you commit to something, do it even if it is inconvenient. When asked to call if more than fifteen minutes late, call. Don't make excuses or turn the tables on your spouse by portraying them as being unreasonable. If you agreed to it, do it. Clarify and take the initiative to communicate if circumstances change. Manage the expectations of others, and don't just explain after the fact.

Learn to Be Transparent and Vulnerable

If you are naturally quiet, work on being more conversational. Share your day. Talk about what you are thinking. Share about yourself, including the good, the bad, and the ugly. Let others know you. You may be surprised that they will like you despite your faults. Research has proven that those who share their shortcomings gain more credibility in the eyes of others and are viewed as more approachable. Let's face it—it is not necessary to be perfect to be accepted.

Manage Emotional Triggers and Reminders

When something reminds your spouse of the affair, he or she may get upset or quiet. It is normal to want to avoid, ignore, or react defensively toward them. However, these occasions provide a great opportunity to rebuild trust by taking the initiative to find out what your partner needs from you. Say, *"I'm sorry you are feeling badly again. How would you like me to support you?"* The choices generally are (1) talk about it and be understanding, (2) leave them alone a while, (3) sit quietly with them, or (4) touch or hold them in a comforting way. Let your spouse tell you what they want at that time. Most spouses report that they appreciate their wayward spouse hanging in there with them during these trying moments.

Say Yes When You Mean Yes and No When You Mean No

When spouses are discovered cheating, most couples try to work out the marriage. However, it is not uncommon for the offending spouse to just go along with whatever their partner wants in order to make peace. They may agree to things they ordinarily would feel differently about just to appease the wronged spouse. It doesn't take long for the betrayed spouse to realize that their accommodation isn't truly genuine. It is not uncommon to conclude that this is just another example of why they cannot be trusted because they don't tell the truth.

Sam was engaged when a friend of his fiancé's observed him kissing another woman. After a great deal of drama and "gnashing of teeth," Sam tried his best to make it up to his fiancé. He went along with everything she said, bent over backward to do things her way, and became a yes man. This tactic backfired and only made his fiancé question him more. Sam was not being honest with himself or his fiancé by not sharing his preferences and feelings. One of the issues within this relationship was that Sam was easygoing, and his fiancé was very opinionated and had a strong personality. Their task as a couple was for Sam to learn to speak up more and for his fiancé to learn to share the stage and realize it wasn't all about her.

In order to build credibility, it is important for the betraying spouse to honestly share their feelings about differences in preferences and opinions they may have with their spouse. Trying to avoid a conflict by being too agreeable eventually backfires.

Apologize and Take Responsibility When You Make a Mistake

Too err is human, to forgive divine. We all make mistakes. Accept this and work through it. Making excuses only diminishes our credibility, and blaming other things or other people is perceived as a cop-out. We will receive less criticism if we quickly take responsibility and try to learn from the mistake rather than defending our actions. If we are not making mistakes, we are not taking chances that help us grow and be the best we can be. Life is not a straight line, but a series of midcourse corrections that teaches us at every turn what to do next. See it as a learning opportunity. Make adjustments and keep on growing. Don't try to hide, minimize, or blame-shift mistakes. Quickly admit them, apologize, and set about to make things right. This is how character and trust are developed.

Maintain Agreed-Upon Boundaries with Others

Understanding proper boundaries in relationships begins in childhood within our families of origin. If your parents were strict and disciplinarians, chances are you are very aware of where the boundaries and expectations lie in most situations. If your parents were permissive, indulgent, and hovering, you may have grown up believing that rules do not apply to you and that you should be able to do things your way.

Building trust in a relationship requires being able to act in situations as if your spouse were right there with you, even when they are not. It is easier to maintain agreed-upon boundaries when we think about how this would affect our spouse if they knew what we were doing. When we are not trustworthy, it affects our sense of connection with our spouse. We become more self-protective and distant to avoid detection. When we act in a trustworthy manner, we have nothing to hide and are naturally more open and spontaneous with our spouse.

Give More Than You Get
The secret to a happy marriage is when both partners feel they are getting more than they are giving. This may seem like an impossibility, but it represents a relationship where each person is meeting the needs of the other in a satisfying way. The single most difficult thing to do in a marriage is to shift from *thinking like an individual to thinking like a team.* Individuals take care of themselves. Teams sacrifice for the good of all.

> "It is more blessed to give than to receive."
> Acts 20:35 (NIV)

One paradox of life and marriage is that when we give to our spouse, we always receive more back. Not that our motive is to get more back, but it is a natural principle of life that those who give of themselves are often given back to in many intangible ways.

Be Patient and Kind
Patience and kindness are two of the most important ways to build trust, connect, and create a safe haven in your relationship.

Treating your partner the way you want to be treated is central to this. People who are treated with patience and kindness are more secure and confident. The acceptance they feel from others helps them accept themselves. Those who live in a relationship with impatience and anger doubt themselves and questions their worthiness.

THE FOUR AS OF INTIMACY: ATTENTION, AFFIRMATION, AFFECTION, AND ATTITUDE

If you were born since the 1980s, during the advent of the Internet, your ideas about true intimacy have most likely been strongly influenced by social media. Appearance, youthfulness, sensuality, body type, proportions, and seductiveness have been touted as the most important factors to focus on if you really want to be attractive and desired by others.

However, intimacy isn't about attractiveness or sex. If you have been seduced by the idea that you have to look and act "sexy" to turn someone else on, you may be painfully surprised when the allure fades later in the relationship. Though we all notice someone who is attractive and who takes care of themselves, form that lacks content becomes boring and eventually unsatisfying.

So what keeps a spouse "tuned in" and "turned on" for a lifetime?

The primary catalyst for fostering connection in a relationship is paying **attention** to your partner. When you first met, you successfully cultivated interest by paying attention to him or her. Once you caught their eye, you did your best to make a good impression by listening attentively to what they said, what they liked, how they felt about things, and what was important to them. In life, *what we focus upon, we strengthen*. Our laser focus was upon finding out more about who they were, and it endeared us to them. Seizing opportunities to be around them often only increased our significance in their eyes if we made them feel important.

Sadly, too many guys put on a full-court press to catch a lady—only to ignore her after they have her. This bait-and-switch tactic eventually breeds resentment and regret later on in a significant other. Spouses will stay interesting if we stay interested. Giving our complete attention shows them how important they are to us. This action more than any other validates our lover, and the return on this investment provides the sparks for a continual, mutual flame together.

Secondly, a person who sees our worth and acknowledges us finds a place in our heart. This is why *affirmation* develops positive regard between two people. If he thinks you are great and reminds you of it often, you will eagerly anticipate his company and shine in his presence.

Mutual admiration and expressions of appreciation ignite excitement and fuel passion. Many people have experienced the idealization of the other person in the initial infatuation stage of a new relationship. This continued affirmation is what keeps love intense as the years go by in a marriage. *Catching people doing things right* is not just a motivational strategy. It is the lifeblood of staying connected to your spouse. It reminds them that no one cares more than we do.

Serve up that praise and adoration generously, because it will be returned to you many times over and fuel a fire between you that will always burn hot.

Next, use *affection* to say those things that words cannot adequately express. Learn to be hands on, not hands off. Being touched warmly can be more affirming than kind words and praise.

I talk to clients regularly who were brought up in unaffectionate families. They are either very needy and crave constant attention, or they are so self-sufficient, they act like they need nothing. They are often difficult to get close to, but almost all of them deeply desire some type of physical connection.

Couples who have lost the motivation to reach out and connect regularly fade into distant, separate lives of unsatisfied longing and apathy. These are the couples who appear to have it together and suddenly without warning are divorced. Others around them will invariably say, *"I thought they were the perfect couple."* Their outward compatibility was just a show—a face put on for the public. Their candle for each other burned out long ago.

Couples who develop daily rituals of affection will find that they will stay connected more sincerely to each other. Daily physical contact in a relationship helps a couple stay playful together. Examples of rituals of affection may include hugs, kisses, regular times together talking, "I love yous," cuddling, playfulness, calls, texts, being happy to see each other, greetings, smiles, sharing your day, checking in with each other, and words of appreciation.

Last but not least, having a cheerful, upbeat **attitude** toward life helps us realize how blessed we are. My wife is the most positive person I know, and she has grown more that way over time. Even though her life has had its share of loss and disappointment, she has come through these times with an amazingly hopeful perspective. She is living proof that *sometimes the bad things that happen in life place us directly on the path to the best things that will ever happen to us.*

She has helped me appreciate the importance of learning from mistakes instead of being defeated by them; not dwelling on the negatives; enjoying the moment instead of living for the future; and seeing the unique beauty of a sunrise, sunset, and full moon, which I was often too busy to notice.

The one decision of choosing to be the right kind of person will determine 90 percent of our happiness or misery in a relationship. Some people have given up on being the right person and are just trying to be right. They end up engaging in criticizing, blaming, and finding fault with their spouses. This either defeats their spouse or causes them to redouble their efforts to defend themselves. The resulting impasse makes the relationship seem hopeless when it really is not. Being right is overrated and not as meaningful as being close. Treating people the way we want to be treated is the key to freeing ourselves from impasses with others.

Lastly, our attitude will determine our altitude in our marriage. It will either deepen or destroy our intimacy together. This one decision to be the right person will determine whether we will be content or discontent in our relationship.

HOMEWORK EXERCISE

Sometimes it is the little things we do for each other that make the biggest difference. This reconnection exercise requires couples to look more closely at the demonstrations of love and generosity that bind them together. Even if the overture is a small act of giving, it represents unique ways that we can give to each other.

Little Things I Would Enjoy You Doing for Me

There is an endless list of little things that individuals in a relationship enjoy having done for them that make them feel loved and cared for. It might be getting your spouse a cup of coffee, bringing home dessert, a massage, a shower together, or a spontaneous dinner out. Make a detailed list of all the things your spouse could do for you that would make you feel most cared for and thought of.

Both individuals *should make up this list of twenty or more items and give a copy of it to each other. Then, regularly at your discretion, surprise your spouse with one of his or her little things, and see how that adds more connection to your relationship.*

HOMEWORK EXERCISE

Touch builds bridges, breaks the ice, speaks in a language words cannot express, adds playfulness, and facilitates affection. What rituals of affection would you like to add to your relationship?

Checklist: Rituals of Affection

Please check the specific Rituals of Affection that you wish occurred more in your relationship.

- ○ a kiss when we wake up
- ○ a hug in the morning
- ○ holding hands
- ○ regular times to talk together during the week
- ○ coming to find me when you get home
- ○ a warm greeting upon seeing me
- ○ cuddling in bed in the morning
- ○ playful pats
- ○ cuddling before going to sleep
- ○ saying "I love you" daily
- ○ a pet name
- ○ get me a cup of coffee
- ○ a smile when you see me
- ○ an "I'm thinking of you" text
- ○ asking me how my day was first
- ○ saying thank you for what I do for you
- ○ sharing your day with me
- ○ being patient when I'm irritable
- ○ watching my kind of movie with me
- ○ a kiss goodbye
- ○ a kiss hello
- ○ a kiss good night

HOMEWORK EXERCISE

Reconnecting means that we are doing more of the things that bind us together and make us to feel closer. Identify the things you do currently that make you feel connected. Next, add those activities that would enhance your emotional intimacy.

Elements of Emotional Intimacy

*First **circle each number** that currently characterizes your relationship. Then, **place a check** by each number that you would like to see more of in your relationship.*

1. You reserve regular times to talk and connect together.
2. You share regular routine rituals of affection (hugs, kisses, touch, handholding).
3. You identify each other's needs and meet them.
4. You compliment each other often.
5. You share "I love you" regularly.
6. You talk about things when they bother you.
7. You do little things for each other whether asked for or not.
8. You make repair attempts and apologize when you hurt each other.
9. You look forward to sharing your day with each other.
10. Make phone calls to say hi and touch bases.
11. Call if you are going to be late.
12. Exercise, take walks, ride along, and do things together.
13. Show appreciation and say thank you often.
14. Remember important dates and celebrate them.
15. Make the effort to understand and listen often (even if you disagree).
16. Spend spiritual time together.

17. Share times with other couples.
18. Give support without offering advice or trying to fix it.
19. Have regular date nights together.
20. Talk honestly about your fears and insecurities when they emerge.
21. Have playful exchanges together.
22. Use expressions of endearment toward one another (pet names).
23. Strive to eliminate tension or bickering between the two of you.
24. You can talk easily with each other even about difficult issues.
25. You continually try to eliminate resentment and regret within the relationship.
26. You have regular, rewarding lovemaking.
27. There is an absence of intimidation, walking on eggshells, or criticism.
28. You can enjoy each other's company despite the activity in which you are engaged.
29. You still do thoughtful things for each other.
30. No secrets exist between the two of you.
31. You can have fun together.
32. You are still attracted to each other.
33. You both feel you get more than you give in the relationship.
34. Demonstrations of irritation, impatience, or annoyance are rare.
35. You are a united front to your children even if you disagree at times.
36. Conflicts are addressed in a timely manner and resolved.
37. Conflicts bring you closer.
38. Petty, punitive punishments are not part of your relationship.
39. You share similar values, morally and spiritually.

40. You appreciate each other's difference versus being at an impasse over them.
41. You disagree agreeably.
42. You would rather be close than right.
43. You allow the other to save face rather than embarrass them.
44. You are not judgmental toward each other.
45. Consideration and respect are clearly demonstrated between you.
46. You treat each other as equals.
47. There is an absence of emotional, verbal, or physical abuse.
48. You admire one another for the special qualities you possess.
49. You are still friends and lovers as well as parents.
50. You show warmth, acceptance, and enthusiasm when you greet each other.
51. You never use "the D word" when angry or to shock the other.
52. You understand and fulfill your partner's primary need (and you know what that is).
53. You touch, pat, tickle, stroke, rub, and caress one another often.
54. You still flirt with each other.
55. You do what the other wants to do when they feel more strongly about it.
56. You stay flexible so either one can lead or follow depending on your strengths.
57. You spend quality time together as defined by what your partner prefers.
58. You are able to listen, attend, stay on one issue at a time, and help your partner feel truly understood.
59. Your immediate response to each other is to find common ground and points of agreement versus expressing a different position.

60. You give your spouse your full attention during a conversation without doing something else simultaneously.
61. You do not feel lonely in your relationship.
62. The relationship is deepening and still interests you.
63. You would do it all again.
64. You are a better person because of the other.

ACTION STEP TWELVE: REUNION AND RECOVERY

Reunions are a time when a friendship is resumed where both people have had some time apart from each other. In the best relationships, it may seem like it was only yesterday, even if it has been years. A marriage that has recommitted and reconnected feels this way. This couple has genuinely missed one other and is grateful to have another chance to be together.

Recovery represents a fresh start in a new direction for the person who has been self-destructive and gotten off track in his or her life. This second chance enables them the opportunity to turn things around in a healthier direction. Marriages that survive infidelity experience the pain of defeat, but also the hope of rebuilding a better relationship than existed previously.

Couples realize what they have been missing when they slowly deepen the relationship in ways that may have never been a part of their marriage before.

- Regular times as a couple without interruption for even brief periods each week are essential.
- Learning to move communication from small talk to emotionally intimate talk is a means toward deepening their closeness.
- Establishing nonsexual rituals of affection introduces affirmation, physical contact, and playfulness between them.
- Facilitating the art of conflict that brings closeness enables couples to solve the reoccurring problems that sometimes erode relationships.

All these areas and more have to be introduced into the relationship if closeness and connection are to occur. Successfully navigating through these stages can often ensure a happy ending to an otherwise bleak prognosis in a broken relationship.

Doesn't every relationship or marriage deserve that opportunity?

BETRAYED BUT UNBROKEN: A CASE STUDY OF THE FOUR-STAGE, TWELVE-ACTION-STEP PROCESS

Jack and Pam had been married for almost twenty-one years when she suspected that Jack was having an affair with a woman in his company. Jack had always worked long hours, so Pam eventually turned her attention toward the children, who were almost all grown and gone. Pam did not want to believe what the evidence was telling her, so she decided to watch, wait, and document (recognition).

On occasion, she would question him about inconsistencies regarding his whereabouts, but Jack would have an explanation or dismiss her concerns. He eventually began getting impatient and irritated at her curiosity, which made her even more suspicious. Finally, she confronted him with the evidence she had collected, and he admitted to a minor involvement only. Shortly thereafter, Pam asked him to move out of the house and separate (reactions of the offending spouse).

After pressing him more about the information she had, Jack finally capitulated and told her about the affair. Pam was heartbroken, and Jack finally began facing the damage he had done to their marriage. They began the arduous task of discussing all that had occurred between them (taking responsibility).

Pam asked him to end the affair immediately by a phone call that she listened to, inform her if any further contact occurred, set limits on his work schedule, provide open access to all his communication devices and technology, and begin counseling with her (relapse prevention).

Jack began to see more fully how devastated Pam was by his affair. He realized the betrayal was not only of her, but his children, the people on his job, and the values and faith for which he had always stood. He was squarely facing how he had let himself down, and in the process, risked destroying all he had worked for his entire life (experiencing remorse).

Once in counseling, they discussed factors that contributed to the affair, such as his long hours, relaxed boundaries with other women, a loss of the proper priorities in his life, feeling bored in his marriage, the erosion of his values and spiritual life, and a desire to feel excitement again. He even blamed Pam for not appearing to want him any longer. She admitted her preoccupation with raising children and caring for her aging parents, but she had never given up on their marriage. She was able to see how living with the status quo without voicing her unhappiness was only avoiding what was going on their marriage (realizing the whys).

Both of them began working on the process of forgiving each other for the real and imagined offenses that had occurred in the marriage. It was admittedly harder for Pam to begin this journey because she was still in so much pain, and Jack had been so deceitful to her. They were able to apologize to each other for letting one another down in their respective ways. They remembered what they had once had together and promised to rediscover that *(reoccurring forgiveness).*

Pam had to face her fears of being hurt again by staying in the marriage. Each of them had to evaluate what they needed to do differently if their relationship was to go forward. They examined their individual insecurities and faults and how those impacted the marriage. What would they each need to change in order to be better partners? *(reevaluating expectations).*

Jack knew he had to make specific personal changes to repair this relationship. He made amends by following through with Pam's need for reassurance whenever she had a difficult day. He cooperated with her requests for accountability willingly without becoming annoyed by her questions. They both agreed to focus on doing what was best for the marriage, despite how it interfered with their individual preferences *(repair and restitution).*

Eventually, it was time for each of them to decide whether to stay together and make the marriage work or not. They decided they wanted to make it work, no matter what. Pam asked Jack to move back into their home, so he did. Demonstrations of gratitude and daily affirmations helped them to balance their previous focus on their problems *(reconciling and recommitting).*

Jack was consistent in keeping his word, being open and honest, maintained appropriate boundaries with others, and gave more than he expected back. They initiated rituals of affection and learned better ways of deepening their emotional intimacy with regular times together uninterrupted by technology or busyness. When they had conflicts, they brought up their concerns and differences and worked toward acceptable solutions instead of sweeping them under the rug *(rebuilding trust and reconnecting).*

Jack and Pam rekindled their interest in each other by doing things together regularly. They dated, took dance lessons, went out of town for the weekend every month or two, and learned to have fun again. Though their sex lives had been lackluster for years, they made it a priority to become playful with each other and gradually introduce intimate times again. Their progress was often three steps forward and two steps back, but they intentionally kept working on building a better future together. Within a couple of years, they were happier in their marriage than either of them could ever remember. Even though there were brief periods of sadness and regret, they continued to make their relationship the priority it had not been previously (reunion and recovery).

HOMEWORK EXERCISE

Emotional-Intimacy-Relationship Rebuilding

Reserve some uninterrupted time to be together to talk about your responses to the following incomplete statements about your relationship. Feel free to spend time adding more feedback, context, or feelings to elaborate upon what you mean about each item. Both of you should take turns answering or responding about the statements, reflecting upon your feelings and experience within the relationship.

1. The first time we met I felt . . .
2. It seems like we have known each other . . .
3. The kind of relationship we have is . . .
4. One adjective to describe our relationship would be . . .
5. One way in which we are alike is . . .
6. One way in which we are different is . . .
7. If our relationship were a film, it would be called . . .
8. A peak experience in our relationship was . . .
9. A place I would like to share with you is . . .
10. I find your friends to be . . .
11. When we meet new people, I . . .
12. When I am with you in a social situation, I feel . . .
13. One of the most fun things we ever did was . . .
14. The needs you satisfy in me are . . .
15. Some of my needs that are not being completely satisfied are . . .
16. Right now, I feel . . .
17. A song that reminds me of you is . . .
18. The amount of time I spend alone is . . .
19. One of your greatest assets is . . .
20. I am proud of you when . . .
21. Something you have helped me learn about myself is . . .

22. One of the feelings with which I have the most trouble is . . .
23. I feel indecisive when . . .
24. I am most suspicious of you when . . .
25. I assume you know that . . .
26. If I could make you over, I would never change . . .
27. You are most helpful when . . .
28. I am afraid . . .
29. I like it when you . . .
30. You annoy me when you . . .
31. One thing I regret having done is . . .
32. A habit of mine that bothers me most is . . .
33. Your greatest strength is . . .
34. I do not like it when you . . .
35. Something I dislike about you that we seldom talk about is . . .
36. I have the most fun with you when . . .
37. If I had all the money is the world, I would . . .
38. A frequent fantasy I have about you is . . .
39. When we have an intellectual discussion . . .
40. You tend to talk a lot about . . .
41. When I don't want to answer questions, I . . .
42. When I can't express something to you, I . . .
43. This experience to me is . . .
44. A thing that helps us grow closer is . . .
45. The things I most like to do with you are . . .
46. I tend not to tell you about . . .
47. Something I am usually reluctant to discuss is . . .
48. Something I have always wondered about is . . .
49. I think you avoid me when . . .
50. An area in which I would like to feel more equal to you is . . .
51. I feel inferior to you when . . .
52. I feel rebellious when . . .
53. I need you most when . . .

54. To keep from being hurt, I . . .
55. It hurts me when . . .
56. When I hurt you, I . . .
57. I get discouraged or frustrated when . . .
58. I think you are unfair when you . . .
59. When you are pouting, I feel . . .
60. The things that hold us together are . . .
61. The habit you have that bothers me most is . . .
62. I become most defensive when you . . .
63. I am most angry with you when . . .
64. When we fight . . .
65. When I feel as if I have lost, I . . .
66. Right now, I am feeling . . .
67. I think that you do not give me a chance to . . .
68. An important thing or issue between us right now is . . .
69. I find that being open with you is . . .
70. One thing I have always wanted to talk more about is . . .
71. I wish you would let me know when I . . .
72. I think it would be fun to . . .
73. If I wanted to make you laugh, I would . . .
74. A pattern I see in our relationship is . . .
75. The part of my body that I like the most is . . .
76. The part of my body that I like the least is . . .
77. What I like most about your body is . . .
78. The ways I like you to touch me are . . .
79. Right now, I am feeling . . .
80. I feel jealous when . . .
81. I feel most tender toward you when . . .
82. One of the times that bothered me most in our relationship was . . .
83. What I like best about our relationship is . . .
84. In the future, I would like our relationship to become more . . .

85. The type of relationship I do not want to develop with you is . . .
86. The thing I value most in life is . . .
87. I believe in and am committed to . . .
88. In five years, I see us . . .

Can you still have fun together? Enjoying each other's company is still one of the most important qualities a relationship can possess. Couples who actually like being together, no matter what they are doing, tend to be the most content. The activity spices up the occasion and makes it memorable.

HOMEWORK EXERCISE

Fun Things We Would Like to Do

There are things couples should do on a regular basis purely for fun and enjoyment. These may be activities you did when dating or on vacations that energized the relationship and reminded you of why you were together.

Make a list of all the things that you would like to do . . .

- that you currently do
- that you used to do in the past
- that you have always wanted to do

HOMEWORK EXERCISE

Here is a way to get an update on how you are doing as a couple. Periodic feedback is essential for a relationship to continue to grow and change for the better. Ask these questions to each other, and be honest about what you feel and what else you would like to occur.

Marital Status Update

1. How do I feel the relationship has progressed up to this point?
2. Am I satisfied with where our relationship is at present?
3. What else would I like to see happen between us?
4. What am I willing to do individually to keep improving?

HOMEWORK EXERCISE

What stage is your marriage in the infidelity-recovery process? **Circle all stages you have worked through.**

Infidelity-Recovery-Stage Assessment

1. Recognition
2. Typical Reactions of the Offending Spouse
3. Taking Responsibility
4. Relapse Prevention
5. Experiencing Remorse
6. Realizing the "Whys"
7. Reoccurring Forgiveness
8. Reevaluating Expectations of Each Other
9. Repair and Restitution of the Relationship
10. Reconciling and Recommitting
11. Rebuilding Trust and Reconnecting
12. Reunion and Recovery

CHAPTER 16

THE BEST WAYS TO AFFAIR-PROOF YOUR MARRIAGE

"A pretty face gets old, a nice body will change, but a good heart will always remain."

—Olubayo Adebiyi

During the first week of my junior year at Clemson University, I walked by the most beautiful girl I had ever seen. We noticed one another, smiled, and said hi as we passed each other. Later that week, I saw her again in Harcomb Commons dining hall and mustered up the courage to walk over and introduce myself. Dru-Ann was warm, friendly, energetic, and vivacious! It was love at first sight, and later, I was to discover she felt the same way, too. Within a week, we had our first date, and I was hooked!

Ironically, another girl I had been interested in for over a year ended up in one of my classes. Susan had just broken up with her long-term boyfriend and began showing a greater-than-friendly interest in me. During that first week, she asked me for some material related to our class. When she came over to my dorm room at the fraternity house to get the syllabus, she was quite warm and attentive. Before too long, we were in an embrace and kissing.

At the same time that this was occurring, a thought popped into my head: How would I feel if Dru-Ann, whom I had just gone out with a couple of days before, was doing the same thing I was doing with another guy? Immediately, I knew that it would not be okay with me, even though we were not dating exclusively yet. So I discretely but quickly wound down the exchange of affection with Susan, gave her the material she came over to get, and told her I would see her in class the next day.

After class the next day, Susan caught up with me and we walked back across campus toward our dorms together, chatting. I called Dru-

Ann that night and, as luck would have it, one of the first things she asked was, "Who was that pretty blonde you were walking with near the post office today? You didn't even speak to me when I walked by!" I was busted, and I immediately felt guilty. I had not even noticed she had passed me on her way to class. So I told her who Susan was but assured her that she was really the girl I wanted a more serious relationship with, not Susan.

I was relieved that the exchange between Susan and me had not gone any further than it did. That incident was a distinct point in time when I decided to pursue a committed relationship with Dru-Ann without seeing other people.

One year and a half later, we were married.

FIVE PRINCIPLES THAT ENSURE FAITHFULNESS

Although stories of love at first sight are suspect at best, it is possible to have an immediate connection, a strong attraction to, and compatibility on many levels with another person recently met. Time together and getting to really know the other person will either confirm or disconfirm those original feelings. It is generally recommended that couples date each other for a year before deciding to get married. The wisdom behind this is that most people can remain on their best behavior for six to twelve months or less. The closer most people get to the end of this period, the more likely it is that both individuals will show their less desirable sides.

Principle 1: *Marriages Are Made, Not Born*

The first year of a marriage is like the opening line of *A Tale of Two Cities:* "It was the best of times. It was the worst of times." It is an incredibly exciting time in the lives of a couple, and yet it can be difficult learning to live with another person who doesn't do things the same way you do. Marriage takes consistent time and effort to become a strong relationship. It takes working at it every day, even though it should not be hard work. Couples who struggle to get along from the beginning of their dating relationship and never show much improvement generally should never get married in the first place.

The goal of the early years of a marriage is to transition from *thinking like an individual* to *thinking like a team*. An individual thinks about what he or she personally wants. A team thinks about what is best for everyone. A couple's willingness to submit to each other out of reverence for Christ (Ephesians 5) is the key to this dilemma.

Most couples do not realize that it takes between five to seven years after the "I dos" to become a strong team. So it does not matter how long you have known each other or even if you have lived together previously. The clock does not start ticking until both individuals have demonstrated a complete commitment to each other in marriage before this will occur. Being in the same house does not assure this type of bonding will occur. It is only when a commitment to look out for the best interests of the other for a lifetime is made and the official "I dos" are promised that the process of becoming a strong team begins. Anything less is just a test drive or "playing house."

Recently, the adult son of our next-door neighbors commented to my wife that he had been watching our relationship for several years. He went on to say he hoped to someday have a marriage that reflected the love and respect that he saw between us. It has indeed taken years to make our relationship what it is today, and all the hard work has been worth it. Marriages are made, not born.

Principle 2: **Treat Your Spouse the Way You Want to Be Treated**

Almost everyone agrees with the first part of the Golden Rule: *treating others the way we want to be treated*. The problem most of us have is realizing when we are not doing this. It is easy to become conditional in the way we treat our spouse. It is human nature to take the position that "I'll do this for you if you do this for me" or "I'm not going to do this for you unless you do this for me."

True security and trust is deepened when our experience has been that our spouse places our needs and interests before their own. It's not that we do not ever think about ourselves first, but that we learn to put our partner first. This, in turn, motivates our partner to reciprocate and look out for our best interests as well. When you are married to someone who cares about how you feel, you learn to care about their feelings as well.

How would I feel if I were spoken to like that?
How would I feel if I were treated that way?
What if my feelings were not considered?

When we anticipate how a decision we make might affect our spouse, we will take actions that generally meet the needs and expectations of us both.

One of the most common questions betrayed spouses ask when infidelity has been uncovered is, "Didn't you think about me when you were with her? How could you have not considered how this might hurt me?"

The second part of the Golden Rule concept is to treat your spouse the way he or she wants to be treated. This treatment toward them may be in ways that have never occurred to us before.

Examples might include:

- Being on time or calling if we are going to be late
- Greeting our spouse upon their or our arrival or seeking them out if they are in another part of the house
- Spending some initial time sharing our day and finding out about their day before retreating to the computer, television, paper, or elsewhere
- Asking them if they need anything when we go to get something for ourselves
- Calling or texting during the day if that is important to our spouse
- Watching the shows or movies or doing the things that they like to do instead of just what we want to do.
- Picking up after ourselves and being sensitive to the general state of the house
- Walking on the outside of the sidewalk if you are a guy and opening doors for your wife. Chivalry is still alive, and it works!

- Being aware of moodiness, irritability, and impatience within ourselves and making attitude adjustments so we are easier to be around
- Learning to apologize and be the first to take responsibility for our part of a problem even if we believe our role is a minor one
- Showing the level of affection that our spouse needs
- Becoming aware of the little things that mean the most to our spouse

God wants us to have a happy marriage. When we experience this, we are a force for good in this unhappy world. Other people notice how we treat each other, and our children have a model for how to carry on in their future relationships. You might be surprised by who is watching the two of you together and how you treat one another.

Satan does not want our marriage to make a difference. When we are dissatisfied with each other, it neutralizes our spiritual influence on others. They do not see that we have anything that they would want to emulate. It sets precedence on the type of marriage our children will most likely have. It diminishes our motivation to grow spiritually as well. Much of the depression people experience today is because they are in a marriage in which one or both parties have quit trying. They have stopped treating each other the way they want to be treated. I see college students from the University of Georgia who experience depression that is, in part, related to the unhappy marriages they have grown up in with their parents. They are reluctant to get into a committed relationship themselves for fear it will not last.

Approximately one-third of the marriages today could be labeled as coexistent. These are marriages that stay together because of habit, lifestyle, the children, or fear of being alone. Just because a couple subscribes to "divorce is not an option" doesn't mean they do not view their marriage as a prison sentence. Living in a coexistent marriage compromises our vitality, our spiritual enthusiasm, and steals our joy of life. It likewise causes others to think, *If Christianity is real, why isn't your marriage any better than it is?*

Treating our spouse the way we want to be treated allows us to put ourselves in their place when we consider our actions toward them. Treating our spouse the way they want to be treated requires that we intentionally know and understand what is important to them.

Principle 3: ***Ask for What You Want***

Most of the couples who come into my office are locked in a mutual blame cycle, pointing out what the other does that is wrong. They have become experts at what is wrong with their partner but a little vague about what they bring to the party. Their criticism has become an ineffective default for trying to get their spouse to change. However, it only entrenches the pattern and polarizes them from each other. They each can easily list multiple faults in their spouse and recite their mistakes as if they had repeated the script a hundred times before. The endless loop of "he said, she said" only redoubles their efforts to prove how wrong the other is and intensifies their animosity toward one another. They live in the past instead of learning from it. They are stuck at an impasse, but oddly enough, neither is asking for what they really want.

Asking for what we want requires the willingness to be vulnerable and risk being hurt or disappointed again. Maybe we have asked in the past and did not get what we needed. The rejection we felt caused us to avoid taking that chance again. However, if we don't ask for what we want, we will end up hurt, angry, and resentful toward the very person who is supposed to be meeting our needs but isn't. We will eventually become critical of them for not giving us what we want.

Criticisms make our spouse feel attacked and defend themselves. They may try to explain the reasons for their actions or even resort to pointing out our faults as well. The result is that neither person feels understood, nor do they get what they need from each other.

What causes this criticize-counter-criticize pattern between two people who really love each other?

Three of the biggest problems that men have are (1) we don't listen well, (2) we often don't remember what our wives tell us, and (3) we tend to retreat and withdraw during conflicts.

Three of the biggest problems women have are (1) they are more easily hurt, (2) they can be moody, and (3) they become critical when they feel taken for granted.

A woman's greatest need is to feel loved and believe that they are the most important person in their husband's life—their top priority, behind Christ of course. If men do not listen or remember what their wives say, how significant do you think that makes them feel? When this happens, most women will feel taken for granted, unimportant, or a low priority. So when our wives ask for something or share things that are important to them, it is essential that husbands listen, remember, and act upon them.

A man's greatest need is to feel respected by his wife. He longs for her to think he is the greatest, that he can do anything he puts his mind to, and that she is his biggest supporter. When he is criticized long enough, he may feel he can never measure up, so he may quit trying.

If wives don't get the expected response from their husbands by asking, they will often try to get their attention by being more direct. If this fails to get the desired response, they may resort to criticizing. When men feel criticized, they get defensive, pull back, and protect themselves. They may feel disrespected, mistreated, and resentful. They then find fault with their wives, and eventually the criticize-counter-criticize pattern will begin between the couple.

When these types of impasse occur in a marriage, it is not uncommon for husbands and wives to discover a sympathetic ear from someone who treats them more kindly than their own spouse does. This impasse provides a temporary crack in the marital veneer. It becomes an opportunity for an understanding and sympathetic colleague or neighbor to be there for an unhappy spouse. This person may seem to appreciate them more than their own partner does.

This is why asking for what we want instead of criticizing or withholding is a simpler, though more vulnerable way to get what we need. Asking for what we want takes some patience, humility, skills of negotiation, and willingness to give and take. It is a much more constructive way of building the strength in a relationship than being critical or withdrawing. It engages your spouse to meet your needs instead of resorting to the risks of allowing someone else into your marriage.

Principle 4: ***Don't Let the Sun Go Down on Your Anger***

When a conflict, an argument, a misunderstanding, or a fight with a spouse occurs, try to work it out quickly. It is best not to remain at an impasse, *sweep it under the rug*, hold a grudge, or passive aggressively punish each other with silent treatment.

When a conflict occurs with someone else, we come to a decision-making crossroads. That crossroads offers two options. The first option is to assume the worst and risk jumping to conclusions about their intentions. When we assume the worst of others, we may or may not be correct. If we are right, we may accuse, try, and convict them without giving them an opportunity to explain themselves. This is hardly a fair trial. If we are wrong, we have insulted them because we assumed the worst and they may have been innocent. Anyone would be insulted by this type of treatment.

The second option is to give the benefit of the doubt, which Andy Stanley calls *believing the best in others*. When we give the benefit of the doubt, we begin by telling ourselves that our assumptions could be right or they could be wrong. What we decide to do is withhold judgment until we get their input. We then ask them questions and give them an opportunity to explain their intentions. This act of grace shows respect, and if our initial assumptions were wrong, we avoid looking like an unjust judge. Our perspective may be widened enough to truly understand what happened, and we can proceed armed with greater understanding. We have also treated the other person the way we would have wanted to be treated.

When Dru-Ann and I were newlyweds and occasionally argued, I would always try to be right. I would point out her mistake and try to get her to see it from my point of view. She, of course, had a different perspective, and we would not be able to find a solution we could both agree upon. She would call me "Mr. Perfect" and I would call her "stubborn," but that only made matters worse. Finally, out of frustration, we would part ways and not talk for a while. I was a clueless young husband who thought my good intentions should be enough. She felt I did not treat her with kindness or sensitivity. I would eventually apologize, even though I often felt she was more in the wrong. She was not ready to let it go and stayed mad for days at a time. We would finally talk and make up, but it was always very upsetting during the time we were at odds with each other.

Someone once said that the secret to a happy marriage is turning mountains into molehills and not letting molehills become mountains.

There is a lot of truth to this because most of us do not remember the cause of an argument after it is over, but we do remember how we felt about it. We also remember how we were treated by our spouse. When we can't find points of agreement, we start to question what we have in common together or why we are together. This is also a point at which we may be more susceptible to noticing how considerately others treat us in contrast to how our spouse regards us.

The Song of Songs in the Old Testament talks about the "little foxes" that spoil the garden when they invade the area. Unresolved resentment can spoil a marriage and cause us to only think about what is wrong in a relationship. There may be more good than bad in a marriage, but unresolved resentments can blind us to that.

According to Terry Real in *The New Rules of Marriage*, the five most harmful barriers to problem solving in a relationship are:
1. Trying to be Right (which means your spouse is wrong)
2. Being Controlling (being rigid instead of flexible)
3. Unrestrained Verbal Expression (verbal abuse)
4. Withholding and Withdrawal (not giving to the other person)
5. Retaliation (punitive behavior)

Would You Rather Be Right or Close?

There is an interactional pattern that is reoccurring in the world of marital relationships. It is the need to be right. When a problem occurs between two people who genuinely love each other, they often both insist that they are *right*. Being "right" takes on such importance and intensity that the other's point of view is treated as if it is *wrong*! Both parties try so hard to make their individual points that neither side feels understood or heard. The result is frustration and anger from feeling misunderstood, ignored, and wronged!

What does this type of communication do to a relationship? It makes both parties feel invalidated and it alienates them from each other. *So what can be done about this unrewarding pattern of interaction?*

Try asking yourself this simple question: **Would I rather be right or close?**

Having to be right all the time means someone else has to be wrong. This creates defensiveness, distance, and separation in the relationship. Being right is overrated, anyway. It is at best a hollow victory because of what it costs the relationship in feelings of closeness.

Closeness occurs when we begin by admitting that our partner has a valid point. In other words, begin by first identifying what you can agree with, not with what you disagree. Each of us wants our particular position acknowledged because we desire affirmation from the person that we love. Promoting closeness comes from demonstrating that what our partner says has merit, even if we have a different point of view. When others feel understood and listened to, they drop their guard and demonstrate the Golden Rule of treating others the way they want to be treated. This means that when you listen to them, they actually want to hear what you have to say as well. Practice this with your partner and you both will be right and close!

Dr. John Gottman is a psychologist who studied seven hundred couples for twenty years to find out what made marriages succeed and last. His results are cited in his book, *The Seven Principles for Making Marriage Work*.

One of the three conclusions he discovered was that:
- *"couples who continued to work on their problems no matter how long it took were more likely to stay together the longest."*

The second conclusion was that:
- *"when both individuals made amends or repair attempts toward one another, they were more likely to get along better."*

The last conclusion he found was that:
- *"when both individuals accommodated each other even if slightly, they were more likely to find mutually acceptable solutions."*

So seek solutions to conflicts, because conflicts should bring us closer.

Principle 5: **No Secrets**

Secrets from our spouse are generally not a good idea unless it is for the purpose of a gift, a surprise, or some other special function done on his or her behalf. If we have to hide something, we probably should not be involved in it. Similarly, if the issue in question cannot pass the how-would-my-spouse-feel-if-they-knew-about-this test, it is generally not a good idea. When in doubt, do without!

John was planning to take his daughter out trick-or-treating with her best friend on Halloween. He had not expected her divorced, single mother to accompany them as they canvassed her friend's neighborhood. After they were finished, the daughters were hungry and wanted to go out and get something to eat. John was in a dilemma, as his wife was expecting them home soon. He called his wife and told her that he was taking the daughters to get something to eat. He failed to mention that this single mother had not only walked with him while the girls collected candy, but was accompanying them to the restaurant. A friend of his wife saw John and the other woman having dinner with the children and relayed that information within minutes. You can imagine the argument that ensued when John arrived home later.

Keeping things from our spouses supposedly for their own good does not take into consideration what they would prefer. Most of the time, avoiding an issue to keep from creating undue conflict only belies a much more serious problem. "What she doesn't know won't hurt her" is flawed reasoning and sets the stage for major trust issues in a marriage.

- *What should we do when an old flame e-mails, calls, or texts us?*
- *Should we tell our spouse if someone is flirting with us at the office?*
- *Is it a nonissue to have lunch with an opposite-sex colleague or not?*
- *If you have a mixed-double tennis partner, is practicing alone together wise?*

If we have questions to a particularly unusual predicament, the best thing to do is be transparent and ask our spouse about their comfort level with the situation. Talking to one or more of our same-sex friends about what they think is another good checks-and-balance approach.

The Video Cam Test

One of the best ways to determine if any situation is appropriate or not is to use the Video Cam Test. Imagine that wherever you are, whomever you are with, or whomever you meet, there is a video camera attached to your shirt or blouse, transmitting whatever is said or done directly back to your spouse. How would that change the way you might handle the situation? If it would, you may be ignoring an important boundary that could negatively affect the security and trust within your marriage.

WIN THREE PERSONAL BATTLES WITHIN

"Be guided by your faith and your principles and not your feelings."

Dave Willis

There is a major affront facing the institution of marriage. It is being levied by those who believe that marriage is outdated and has lost its relevancy. Some view marriage as men's way of enslaving women. Young people today appear to be so afraid of divorce that they have postponed getting married and have embraced living together as a safe alternative. The flaw in this compensatory strategy is that cohabiting couples are just as likely to end their relationship as non-cohabitating couples. Even if they do eventually marry, they are more likely to divorce than married couples who did not initially live together.

The problem is not with the institution of marriage, but that we have placed the rights of the individual above the importance of the relationship. The success of a marriage depends upon making both a total commitment to our partner as well as making a conscious choice to forgo some of our personal rights as individuals. We do this in exchange for the privilege of living exclusively with a person who makes our life better than it would have been alone. Marriage enables us to realize that our lives are much more enriched by having a partner by our side than being by ourselves. We also regard that relationship as something we do not just casually opt out of if it isn't what we expected. Marriages are not perfect because people are not perfect. Relationships will experience difficult times, but that doesn't mean that there may be someone better out there. "There" is not necessarily better than "here."

The secret to maintaining fidelity in marriage lies in winning three personal battles within ourselves:

- The battle of attraction and desire
- The battle of the mind
- The battle of actions

> *"Each one is tempted when by his own evil desire, he is dragged away and enticed. Then after desire has conceived, it gives birth to sin; and sin, when it is full-grown, gives birth to death."*
>
> James 1:14–15 (NIV)

We will be tempted in life. Many of those things that are appealing to us are actually good for us. Friendships, aspirations, interests, and food are all wonderful aspects that make life fun and worth living. However, there are also unhealthy and destructive things that tempt us as well, and these can steal our joy and ruin our lives.

The Battle of Attraction and Desire

> *"Above all else, guard your heart, for everything you do flows from it."*
>
> Proverbs 4:23 (NIV)

We are all people watchers at heart. Our curiosity causes us to notice other people and admire certain characteristics about them that appeal to us. We naturally identify with what others are doing and sometimes imitate them. The entertainment industry capitalizes on this human tendency financially by promoting beautiful, talented individuals who seem to have it all. They influence us to dress in certain ways, buy certain products, or even embrace a particular lifestyle. These attractive people can cause us to envy what they have or even desire them as well. We might ask ourselves, *What would it be like to actually be that person? Wouldn't life be exciting if I were with them?*

One recent poll with teenagers and young adults asked what they would wish for if given their greatest desire. The majority of these young people wanted to be well known, famous, and rich. They wanted others to be attracted to them and admire them for who they were.

If someone has ever caught your eye and kept you gazing at them longer than you intended to, then you have probably experienced the initial feelings of attraction toward another person. If you couldn't get them out of your mind, then you may have eventually found yourself fantasizing about them. These fantasies can turn into temptations very easily. Temptations do not turn into desires, however, unless we entertain them or replay them. Focusing too long on any image or person can make a strong, lasting impression on our emotions and our minds. Drinking certain images into our minds can be emotionally intoxicating and titillating. The desires these temptations create can make us prone to taking actions we may regret. Steve Arterburn's book *Every Man's Battle* gives techniques such as "bouncing our eyes away" to keep us from inappropriately "dwelling on the opposite sex" for any more than a millisecond. The intention of this strategy is to keep us from sexualizing others and to help us defend ourselves from desiring other people.

The Battle of the Mind

> *"As a man thinketh in his heart, so is he."*
> Proverbs 23:7 (KJV)

"What we focus on, we strengthen" (DCW). Temptation can elicit emotions and desires, but the battle is in our minds. Dwelling on certain thoughts reinforces them and can generate fantasies that make us desire another person. When the desire is strong enough, we will eventually act upon those desires.

We live in a time when people have highly undisciplined minds. They search through the Internet, commercials, and advertisements to find something that stimulates and entertains them. As a result, they feel the need for more input to maintain that high level of engagement and the feelings of excitement. They do not realize that what they expose themselves to can actually adversely affect them. This is why most habitual pornography users are surprised to discover that they have a difficult time emotionally engaging a real, live person in a meaningful relationship.

Many liberally minded people suggest that fantasizing is harmless and only adds spice to their lives. If that fantasy is of someone other than your spouse, it will diminish your desire for your spouse and increase that desire for the other person. If the lack of desire for your spouse tempts you to think of someone else, find out what problem you are having with your spouse and remedy it quickly. Dwelling on the what-ifs of being with someone else will emotionally erode feelings of attraction toward one's spouse. It is naïve to believe that fantasizing about someone else will be a helpful aphrodisiac that benefits your marriage.

We are encouraged to "take captive every thought to make it obedient to Christ" (2 Corinthians 10:5, NIV). We can influence how and what we think about for our good or to our detriment.

- The most discontent people think about all the misfortune that has occurred to them and how unfair life is.
- The most anxious people dwell on everything that can go wrong, and their negativity dominates their thoughts.
- The most peaceful people think about "whatever is true, whatever is noble, whatever is right, whatever is pure, whatever is lovely, whatever is admirable—if anything is excellent or praiseworthy—think about such things" (Philippians 4:8, NIV).
- The happiest and most faithful couples think about how blessed they are to have each other. They intentionally think about the wonderful qualities their spouse possesses on a daily basis.

The Battle of Actions

> "We can't run from our problems, but we don't have to run to them."
>
> Unknown

When temptation leads an individual to think about or desire another person, the next step is inventing reasons to be in closer proximity in order to engage them. Though these actions may initially seem harmless, they often have the ulterior motive of getting the other party's attention. Finding excuses to be around another person will cause anticipation of those chance encounters. We have all seen people who have suddenly started paying closer attention to their appearance, how they dress, and to getting into better shape. It sometimes is an indicator of a new relationship in their lives.

It is only a matter of time before these seemingly innocent interactions will become a planned and anticipated rendezvous. If you are married and you don't inform a trusted friend about the challenges you are experiencing, it will only be a matter of time until something happens to damage your marriage.

> ". . . then after desire has conceived, it gives birth to sin; and sin, when it is full grown, gives birth to death."
>
> James 1:15 (NIV)

Jill was a young professional who was twenty-eight years old and engaged to be married to Hank. Jill was a fun-loving, energetic woman who tended to flirt and be playful with others. She had grown up being in some type of serious relationship most of her high school and college years. If one romance ended, it wasn't long before she was involved again with someone else. She had an eye for the guys and was often overheard with her girlfriends talking about some good-looking stud she had noticed. It was not surprising that Hank would occasionally become jealous at her friendliness toward other guys when they were out together. She couldn't understand why Hank questioned her trustworthiness. In her mind, she was just being social and nice to those around her. What she didn't realize was that her willingness to entertain natural interests in other guys was interfering with her commitment to her fiancé. By allowing herself to indulge her thoughts and feelings about other men, she kept herself from developing a deeper connection and loyalty to Hank. When they went to premarital counseling together, it became apparent that she was always looking for the next-best thing in a relationship. She came to realize that during her upbringing, her mother had left several marriages for what she believed was a better opportunity. Jill was just inadvertently following in her mother's footsteps.

CHAPTER 17

THE MARITAL BOUNDARIES TEST

We live during a time in our society where it is difficult to determine the difference between healthy and unhealthy physical and emotional boundaries in relationships. In our efforts to avoid appearing close minded and intolerant, we may naively accommodate certain unhealthy boundaries to exist that could be harmful for us or others. Many problems that occur in relationships today begin with actions or attitudes that cross healthy, moral lines and lead to poor judgment. When certain emotions or feelings are aroused by careless actions, a slippery slope of moral missteps can generate further indiscretions. The betrayals that ultimately spring from these actions cause deep regrets.

The minister of Atlanta's North Point Church and noted author Andy Stanley talks about the wisdom and safety that "guard rails" provide for us. Although we may believe certain situations are safe and pose no harm, without defined boundaries we may veer off course in life and find ourselves catapulting over the edge into a fatal abyss. The free fall may be initially exhilarating, but the sudden stop at the bottom can be deadly. "Freedom within limits" provides us with security and the room to enjoy our lives securely in combination with the realization that boundaries are there to protect us from harm.

THE MARITAL BOUNDARIES TEST

Each marital partner should take this test separately.

The following scenarios are examples of typical situations that married individuals occasionally find themselves facing. You may have never encountered some of these situations, but give what you believe would be your most likely response.

Choose the answer or answers that best represent how you would actually react or how you would most likely handle the situation. Select the answer that <u>honestly</u> reflects your opinions, preferences, and views, and not what you just think you <u>should</u> do.

After you have completed the questions, compare your answers with your spouse to see how your perspectives align with each other.

Then, view the recommended answers at the end of the questionnaire.

What do you do if:

1. Someone socially or at work makes an inappropriate, sexually suggestive comment to you.
   - (a) Joke back with them because they probably don't mean anything by it.
   - (b) Ignore it.
   - (c) Tell them off.
   - (d) Do not react but let someone close to you know exactly what was said.
   - (e) If it continues, respectfully remind them that their comment was not appropriate.

2. An opposite-sex colleague asks you to have lunch or dinner with them alone.
   - (a) Accept the invitation since it is only a one-time situation.
   - (b) Invite other colleagues to join you.
   - (c) Determine if the reason they are meeting can be addressed during work hours.
   - (d) If the person insists despite your reservations, let them know your preference would be to include other colleagues.

3. You feel attracted to someone else at work or who is a social acquaintance.
   - (a) Ignore it because these types of things happen all the time.
   - (b) Get to know them better as a person to neutralize the attractions.
   - (c) Share those feelings with a friend or your spouse and discuss realistic boundaries.
   - (d) Have nothing to do with them.

4. **You feel comfortable calling opposite-sex friends "just to talk."**
   (a) Don't make a big deal of it.
   (b) Ask your spouse about how comfortable he or she is with these interactions and accommodate their wishes.
   (c) Get the opinion of your same-sex friends to see what they think about it.
   (d) Limit your calls to a designated time frame.

5. **You tend to flirt with the opposite sex.**
   (a) Inquire about how your spouse feels about it and respect his or her wishes.
   (b) As long as you mean nothing by it, it is harmless.
   (c) It is merely your way of playfully influencing others.
   (d) Investigate out how your same-sex friends view your actions.

6. **You have an opposite-sex personal trainer.**
   (a) I don't need to make any changes because they are trained professionals who know how to maintain appropriate boundaries.
   (b) I am only there trying to get in the best shape possible.
   (c) Make sure my spouse has no concerns, and if he or she does, find a new trainer.
   (d) The physical contact we have during a workout is "strictly business."

7. **An opposite-sex friendship no one else knows about develops.**
   (a) It is probably not a relationship I should have if no one else knows about it.
   (b) It is my right to have friendships with whomever I choose.
   (c) We are able to talk about things that I am unable to discuss with my spouse.
   (d) My friends and spouse probably wouldn't understand.

8. **Working late alone regularly with an opposite-sex colleague occurs.**
   (a) It is part of the job and I have to accept it.
   (b) I don't mind the attention my colleague gives me.
   (c) I should discuss appropriate boundaries and enforce those or seek other employment.
   (d) We have become good friends, so it makes the job tolerable.

9. **You fantasize about someone other than your spouse.**
   (a) Comparing your spouse to other people could be damaging to your marriage.
   (b) Discuss this with a close friend who will be honest and direct with you.
   (c) Fantasy is harmless and not the same as acting on the thoughts.
   (d) Fantasy sexually enhances the intimate time you have with your spouse.

10. **An opposite-sex friend or colleague sends you socially oriented texts regularly during off-hours.**
    (a) Make nothing of it since you are friends or colleagues and answer them.
    (b) Consider it a compliment that they are showing interest.
    (c) Tell them to leave you alone and that they are being inappropriate.
    (d) Ignore their texts, and if they persist, ask them to limit their inquiries to business during business hours.

11. **You make suggestive comments to others, just trying to be friendly.**
    (a) Accept the fact that you are naturally a playful person.
    (b) Enjoy the attention you receive as a result of your overtures.
    (c) Talk to your spouse, a friend, or counselor about the appropriateness of your comments.
    (d) Retain the services of a good attorney to protect you from a possible sexual harassment lawsuit.

12. **You sneak a quick peek when a woman bends over (men only).**
    (a) There is nothing wrong with looking. Enjoy the view!
    (b) Look the other way.
    (c) Ask yourself why you feel compelled to look sexually at another woman.
    (d) It is okay if you are not lusting.

13. **Someone other than your spouse unexpectedly tries to kiss you passionately.**
    (a) Stay cool and don't make a big deal of it.
    (b) Ask them what that was for.
    (c) Try to turn your head and offer your cheek.

(d) Let them know that is not okay with you, and inform your spouse later.

14. You keep secrets from each other.
(a) Unless the secret is a gift or surprise, a no-secrets policy is advised.
(b) It is your right to maintain your own privacy.
(c) It minimizes conflicts if you do not see eye-to-eye on a particular issue.
(d) It depends on whether it will hurt the other's feelings or not.

15. One of you has a bank account or credit card the other doesn't know about.
(a) You have a right to manage the finances that are yours any way you would like.
(b) If your spouse is controlling and overly frugal, it reduces conflicts.
(c) It is okay as long it does not negatively impact the family budget.
(d) Both individuals in a marriage should have full knowledge of the family assets.

16. You e-mail or talk to an old flame, and your spouse is unaware of this.
(a) It is harmless and simply about old friends staying in touch.
(b) It would only make him/her insecure or jealous if he or she knew.
(c) If he/she is uncomfortable with it, I will do what is best for our marriage.
(d) I really don't like being told what I can and can't do.

17. You talk about the satisfaction level of your sex life with the opposite sex.
(a) Getting the perspective of the opposite sex can be helpful.
(b) As long as the conversation is with a friend, it is harmless.
(c) It can help me know what others are doing with the same problems.
(d) If I am not happy with our sex life, I ought to start by discussing it with my spouse.

18. **You have an opposite-sex workout partner.**
    (a) If we are both interested in exercise, why not?
    (b) Find out how my spouse feels about it.
    (c) We are just close friends.
    (d) Exercising with a buddy is motivating and ensures consistency.

19. **You secretly view sexually explicit websites.**
    (a) Occasionally viewing sexual images is normal and harmless.
    (b) It is a great aphrodisiac that gets me in the mood for sex together.
    (c) If my spouse found out, he or she would be upset.
    (d) It interferes with my emotional and physical connection to my spouse.

20. **You talk about your marital problems with an opposite-sex friend or colleague.**
    (a) It is helpful to get the perspective of the opposite sex.
    (b) It is okay to talk about your marriage, but not your sex life.
    (c) Limit these conversations to same-sex friends who are supportive of your marriage and will not automatically take your side.
    (d) If they share their marital problems as well, it may help you appreciate your marriage more.

21. **You show cleavage or wear revealing clothing at work (women only).**
    (a) It may detract from your professionalism and the respect others have for your job performance.
    (b) It makes you more interesting and powerful.
    (c) It will help reveal who your competition is on the job.
    (d) It helps your efforts to influence the right people.

22. **You complain publically about something you don't like in your spouse.**
    (a) It will embarrass him or her into making a change.
    (b) It will let him or her know how strongly you feel.
    (c) It will only make him or her more resistant to changing.
    (d) It may highlight your powerlessness to influence him or her to change.

23. You give out or get phone numbers of the opposite sex.
   (a) You really can't have too many friends.
   (b) It is a good way to increase your professional contacts.
   (c) It could give the wrong message to others.
   (d) If your spouse is uncomfortable with it, don't do it.

24. You engage in full-frontal body hugs with the opposite sex.
   (a) It is harmless if you are just being warm and friendly.
   (b) No one ever gets enough affection.
   (c) What might be innocent to you may be arousing for someone else.
   (d) Learn to give A-frame or side hugs.
   (e) This is generally reserved for your significant other.

25. Someone is too "touchy," and their physical contact seems too familiar.
   (a) If you are good friends, it should not matter.
   (b) Physically block their advances if they become too familiar and ultimately correct their inappropriateness—verbally, if necessary.
   (c) Some people are just very touchy and show their warmth that way.
   (d) Adjust your body position, distance, and personal warmth to reflect your level of receptivity.

(1) d, e (2) b, c, d (3) c (4) b, c (5) a, d (6) c (7) a (8) c (9) a, b (10) d (11) c (12) b, c (13) c, d (14) a (15) d (16) c (17) d (18) b (19) d (20) c (21) a (22) c, d (23) c, d (24) c, d, e (25) b, d

The MBT is merely an exercise to facilitate conversation and a healthy exchange of ideas on preferred boundaries in relationships. It is not intended to portray or represent itself as a standardized test.

CHAPTER 18

THE PROCESS OF BECOMING ONE

MATURING INTO A MARRIAGE MINDSET: BECOMING A TEAM

Who do we think about the majority of the time? Why, ourselves, of course, because we are with ourselves all day long, every single day of our entire lives. We think about how we feel, what we want to eat, how we are going to spend our day, what we want to wear, how we look, and what we want to do. So it is not surprising that when we first get married, we still think like an individual. Hopefully we have begun integrating our significant other into our daily thoughts and actions, but we are still inclined to think about ourselves.

In fact, it literally takes a full five to seven years from the initial "I dos" to truly think like a team. This doesn't mean we don't think a great deal about our spouse, if we are truly in love. It just means that we are still not out of the natural habit of thinking about ourselves first more than we think about our spouse.

The majority of first-time marriages either end the first year of marriage or by the seventh year of marriage. Those couples who divorce after the first year of marriage become painfully aware that the relationship is fraught with problems that appear insurmountable. Perhaps the couple was a poor match or should never have married in the first place. This is not necessarily true, but they feel hopeless or that the relationship can never get better. They do not recognize that marriages are made, not born, so they bail out.

The marriages that end by the seventh year divorce typically because they have not made the shift to thinking like a team.

Their problems may include issues like changing bad habits, adjusting negative attitudes, mutually managing money together, spending appropriate time with one another, or realizing what the specific needs of one's spouse are. The solution to the problems that most couples have together is simply a lack of mutual sacrifice. In other words, learning the importance of "it is more blessed to give than to receive" (Acts 20:35, NIV). This simple but profound paradox is the key to overcoming many conflicts that create impasses within a relationship. It demonstrates "let me give you what you need" with the hopes that you will reciprocate.

HOMEWORK EXERCISE

The Marriage Mindset Quiz

In unhappy relationships, most people feel they are giving more than they are getting. If one person has to be unhappy in order for the other person to be happy, there is a problem in the basic philosophy of the marriage. However, in the best relationships, both people feel they are getting more than they are giving. Below is a contrast of what is necessary to have a marriage mindset.

*Check the items that most **characterize your spouse** in the relationship. Then add the total number of items in each column to determine if your marriage is more team focused or individually oriented.*

Marriage Mindset

- ○ It is about us
- ○ What do you need?
- ○ Delays self-gratification
- ○ You first
- ○ Needs the other in their life
- ○ Is sacrificial and other oriented
- ○ Compromises and accommodates
- ○ Anticipates the needs of the other
- ○ Thinks first, acts later
- ○ Thinks like a team
- ○ Allows self to be influenced
- ○ Makes amends
- ○ Wants to please
- ○ Sensitive to impact upon others
- ○ We have complementary strengths
- ○ Would rather be close
- ○ Apologizes

Total _____ (Team oriented)

Individual Mindset

- ○ It is about me
- ○ What do I need?
- ○ Impulse oriented and self-gratifying
- ○ Me first
- ○ Is self-sufficient
- ○ Takes care of self
- ○ Wants his/her own way
- ○ Doesn't initiate but will respond if prompted
- ○ Acts first, thinks later
- ○ Thinks like an individual
- ○ Stands his/her ground firmly
- ○ Makes a point
- ○ Wants to impress
- ○ Makes an impact on others
- ○ Our differences cause us problems
- ○ Would rather be right
- ○ Eventually acts like everything is okay

Total _____ (Individually focused)

IMPROVING YOUR MARRIAGE BY DEEPENING YOUR FAITH

LOCKED IN AN IMPASSE

The majority of the couples who come to my office for marriage counseling believe that if their spouse would change, their relationship would be better. Many start the first session by citing the faults of their spouse, which is typically countered by their spouse listing their problems as well. They have each become experts at what is wrong with the other, but a little vague about what they bring to the party!

This point-counterpoint, mutual-blame cycle creates an impasse that escalates their anger and makes them both feel powerless to change the relationship. Not easily dissuaded, they often redouble their efforts by bringing up each other's past, despite how entrenched they become. The fact is, we cannot change another person. We can only change ourselves.

Jill and James went to premarital counseling for their conflictual relationship. Both had been married before and wanted this relationship to work. They began their sessions by each pointing out the faults of their significant other, which generated defensive explanations and other past arguments. They were so determined to indict each other to prove their point; they could not step back and listen to what they each legitimately might consider to change personally. This relationship was doomed from the beginning. No amount of redirecting them or trying to focus on what was good about the relationship could occur, and the premarital counseling was terminated. Each was urged to get into individual counseling first to work out their personal issues before returning to couples counseling.

The best tactic for facilitating change is to begin by changing the faults and flaws we possess. If one partner decides to merely focus on what they need to do in order to become a better person, most spouses who sincerely want their marriage to get better will follow suit. The secret weapon for influencing change in others is to first change ourselves!

WE ARE OUR OWN WORST ENEMY

Our worst enemy is not outside ourselves, but it is ourselves. *We are our own worst enemy!* We will all encounter someone in our lives whom we identify as an enemy from time to time. The reality of life, however, is that we do more damage to ourselves than any other person ever can. We shoot ourselves in the foot more often than anyone else ever could. Once we accept this, we will stop looking elsewhere for the origins of our problems.

If we really want to become the best person we can be in our marriage, we have to start by deepening our spiritual lives. We often give attention to our physical life by working out, our emotional life by reading self-help books, or our intellectual life by getting a good education. Unfortunately, we often leave our spiritual development to chance instead of intentionally trying to grow in this vital area.

DEEPENING OUR FAITH

So how can we consciously deepen our spiritual life so we can have the best marriage possible?

1. Be Open to Input from Others

> "All receive advice. Only the wise profit from it."
>
> Syrus

Most of us don't know what we don't know. This is most apparent when observing a know it all. They have all the answers, and if the world would just listen to them, they would straighten it all out. They, however, rarely listen to others. People who actually do know a lot will often admit that the more they know, the more they realize they don't know. They are humble enough to realize that "plans fail for lack of counsel, but with many advisers they succeed" (Proverbs 15:22, NIV). Seeking input and feedback from others who are more experienced than we are is a sign of strength, not of weakness.

When we pray to God to give us direction, knowledge, and insight, we are demonstrating a willingness and openness to His will. Placing our worries and fears on our Lord for support, relief, and answers indicates we know who is in charge, and it is not us.

John Gottman's *The Seven Principles for Making Marriage Work* discovers that one of the factors that keeps a marriage together for more than twenty years is the willingness of a husband to seek and accept input from his wife. Those who are able to adjust their decision-making course to include the needs and the opinions of their wives enjoy a happier marriage.

Most people don't ask for advice, while others take issue with those who try to offer it. Those who seek input will almost always avoid mistakes they would have otherwise made. When I offered direction to my sons when they were younger, I could see their eyes glaze over as they were tuning me out. They often opted to learn from their own mistakes and not mine. Their approach caused them to suffer consequences they could have otherwise avoided. It was very rewarding recently to hear my youngest adult son, David, ask for my insight on a particular issue with which he was grappling. I tried to be respectful and not go overboard on suggestions, but he urged me to offer my input freely. He actually encouraged me to volunteer advice if I saw something that would help him handle his situation better. I think my sons have truly grown up to be mature young men.

Couples who trust and rely on each other to be one another's best friend and critic will avoid many mistakes in life. They will also grow to appreciate each other's respective strengths and welcome the perspective of a partner who has their best interests at heart.

2. *Be Willing to Change When Necessary*
People who refuse to change cannot help changing for the worst. The desire to be better, improve, and grow is in our DNA. Healthy people want to see improvements in their lives. No one employed

in a job says, "I'm making enough of money. There's no need to ever give me a raise again," or "Don't worry about promoting me—I'll be fine in this position indefinitely!" It is normal and natural to want to be better, feel better, look better, and be a better person. When this is not the case, something is wrong. Something has happened that has interfered with our normal inclination to grow and develop.

Life is difficult. We all encounter discouragement, disappointments, mistreatment, and unfairness in life. They can cause us to lose hope that things can be better and cause us to just settle. Giving up is often an emotional state that occurs within us when we can't seem to make a difference. It affects our spirit, and we become unmotivated to try any longer.

God provides us hope that life can be better. When we are experiencing a heavy load in life, He can carry what we can't. We shouldn't forget that God has our best interest in mind and wants us to succeed in the things that important to us. It is necessary for us to realize that we have God's power in our lives if we have a relationship with Him. He is always working in the background for our good (Romans 8:28). God never gives up on us, even when we give up on ourselves.

If we quit growing and changing, it will damage our marriage. We may not intend it to, but giving up and settling causes us to lose vitality and appreciation for the lives we have together. It causes our spouse to have to shoulder the emotional load in the marriage while receiving less from us. Even our children are impacted by our not growing and changing personally. We are always setting an example and a precedent for them. Our kids are taught by us how to manage life. We equip them with the tools they need to face difficulties by staying in the fight ourselves and wrestling with our own problems. They need to see this in us.

Refusing to change is not an option unless we don't mind seeing our marriage become mediocre and boring. Accepting that this is as good as it gets is a precedent for our children to also give up when their marriage encounters trouble. They will follow in our steps. Healthy parents want the best for their children and are willing to make sacrifices, even if it takes them out of their comfort zone.

Remember that God wants us to enjoy the best of life, but it means we have to continue to grow and change. This has always been His plan for us so that we can experience His blessings. Our willingness to claim those blessings requires that we continue to change for the better.

3. Seek God's Will and Wisdom

Unless the Lord blesses our plans, they will eventually fail. Our plans may succeed in some ways, but cause us great pain and anguish in others. This is why we should seek God's will for our lives in all we do, even if those plans appear to be a good decision.

> Now listen, you who say, "Today or tomorrow we will go to this or that city, spend a year there, carry on business and make money." Why, you do not even know what will happen tomorrow. What is your life? You are a mist that appears for a little while and then vanishes. Instead, you ought to say, "If it is the Lord's will, we will live and do this or that." (James 4:13–15, NIV)

Many couples' marriages have suffered by doing what appeared to be a good idea at first, but did not work out as planned. This is why, in all we do together, we should pray for guidance and directly ask God to open and close doors in our lives. He knows the future, and he knows what is best for us. Doesn't your marriage deserve the best?

I really loved the home we had in Atlanta. It was large and spacious, and quite frankly, it had unknowingly become a symbol of success to me—an idol. Our children had grown up and moved out, and we really didn't need a home of that size. My wife kept suggesting that we downsize, get out from under the debt, and enjoy life more. I literally resisted her suggestions for a year. Then, I relented, and we put the house on the market. It sold in one day! This was in 2007. Within six months, a real estate recession occurred that devalued all real estate. It caused many people to lose their homes. This recession went on for eight years. I am so glad that I finally listened to my wife. She had more spiritual insight than I had at the time. She had no way of knowing about the recession, but she did know that we didn't need to live as lavishly as we had been. What would have happened if I had refused to listen to her? What would have happened if she had not used good spiritual discernment in the stewardship of what God had blessed us with?

4. Show Concern for Others

Consider others before yourself (Philippians 2:3). The one resounding theme in the Bible is to treat others as you would have them treat you. Concern for others separates Christians from others in a way that makes a compelling case for demonstrating God working through us. It is better to give than receive because it blesses others and, in turn, we are blessed, often in ways we had not anticipated.

This quality of considering others before ourselves is what makes a marriage work. If two people are putting each other ahead of themselves, they will experience the love God shows us. The best marriages are between two people who both feel like they are getting more than they are giving. Therein lies the paradox of sacrifice. When we give to others, we always receive more back intangibly than we ever thought possible. This does not make logical sense, but it makes spiritual sense.

We can best understand this principle with our children because we give to them sacrificially throughout their younger years. They often do not realize what we forego so that they can have the things they want and need. When our kids are younger, they don't thank us profusely or always demonstrate appreciation necessarily. However, we enjoy seeing them happy, so we do this gladly. When we are providing for those who need help, we are a blessing to God. "Truly I tell you, whatever you did for one of the least of these brothers and sisters of mine, you did for me" (Matthew 25:40, NIV).

The dignity of notice is another way we show that we care about others. Have you ever felt invisible to others? Have you ever gone to a social gathering, meeting, conference, or to church, and felt like no one noticed you? That no one seemed to be interested in who you were? Ignoring others makes them feel unimportant, insignificant, and isolated, even in a large crowd of people. The dignity of notice is about paying attention to others and acknowledging their presence. Caring about others is also demonstrated by not only noticing them, but taking a moment to tune into them. It might require us to move from small talk to level-two talk. Level-two talk is asking questions about them and really listening to their answers. Relationships are forged by showing a genuine interest in others. Marriages remain strong when couples regularly give the dignity of notice.

5. Demonstrate Your Priorities by Your Walk, Not Your Talk

We admire people who live by their principles. We feel compelled to imitate and follow someone who is trying to do the right thing even under dire circumstances. We cheer them on from the sidelines. We want to see good win out over evil and justice served over injustice. Our world needs leaders we can admire and believe in.

One of the most disillusioning things to see is how many of our heroes have fallen into temptations that have caused us to lose respect for them. They may have started off with good intentions, but attention, fame, and fortune eventually corrupted them. Their desire to stay in the limelight and retain their significance has caused them to compromise their values and make poor choices in their lives.

The person who walks the talk will always be more respected than the person who talks the talk. We can impress and fool the people whom we know, but we cannot fool the people with whom we live daily. Our day-to-day actions prove who we really are and others will notice, especially our spouses and our children.

An old fraternity brother from the University of Florida, Dave Matthews, during an online group chat with some other Christian buddies years ago wrote, "Chuck is one man who walks his talk." I was very humbled by his observations and have remembered his sentiments many times. They have motivated me to always continue to try to do the right thing. Someone is always noticing, and they will be influenced by our example.

It is very apparent that who we are determines to a great degree who our children become. The kind of people they become, the interests they have, and the careers they choose are strongly influenced by what their parents do. I have always loved to play music, exercise, and read. Our two sons as adults have adopted those interests and pastimes as well.

Last year, my oldest adult son, Chris, gave me a card that said, You are my role model and the best man I know. He may never know how much that meant to me, because one of my life goals has been to be the kind of person I wanted them to be.

Sometimes parents do the best they can do, and their children do not follow in their footsteps. Our children are individuals who will eventually make their own decisions, with which we may not agree. They have to learn from their own mistakes, and we are not responsible for their poor choices. We can, however, be a positive influence that helps them find their way, even when they get off track in life.

Walking the talk in our marriage means that we treat our spouse the way we want to be treated. When they don't treat us well, we show grace and turn the other cheek. We forgive the times our partner hurts us, and we apologize for the times we hurt them. We manage our feelings and emotions so we don't say things we will later regret. We do what is best for the relationship, despite our anger and wounded pride. It is a strength, and not a weakness, to be the first to try and make peace. The question of "What would Jesus do?" is always a good tiebreaker when both sides think they are right. Lead, follow, or get out of the way is a good philosophy for resolving conflicts in a marriage. Someone needs to set the precedent and not remain part of the impasse. Be that person in your marriage.

6. Show Mercy and Forgiveness

We live in a blame-oriented society where our first impulse is to look for what is wrong in others. We compare, compete, and quickly notice the flaws in others. It is as if we need to assure ourselves of our own superiority in order to feel adequate around others. This self-protectiveness generates both negativity and distrust toward others, while keeping us self-absorbed and primarily looking out for our own interests. The result of this thinking is a judgmental attitude. It leads to assuming the worst in others instead of assuming the best.

Jesus preferred "mercy . . . over judgment" (James 2:13, NIV). Mercy gives the benefit of the doubt instead of assuming the worst. It promotes acceptance instead of skepticism. It wants to believe the best of others instead of assuming that others are guilty. It is the willingness to give others a second chance when they make a mistake. It offers others the opportunity to learn from mistakes.

Forgiveness accepts the fact that we will all make mistakes. We will sometimes hurt the ones we love. We all deserve a chance to redeem ourselves in order to recover from the hurt that we have caused. Mercy and forgiveness are the ultimate acts of hope in others. They demonstrate an ability to turn the other cheek and let go of the offense. They are generosity in action.

Mercy and forgiveness deepen our faith by showing acceptance toward others when it may not be deserved. No relationship would ever survive without mercy and forgiveness. Marriages grow stronger not by the absence of mistakes we make with each other, but by the mercy and forgiveness we demonstrate toward one another.

We will grow in our faith when we:

- are open to input and advice from others
- demonstrate a willingness to change and become a better person
- seek God's will for our lives
- possess a concern for the lives of other
- show our priorities and values by our daily actions
- offer mercy and forgiveness toward others

Mercy and forgiveness will strengthen our character, and we will become a more authentically spiritual person. It will help us become aware of what is most important in life and love others from the heart. We will be a better spouse because we will be treating our husband or wife the way we want to be treated.

CHAPTER 19

REJUVENATING YOUR LOVE LIFE

"He who finds a wife finds what is good and receives favor from the Lord."
—Proverbs 18:22 (NIV)

Pay attention to your love life if you do not want your marriage to be vulnerable to an affair. Never take for granted what you (and only you) share with your spouse. Many couples regret allowing their physical intimacy to become a low priority. Most spouses long for the closeness they once had and expressed to each other through their lovemaking.

There will always be demands that compete for our time and energy. It is understandable that our sex lives occasionally have to take a back seat to the tyranny of the urgent. We all know that the needs in our marriage sometimes have to be placed on hold while we attend to other work or family matters. However, these needs should not remain on hold indefinitely, or the marriage will suffer.

Marriage is the power source that fuels what we do for our family. When a marriage relationship is fulfilling, we are better at all we do. We are kinder, more generous, and can face the demands of life with resilience. Our sex lives are a reflection of that relationship and also a celebration of it.

The more emotionally connected we are, the more likely our sex lives will stay active. When sex is a regular part of our lives together, we become energized, optimistic, and bonded together. It helps us feel secure within ourselves. A regular sex life is a bonding experience that acts like a shock absorber against life's bumps. We are not as inclined to be irritated by each other or annoyed by one other's idiosyncrasies. Those couples who do not have sex together with some mutually agreed-upon frequency react negatively to every little bump that occurs in their relationship. They do not seem to be patient with each other or show tolerance for the inconveniences that occur between them. They lose the incentive to engage each other and drift into doing their own thing.

HOW TO BECOME A BORING SPOUSE

Remember how exciting life was when you first met your future spouse? The spark between you created an invigorating energy that made you want to talk for hours. You may have never met someone so interesting or who brought out the best in you in this way. The excitement of this new relationship generated creative urges that compelled you to try new and different experiences, get out of your comfort zone, and stay up half the night just talking to each other. These are memories most couples reflect upon fondly when reminiscing about when they first met.

Sadly, however, approximately one-third of all couples married over twenty years report their relationship has lost momentum. They describe it as coexistent, like living with a roommate, or as two ships passing in the night. In other words, it's boring!

HOMEWORK EXERCISE

Checklist: The Boring Spouse

Here are some surefire ways to guarantee you too can become a boring spouse.

Check the ones you do.

__ Get into a routine. Do the same things over and over again. Avoid variety.

__ Watch TV, videos, and DVDs nightly as your preferred means of entertainment.

__ Work long hours and bring work home with you at night and on the weekends.

__ Make your family totally child focused to the detriment of couple time together.

__ Give time to your relationship only after everything else has been done.

__ Do not date regularly. Save time together for when you go on vacation.

__ Put off getting that gift for him or her until the last minute.

__ Only have sex when it is convenient, spontaneous, and you are not tired.

__ Do the thoughtful little things only when it is a special occasion.

__ Don't do things that your spouse wants to do if they don't interest you.

__ Insist that things be done your way because you are often right.

__ Keep your thoughts and feelings to yourself. Only speak if it is necessary.

__ Take a job that has you traveling more than 50 percent of the time.

___ Define your success by your salary, status, and possessions.
___ Since you are naturally forgetful, have your spouse remind you about things often.
___ When you have a disagreement, let it go, get quiet, and sweep it under the rug.
___ Keep the peace by always being reasonable, accommodating, and agreeable.

Total ___ (five or more qualifies as boring)

Becoming a boring spouse does not occur overnight. It takes practice and focusing our attention elsewhere. You too, however, can excel at coexistence if you consistently execute the activities listed above. For additional pointers, go to: *www.imabore.com*.

EMOTIONALLY DISCONNECTED: THE KEY TO A SEXLESS MARRIAGE

Tina and Tim were a couple who had been married over twenty-five years and had very infrequent or almost no sex for half their marriage. They were nice people for the most part, but they had drifted apart and were emotionally disconnected from each other. He worked a lot and she was more involved with her grown children and grandkids, and consequently, their marriage had become a low priority over time. He got involved in pornography and sexual fantasy games in his private time, and she seemed content just doing what she wanted by herself. They both let themselves go physically, adding another dimension of unapproachability to their relationship. They rarely ever fought. He just did what she told him to do generally.

Though this story may seem sad, it is being reenacted in many marriages today.

Of the marriages that do survive divorce, almost half suffer some type of emotional disconnection, drifting apart, or coexistence. They may not be openly unhappy together, but they aren't happy couples together. You see them every day in public acting the part, but when they get home, there is not much emotionally going on between them.

One of the partners may even eventually come in for individual counseling reporting vague feelings of depression or anxiety. When I dig deeper, many will acknowledge some level of dissatisfaction with their marriage, but do not really believe it can change much. They have decided that this is as good as it gets, and they don't really want to risk ending things together. There are enough other benefits they have accrued during their time together that it would create too much of an inconvenience to draw a line in the sand.

Sound familiar?

Settling for mediocrity in your marriage is a sure way to just accept unhappiness and a lifetime of loneliness. It will almost always be reflected in our sex lives or the lack thereof. Conflict avoidance is the deadliest of the three types of conflict that exist in relationships (destructive, constructive, and avoidance). It will undermine our motivation to try and make things better. It will cause us to look at our spouse's faults, instead of what we are responsible for or capable of doing differently. It will cause us to feel deep resentment, but we may minimize it by rationalizing that other things are more important now. Our feelings will be internalized and ignored to the point of oblivion. It may even cause us to find someone else who appreciates us more and makes us feel alive again.

What's Done in the Dark

HOMEWORK EXERCISE

No one plans to drift apart emotionally, but it happens at some time or another in most marriages and relationships. Perhaps it occurs for a brief period or for years at a time. Sometimes it occurs because of a new job, a new baby, or because of school. Whatever the cause, it can have an insidiously damaging effect on the love you hoped would last forever.

Checklist: Drifting Apart

Here are some tactics to ensure that it will happen to you:

Check the ones that apply to your marriage:

   ___ 1. Assume that what you want is what she wants (self-focused).

   ___ 2. Ignore a recurrent problem in hopes it will go away on its own (denial).

   ___ 3. Refuse to talk about things, withdraw, and shut down (stonewall).

   ___ 4. Counter concerns about you with what he/she does wrong, too (blame shift).

   ___ 5. Accept the status quo (avoidance).

   ___ 6. Be relentless in pointing out faults, and don't give him/her time to think about it—after all he/she has had enough time to change (critical parent).

   ___ 7. Don't talk for a day or two to let your partner know how wounded you are (narcissistic retaliation).

___ 8. When your spouse brings up something that is a problem for them, always have a reason why it happened that way (deflection by excuse).

___ 9. When your unhappiness with the relationship continues long term, get depressed; give up trying; self-medicate with pills, pot, food, alcohol, or pornography; complain often to others; gain weight; or spend money excessively (passive aggressiveness).

___ 10. Blow up and finally say all the things you have been thinking about your spouse directly to him/her (verbal abuse).

Having identified some problems that are occurring in your marriage, what are you going to do about them?

ENHANCING EMOTIONAL INTIMACY BY MEETING THE NEEDS OF YOUR SPOUSE

How do couples learn to enhance their emotional intimacy together?

Emotional intimacy is not about sex, but *showing fondness and interest.*

It is about *truly knowing and being known* by your partner. Emotional intimacy is about giving the kind of *genuine, undivided attention* you gave the first time you met or when you realized you were in love. Emotional intimacy grows through sharing time together. It is not just about doing things, but *being fully present when you are with each other.*

It involves *caring more about the other person's feelings* than trying to be right.

It is about *listening* and *giving support* instead of giving advice.

It is about *delivering affirmations* instead of leveling criticisms.

It is about *offering apologies* instead of providing justifications.

Emotional intimacy includes *sharing your hopes and dreams with each other* no matter what age you may be, and then encouraging the pursuit of them.

It means *making memorable moments together* now, because you may not have tomorrow. Emotional intimacy is being with someone who enables you to experience all the fullness that life has to offer.

HOMEWORK EXERCISE

Checklist: Emotional Intimacy

*Answer the following questions by circling **Y** for yes and **N** for no.*

1. Do you feel emotionally intimate with your spouse?
   Y / N

2. Are you closer now than you have ever been?
   Y / N

3. Does the time you spend together satisfy your need for connection?
   Y / N

4. Are you able to talk openly about your insecurities and weaknesses, no matter how embarrassing?
   Y / N

5. Do you agree to have no secrets between you?
   Y / N

6. Are you soul mates?
   Y / N

7. Is there no one else with whom you would rather be?
   Y / N

8. Do you still have fun together?
   Y / N

If you can say yes to all these questions, you have a unique and enviable relationship that not many couples experience. If you can't, talk about how to make that particular area better and work on it. There is always hope that your marriage can deepen in this vital area.

TAKING IT SLOWLY: RESUMING SEX AFTER AN AFFAIR

> *"Show me a couple who isn't having sex more than once a month, and I'll show you a couple who is angry with each other."*
>
> DCW

A spouse who has been faced with infidelity encounters a similar form of trauma that soldiers experience in combat, albeit on a different level and to a different degree. The threat to security, the shock that occurs upon discovery, the loss of trust, and the sense of vulnerability are all very similar. Infidelity always negatively impacts a couple's sex life.

Some betrayed spouses immediately stop all sexual contact and refuse to be intimate with their partner for months or even years after the discovery of an affair. They are so hurt and angry that they do not want to be that vulnerable with this person again. They imagine their spouse having sex with someone else, and the reminders are overwhelming. On one hand, they are protecting themselves, but there is often a retaliatory element present as well. *"If you want sex, go find your whore"* is the sentiment some betrayed wives convey. While this reaction may seem deserved, it sometimes inadvertently sends the offending spouse back to his or her lover.

Other betrayed spouses react by increasing the frequency of sex with their partners to a level never before experienced. They seem to be trying to reconnect emotionally by stepping up their previously lackluster physical life together. This sexual, full-court press may provide immediate comfort to the marriage at first, but the pain and hurt of the infidelity issues still must be addressed. Once the fear of abandonment passes, the hurt and pain of the affair will return with a vengeance.

Most couples will experience an interruption in their sex life as they regroup to try to understand how the affair has impacted them emotionally. This is clearly not a problem that just having sex together again will help. Their love life together does not easily resume, even when a couple takes the time to evaluate what happened in the affair and what weaknesses within the marriage contributed to it. When they do try to become sexual again, flashbacks of their spouse with the other person often interfere with those efforts. Fear of being hurt again can override attempts to rebuild the intimacy in the marriage as well. It is important not to force the emotional or sexual reconnection, but to allow it to naturally occur. Healing can only occur if a couple agrees to move forward with time together, being attentive, and offering affection and comfort. Dating again, learning to have fun together, making new memories, and time away together will help them start a new chapter in the marriage.

Living in the past will only sabotage the future, so learning from the past is what is necessary. The immediate past becomes a distant past when couples work on reconnecting and adding new memories to the present. The passing of time, recurrent forgiveness, and conscious efforts to repair the marriage with regular experiences together are the best prescription for healing.

HOMEWORK EXERCISE

Sensate Focus

This is a nonsexual, physical, touching, and massage exercise that helps couples break through the distance, discomfort, anxiety, and anger associated with difficulties they have experienced in their relationship.

The purpose is to reacclimatize to close proximity and contact without the threat of sexual involvement.

The activity involves each person taking five minutes to massage the hands, arms, shoulders, head, and feet of their partner. This is a clothes-on exercise and should not include any sexual over- or under-the-clothes contact.

Each person should take turns and spend five minutes providing the touch and massage to the other. Feel free to instruct the partner providing the massage about what is relaxing to you, and to ask them to make adjustments based on tactile pressure, pace, and comfort level.

(Please do this at least three times per week for each other.)

YOU NEED TO FEEL LOVED TO MAKE LOVE

I have told couples for years that men need to make love to feel loved, and women need to feel loved to make love. While this is fundamentally true, it only partially reflects how many men and women approach sex. The reality is that both sexes really need to feel loved to make love, if their love life is going to deepen.

Many women have lost their desire to have sex with their husbands. This is because they do not experience the emotional connection, consideration, thoughtfulness, and specialness they desire. Likewise, many men have lost their desire to pursue their wives and give them what they need emotionally. This is because they feel last on their wife's list or just another obligation to check off. *Not a very romantic way to live your life, is it?*

So, gradually, the routine and boredom turns into drifting apart. Years later, they may come into my office and say, "We love each other, but just don't feel 'in love.'" Surprise! Surprise! Their relationship is running on fumes, and they are not sure why the tank is empty.

A satisfying, regular sex life is not necessarily what marriage is all about. However, our sex lives are a reflection of our love for each other and, therefore, a celebration of the kind of relationship we share. Generally, when a couple describes the quality and frequency of their sex life, I can surmise a great deal about their emotional life together, for they closely parallel each other.

Early in a marriage, both people are interested and motivated to be intimate on a reasonably regular basis. They are still validating each other and attentive in many important ways. Within a few short years, this specialness may wane or other things may compete for the time and energy that used to be given to their spouse. If a couple permits outside demands to turn their love life into a routine or a servicing of each other only, dissatisfaction and disinterest will set in. Allowing our relationship to become a low priority will cost us in the long run.

Burke and Young reported in *The Journal of Sex Research,* Volume 49, 2012 that couples were happier and experienced greater satisfaction within their relationships when they had sex more frequently.

Dr. Neil McArthur is an associate professor of philosophy at the University of Manitoba and teaches sexual ethics classes. He wrote an article entitled "Should We Have Sex Just Because Our Partner Wants To?" He cites that having sex with your partner sometimes when you don't feel like it is equivalent to participating in an activity because they wanted to. You might not have preferred to engage them at first, but afterward, you are glad you did.

Dr. Pat Love, a noted sex researcher and the author of *Hot Monogamy: Essential Steps to More Passionate, Intimate Lovemaking,* discovered that many women in her studies admitted that they often did not feel like making love until they were making love.

Hayley Wright, a researcher in cognitive aging at the Centre for Research in Psychology, Behavior, and Achievement at Coventry University in England studied 6,800 men and women ages fifty to eighty-nine. She found that those who were sexually active scored higher on cognitive tests or memory skills than those who were not. Men actually showed higher scores on planning, solving problems, and paying attention.

It is important to maintain our sex lives through good times and bad times, because

our sex lives provide a cushion against the everyday stresses we experience. They are the shock absorber that allows us a margin of relief against other disappointments that we all inevitably encounter. When we know things are good at home, the assaults on our self-esteem don't seem to injure us as deeply. It also serves to generate within the relationship a reserve of patience against the minor annoyances we sometimes feel toward each other because of insensitivities, habits, or eccentricities we all possess to some degree.

Ask yourselves:
What parts of our lovemaking do I enjoy most?
What could make it better?

LISTENING LIGHTS UP THE SHEETS

"Never miss a good chance to shut up."
                                    Will Rogers

Talking is a talent, but listening is an art. No one ever got in trouble by listening closely to their spouse. They may have actually learned something that they did not realize was so important to them. Generally speaking, we aren't learning much when our lips are moving! Though most of us prefer to talk, wisdom is what we get from a lifetime of listening. Yogi Berra once said, "You can see a lot by observing."

Why is being listened to such an aphrodisiac?
It often means that the other person is genuinely interested in what we have to say. We feel important to them, and it makes us want to open up more. Their undivided attention causes us to drop our guard emotionally, and the self-protective walls start coming down. We gradually become more transparent and genuine with them. There is nothing more affirming than someone who listens and wants to spend time with us.

Everyone needs someone who takes the time and makes the effort to understand them completely. Stephen Covey writes, "Most people do not listen with the intent to understand, they listen with the intent to reply." In fact, most people are preparing what they are going to say in their heads while the other person is talking. This is not complete listening, but half-an-ear listening. It is often ineffective because the person speaking notices that we aren't really understanding them. They may redouble their efforts to restate what they are trying to communicate, but it detracts from the meaningfulness of the exchange. The result is that they don't feel as close to us as would have been the case if we just focused on them. It often contributes to arguments and frustration because they just do not feel understood or cared for.

Jim and Jen were an engaged couple who were seeking premarital therapy for their relationship. They had both been married before. Though they appeared to be in love, Jim could not stop "yes, but"-ing much of what Jen said. Whenever she had something to say, he felt compelled to add, challenge, or correct some part of it. As you might imagine, this led to a number of arguments between them. His strong need to be right cost him the closeness they initially had. Instead of finding points of agreement and building upon those, he took issue with and focused on their differences. Jim could not share the stage with other people because he had "Yes, but" listening. He needed to have the last word, but it almost always cost him closeness in the relationship.

Complete Listening

"A closed mouth gathers no foot."

Unknown

Complete listening requires us to do the following things:

1. Quiet your mind, eliminate distractions, and be fully attentive to the other person.
2. Refrain from preparing a response in your head. Just listen and focus.
3. Keep your agenda out of the exchange. This is about the speaker, not us.
4. Attempt to understand in a way that your partner knows you understand.
5. Ask questions when you need clarification.
6. Don't interrupt. Wait for them to stop, or use your body language to create a pause.

7. Don't change the subject, add to what's been said, or self-reference because that response represents this-relates-to-me listening.
8. Wait for them to finish speaking, ask you what you think, or invite your perspective.

To be kind is more important than to be right. Many times what people need is not a brilliant mind that speaks, but a special heart that listens.

> *"Everyone should be quick to listen, slow to speak, and slow to become angry."*
>
> James 1:19 (NIV)

FOR YOUR EYES ONLY: HOW EXCLUSIVITY HEIGHTENS ATTRACTION

> *"May your fountain be blessed, and may you rejoice in the wife of your youth. A loving doe, a graceful deer—may her breasts satisfy you always, may you ever be intoxicated with her love."*
>
> Proverbs 5:18 (NIV)

God's original plan was for each person who wanted to be married to find one person with whom to spend their lives. He realized being alone wasn't a good thing, except for people who enjoyed being on their own. Some people believe that the idea of being with one person for life is unrealistic and boring, if not impossible. They ignore and neglect what they originally worked so hard to get. Then, they spend their time wishing they had something else.

We are people watchers by nature. Most of us are curious about others, their interests, what they like, and what they are doing. We are also imitators. If we see someone doing something that looks like fun or is interesting, we want to do the same things. We are also envious. When someone has something that we don't have, we want it. What we have seems less valuable until we are able to get what we think is better. All this breeds a general sense of dissatisfaction and discontent within us. Therefore, we spend our time and resources chasing after the next-best thing, hoping that it will finally make us happy and content. We do this in relationships as well.

The most significant reason couples lose interest in each other is because they don't work on their relationships. They fail to stay emotionally and physically involved; therefore, their marriages become mediocre and coexistent. Everything worth having is worth taking care of. It doesn't matter whether it involves exercise for our bodies, maintenance on our houses and cars, or nurturing for our relationships. They all need regular attention to operate at their best.

The second reason couples lose interest in each other is that they compare their spouses to other people and view them as lacking in certain areas. Everyone looks better from a distance, and in the same way, familiarity breeds contempt. Believing that what others have is better than what we have is a mistaken assumption.

Tim and Sandy had been married for almost twenty years and had three children. Tim's job required that he travel and entertain different customers. Sandy was the steady rock of the family who handled everything while Tim was gone. One day, out of the blue, Tim asked Sandy, "Have you ever thought that there could be someone better out there for us?" Sandy was shocked, but Tim was serious. He had been thinking about how much better his life might be if it were different. He wondered what it would be like to be single again. What if he had made different choices earlier in his life? Tim had fallen victim to the false belief that "there" is better than "here."

In life, what we focus on, we strengthen. The arm we use the most is usually the stronger arm. We are best at what we spend most of our time doing. The same is true in relationships. When we focus primarily upon our spouse, he or she will grow to mean more to us. This is why older couples, who have been together for years, still think that their spouse is the most beautiful or handsome person they know. It is by design that we can be more in love with and attracted to our spouse when we have made them the entire focus of our attention and affection. When we express gratitude and appreciation regularly to our spouse, we strengthen our fondness toward them. They, in turn, feel the validation they need in order to feel important.

Men who look at other women and think about what it would be like to have a relationship with someone else are at risk of harming their own marriage. Women who compare their husbands to other men and find them lacking will start experiencing and expressing discontent at home. This is one of the main reasons coveting or mate-poaching affairs occur. When someone tells themselves, "I wish I had a wife (husband) like that," they are emotionally venturing into dangerous waters.

This is precisely the reason pornography is having such a devastating effect on the ability of an individual to be emotionally present and connected with one's own spouse. Comparing and coveting what we do not have erodes the enjoyment and celebration of what we already possess. It deceives us into thinking there might be something better. It distracts us from giving our all to the one we chose long ago. In order to make our relationship the best, we have to give our best.

Tom came to counseling reporting feelings of depression and difficulty staying motivated in his day-to-day responsibilities. He had seen psychiatrists and tried a variety of different medications, but nothing seemed to help him for long. He was not attracted to his wife any longer and seemed to find little pleasure in life. Eventually, he disclosed that he had a secret affection for an old girlfriend he had known in college. He had kept up with her on social media, watching her life from a distance and wishing he were a part of it. His focus on what might have been was robbing him of what was. He was sabotaging the happiness and contentment he could have in his own marriage by thinking that the grass was greener elsewhere. When he finally started working on his own marriage, his depression lifted.

The lyrics in Michael Martin Murphey's song "What's Forever For?" question what the purpose of the future is if people will not show love and commitment to each other forever.

Gratefully appreciating the positive attributes of the person we have in our life, in my opinion, is the single most important determiner of a happy, satisfying relationship. *Marriages are made, not born.* They require a great deal of time and attention if they are going to be the best they can be. Dance with the one you came with, and don't waste time wondering what else is out there. You will be happier and more content if you do.

"It's never too late to be what you might have been."
George Eliot

HOMEWORK EXERCISE

Below is an exercise that, if done daily for one month, could change the way you feel about your spouse.

Prayer of Gratitude

Every morning, take special time to say a prayer of gratitude for your spouse. Include in that prayer all the good qualities of your partner, how he or she has made your life better, the ways they have helped you in your life, when they have been there for you during difficult times, and how they have motivated you to be a better you just by being there.

EPILOGUE

Okay, I admit it. I'm a romantic. My heart's desire is for people to get along and live happily ever after. I have made a profession out of being a peacemaker. Seeing couples find the magic in their relationship and deepen their appreciation for each other gives me great satisfaction. Helping people repair their damaged relationships and have a happy marriage has been my mission in life.

Why has this been so important to me?

I have personally been so blessed in my own marriage that I would like others to experience what a good marriage can be. Our marriage has not been perfect. We have worked on it steadily over the years.

During our first five years of marriage, I was working full time, attending graduate school, attending church services and functions four times a week, and building a part-time private practice at night. We hadn't even had children yet! I was burning the candle at both ends. My wife was getting very little of my time, and what time she did get was not very emotionally fulfilling. You might say my mistress was my career.

At one point, Dru-Ann wrote me a letter acknowledging my drive, hard work, and desire to succeed. She also said that she wasn't sure that she was the person I needed to be married to. In other words, I needed someone who did not need me so much. She needed someone who would make her a priority and share her life. I was devastated, to say the least! I thought I was doing all of this for us, but she felt it was mainly for me. She was probably more right than I was ready to admit. However, I got it. She wanted a husband who was involved, around, and cared about meeting her needs.

Now this would have been an opportune time for her to have an affair. She could have easily found someone else, as she was and is a very beautiful woman with a fantastic personality. I suppose I could also have found someone more sympathetic to the sacrifices I believed I was making and had an affair as well. Had either one of us done this, it might have been a death blow to the marriage. Instead of resorting to mutual-blame tactics or retaliatory affairs, we decided to make some serious changes in our marriage.

We decided to set aside regular times to talk and be together. We shared the experiences from our day when we came home with one another. We did more fun things together. We had sex regularly. We learned to ask for what we wanted from each other without criticizing. We apologized when we hurt the other's feelings. We did what we said we were going to do, or informed one another if circumstances changed. We made Christ the center of our lives and deferred to Him when we needed a tiebreaker during a conflict. We became best friends again. Within five years, we had both of our sons, Chris and David. What a blessing they were to us.

None of the rebuilding we experienced was by accident or luck. It was intentional. It did not happen overnight but gradually over time, and it was worth it all. We are grateful to now have a marriage that others often positively comment upon and admire. We are just glad to know we will be best friends and lovers forever.

BIBLIOGRAPHY

Arterburn, Stephen and Fred Stoeker. *Every Man's Battle: Every Man's Guide to Winning the War on Sexual Temptation One Victory at a Time* (New York: Waterbrook Press, 2009).

Blankenship, Richard. *Spouses of Sex Addicts: Hope for the Journey* (n.p.: Xulon Press, 2011).

Brown, Emily. *Patterns of Infidelity and Their Treatment* (Philadelphia: Brunner-Routledge, 2001).

Burke, Tricia and Valerie Young. "Sexual Transformations and Intimate Behaviors in Romantic Relationships." *The Journal of Sex Research*, Vol. 49, Issue 5 (2012): 454–463.

Carder, Dave. *Torn Asunder: Recovering from an Extramarital Affair* (Chicago: Moody Press, 1995).

Covey, Stephen. *The 7 Habits of Highly Effective People: Powerful Lessons in Personal Change*, 15th ed. (New York: Free Press, 2004).

Currin, Liz. *The Essential Guide to Surviving Infidelity* (London: Alpha, 2012).

Dew, Jeffrey, Sonya Britt, and Sandra Huston. "Examining the Relationship between Financial Issues and Divorce," *Family Relations*, Vol. 61, Issue 4 (2012): 615–628.

Dobson, James. *Love Must Be Tough: New Hope for Marriages in Crisis* (Carol Stream, IL: Tyndale House Publishers, 2007).

Glass, Shirley and Jean Coppock Staeheli. *NOT "Just Friends": Rebuilding Trust and Recovering Your Sanity After Infidelity* (New York: Free Press, 2003).

Gottman, John and Nan Silver. *The Seven Principles for Making Marriage Work: A Practical Guide from the Country's Foremost Relationship Expert* (New York: Harmony Books, 2015).

Harley Jr., Willard and Jennifer Harley Chalmers. *Surviving an Affair* (Grand Rapids: Revel, 2013).

Hertlein, Katherine. "Therapists' Assessment and Treatment of Internet Infidelity Cases," *Journal of Marital and Family Therapy*, Vol. 34, No. 4 (2008): 481–497.

Kador, John. *Effective Apology: Mending Fences, Building Bridges, and Restoring Trust* (San Francisco: Berrett-Koehler Publishers, 2009).

Kendrick, Stephen Alex Kendrick. *The Love Dare* (Nashville: B&H Publishing Group, 2008).

Love, Patricia and Jo Robinson. *Hot Monogamy: Essential Steps to More Passionate, Intimate Lovemaking* (n.p.: CreateSpace, 2012).

Lusterman, Don-David. *Infidelity: A Survival Guide* (Oakland: New Harbinger Publications, 1998).

Maltz, Wendy and Larry Maltz. *The Porn Trap: The Essential Guide to Overcoming Problems Caused by Pornography* (New York: HarperCollins, 2009).

Marin, R., Christensen, A. and Atkins, D. "Infidelity and behavioral couple therapy: Relationship outcomes over 5 years following therapy," *Couple and Family Psychology: Research and Practice*, Vol. 3, No. 1 (2014): 1–12.

McArthur, Neil. "Should We Have Sex Just Because Our Partner Wants To?" *Psychology Tomorrow Magazine,* Issue 12 (2014).

Neuman, M. Gary. *The Truth about Cheating: Why Men Stray and What You Can Do to Prevent It* (Hoboken: John Wiley and Sons, 2008).

Pittman, Frank. *Private Lies: Infidelity and the Betrayal of Intimacy* (New York: W. W. Norton and Company, 1989).

Real, Terrence. *The New Rules of Marriage: What You Need to Know to Make Love Work* (New York: Ballentine Books, 2008).

Shain, Merle. *Hearts That We Broke Long Ago* (New York: Bantam Books, 1983).

Snyder, Douglas, Donald Baucom, and Kristina Coop Gordon. *Getting Past the Affair: A Program to Help You Cope, Heal, and Move On—Together or Apart* (New York: Guilford Publications, 2007).

Spring, Janis. *After the Affair: Healing the Pain and Rebuilding Trust When a Partner Has Been Unfaithful* (New York: William Morrow, 2012).

Stanley, Andy. *The Principle of the Path: How to Get from Where You Are to Where You Want to Be* (Nashville: Thomas Nelson, 2008).

Steffens, Barbara and M. A. Marsha Means. *Your Sexually Addicted Spouse: How Partners Can Cope and Heal* (Far Hills, NJ: New Horizon Press, 2009).

Wright, Hayley. "Sex on the brain! Associations between sexual activity and cognitive function in older age." *Age and Ageing*, Vol. 45, No. 2 (2016).

ABOUT THE AUTHOR

D. Charles Williams, PhD, is a licensed psychologist, marriage and family therapist, AAMFT-approved supervisor, and executive coach. He practiced in Atlanta for over twenty years and currently has a private practice in Athens, Georgia. Visit Dr. Williams's website at www.drwilliamscoach.com.